FIC
TRE

Trenhaile, John

A view from the
square

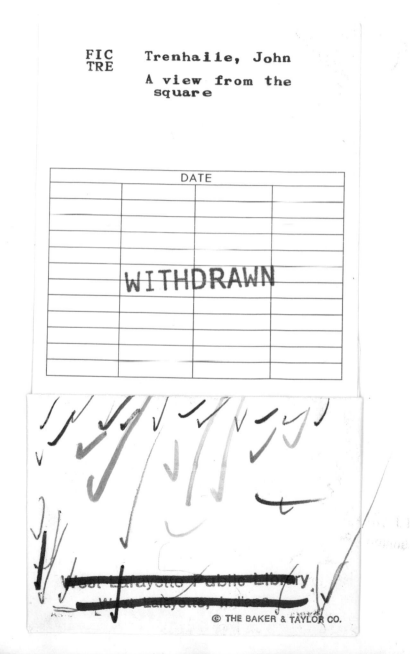

DATE		
WITHDRAWN		

A VIEW
FROM THE
SQUARE

ALSO BY JOHN TRENHAILE

The Man Called Kyril

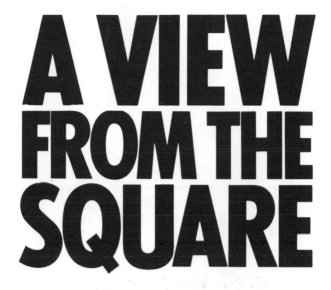

JOHN TRENHAILE

CONGDON & WEED,

Library of Congress Cataloging in Publication Data

Trenhaile, John.
A view from the square.

I. Title.
PR6070.R367V5   1984   823'.914   83-26997
ISBN 0-86553-115-3
ISBN 0-312-92892-0 (St. Martin's Press)

Published by Congdon & Weed, Inc.
298 Fifth Avenue, New York, N.Y. 10001

Distributed by St. Martin's Press
175 Fifth Avenue, New York, N.Y. 10010

5/84 B+T 8.86

First published in Great Britain 1983
by The Bodley Head Ltd, London

For Francis, my friend, with love

DANFORTH: This is a sharp time, now, a precise time – we live no longer in the dusky afternoon when evil mixed itself with good and befuddled the world. Now, by God's grace, the shining sun is up . . .

ARTHUR MILLER, *The Crucible*

To live a life is not so simple as crossing a field.

Russian proverb

Lines from *The Crucible* by Arthur Miller reproduced with permission.

1

Gerald Gilchrist came out of the Brasserie Monopole, buttoning his coat collar against the wind, and glanced quickly up and down the street for a taxi. He was late. In the poky little annexe off the Rue Théodore, Harding, his boss, would already be looking at the clock and wondering where the hell he'd got to. How long before he resorted to amber procedures? Gilchrist couldn't remember. Stung by the thought he began to walk rapidly in the direction of the lake, every so often looking over his shoulder in search of a cab. The weather was against him. He looked in vain.

While he was at lunch it had begun to snow, so that by the time he reached the *quai* the soles of his shoes were saturated with slush and his feet were starting to go numb. No point in a taxi now; a few minutes' brisk walk would bring him out behind the cathedral and from there it was only a stone's throw to the office.

But ahead of him the bridge was blocked. Motor-cycle police had sealed off both the carriageway and the pavement, and a large crowd was already gathering. Gilchrist swore and looked at his watch. Harding would be seething now. Nothing for it, though. Over the past few days the inhabitants of Geneva had learned to live with street blockades.

He wandered across the *quai* so as to distance himself from the crowd and stared out over Lac Léman. Flat, grey. . . featureless. Like his future.

In the year after Cambridge they had said, Come and work for us. Finish your training as an accountant, the languages are fine but we like our people to have additional skills, something extra, then. . . Then Geneva. First posting. In the grey, snow-flecked light of mid-afternoon the memory of the relief he had felt seemed grotesquely unreal. Not Moscow, not Jiddah, not, oh thank God, praise Allah, Tehran. . .

Switzerland. A state of mind, isn't that what somebody had called it? For Gerald Gilchrist it was synonymous with disillusionment, long-term depression, ennui.

He turned away from the lake to face the bridge. The first car in the convoy cruised slowly across the Rhône, a small red and gold pennon fluttering over its bonnet. Somewhere behind a siren howled briefly and was silenced. Russians. Blinds across the rear windows. That meant the Deputy Prime Minister himself, probably Beletsky as well — the elderly General from the Ministry was rumoured to be on his way up, his years of SALT experience paying off at last. Gilchrist glanced at his watch. Two forty-three. Four-car motorcade, Soviet Deputy Prime Minister and entourage, travelling north-west, probably from or to a plenary session of the conference, to or from the mission, with its high wire fence and white sentry cabin in the woods. Perm any two. That should make them sit up in London. That'd shake them.

The footway was open again, the crowd dispersed, but inexplicably Gilchrist's sense of urgency was gone. Even the thought of Harding implementing amber procedures failed to lift his mood. He turned back to the lake, placed his arms on the wall in front of him, and gazed down at the restless, grimy water. Snow was trickling into his collar, his feet had turned to stone, he was late past all excusing, and suddenly he didn't care about any of it. He didn't give a fuck.

He became aware of a presence near by. Another man had come to stand against the wall, hands folded on the parapet, eyes fixed on the water. If he was conscious of Gilchrist he did not show it, but continued to stare downwards as though intent on fathoming the depths of the murky lake. Something about his profile disconcerted the young Englishman. The ears were long and pointed, like a devil's. Instinctively he began to detail what he could see of the man's face. . .rough, tanned skin, age early sixties, grey hair streaked with white, eyes. . . impossible to tell. Gilchrist widened his sphere of observation.

8

Expensive camelhair overcoat, kid gloves, no hat. Something made him look over his shoulder and see a BMW 735i parked (illegally) by the kerb. The back door was open, revealing a slice of the comfortable interior and the lower portion of a woman. Gilchrist couldn't see her face. It seemed as though the man with large ears had told the chauffeur (Gilchrist belatedly noticed the chauffeur, a hard-faced man wearing a grey fedora) to stop while he took some fresh air. What a place to choose, right on the *quai*. But then if you were rich, and careless. . .

Gilchrist straightened up abruptly and began to walk towards the Pont du Mont Blanc. He was not rich, nor were any of his colleagues in the cramped offices behind the Rue Théodore. They were supposed to be united by a common motive — love of country. Patriotism means a lot to us, they had said. Even today. Come and work for us. . .

In Gilchrist's book, patriotism meant a one room apartment in Châtelaine, a mo-ped, a seat in an office designed for single occupancy but shared with two others, £6,875 per annum, foreign residence allowance (subject to periodic review) and sundry perquisites such as the occasional lunch in the Brasserie Monopole. In Geneva his money went nowhere. Normally he could not have afforded to eat in a restaurant but this was the third day of the SALT conference of Foreign Ministers and Gilchrist, like everybody else in the annexe, had been ordered on to the streets with instructions to listen for the buzz. What buzz? he had asked. Any buzz, snapped Harding. Here's twenty francs. I want some change, mind. You're always complaining that I treat you like a bloody accountant. (This was true. Gilchrist did the weekly accounts and made up the yellow sheets for London Audit. No one else in the annexe was qualified to do it.) Get out on the streets for a change and do some work.

The memory of the man with the BMW obstinately refused to fade. Gilchrist stopped and looked back. The wall stretched away, unoccupied, into the dense white drapes of snow, and the car had gone. Something about the face. . . He frowned, trying to recall the details which seemed so familiar. Grey hair. Early sixties. Ears. . .

He quickened his pace, eager for the fuggy warmth of the

annexe. The snow was coming down harder now. Harding would be livid; he ought to have been back an hour ago, and he had nothing of interest to report. All the places on his list had been crammed with journalists covering the conference, but they talked about nothing except expenses and trouble with the telex machine. Not like Tilsen. Gilchrist screwed up his face. Tilsen shared his office and was a couple of years older. Yesterday he had come back with a 'buzz' that Krilenko's wife was a Colonel in the Second Main Directorate of the KGB, and Harding thought enough of that to cable London Station. But then Tilsen had been fully trained, Gilchrist reminded himself. The remainder of his own training was always promised for next month, after the vacation season, in the winter sometime. . . Harding was meant to take an interest in the youngsters sent out from London, find out their strengths and weaknesses, make recommendations for their future deployment. A bird's eye view of an operational section, that's what he was supposed to be giving Gilchrist. But Harding had favourites and Gilchrist was not among them, so he didn't count.

Panic.

Suppose Harding had already contacted the Embassy? Wasn't that the first step? Gilchrist broke into a run, heedless of the other pedestrians around him, shouldering his way to the edge of the road. He started to cross without looking. A horn sounded, very loudly and very close. He jumped back in fear, catching his heel on the kerbstone as a prelude to an ugly backwards sprawl. The crown of his skull landed on the pavement with an audible crack but no one stopped to help him. Gilchrist strove to sit up, cursing all things Swiss, while he massaged his throbbing head. His sight was muzzy. The pain was enough to make his eyes prick with tears — pain and the cold and anxiety together.

He became aware of a car which had parked opposite the scene of his mishap. The car which had caused it in the first place. Gilchrist started to scramble up, seized with a ridiculous desire to pound on the smooth plate glass, protest, demand compensation for this unwarrantable negation of his own importance.

10

And then he saw that it was a BMW 735i, the back nearside window of which was lowered so that the occupant, a man with large pointed ears and grey hair streaked with white, could look down on him. . .

For what seemed like a long time they stared at each other, Gilchrist's anger giving way to sullen resentment and then, under the cold scrutiny of the other man's narrow eyes, irrational trepidation. The eyes were blue, Gilchrist noticed, blue and strangely penetrating, as if their owner spent much time straining to pierce thick shadows which only he could perceive. In his concussed state they seemed to glow, expand and contract to a steady rhythm.

Then the man sat back and his lips moved; the driver's grey fedora dipped in brief acknowledgement, the tinted window hummed upwards and the car drove off with a swish of wet snow to spatter the already soaking bottoms of Gilchrist's trousers. To his astonishment he found he was trembling. He shook himself roughly and stared after the car for just long enough to memorise the number before once again breaking into a run.

A few moments later he pushed through the swing doors and started to pound up the creaking stairs to the fourth floor. There was no *ascenseur* and the rent was reduced on that account. Because of the noise made by the stairs his prospects of evading Harding were nil. The door to the Head of Section's office was open. Gilchrist squared his shoulders and tried to hurry past, but Harding was on the alert.

'Come in here, Gilchrist.'

Gilchrist entered, praying silently that Harding had not yet implemented the dreadful amber procedures for missing personnel. The office oppressed him at the best of times; today it seemed insufferable. Everyone else was forced to make do with stick-like modern office furniture but Harding had set out to make his room Louis Quinze. As an effect it failed dismally — an incongruous, stuffy, wasteful whim authorised by Gilchrist's predecessor (under protest), disallowed by a furious London Audit, then reinstated on appeal to some nameless authority with whom (or so the rumour went) Harding had trained at Gosport. It was the largest room in the

11

annexe, also the most uncomfortable.

Despite the stuffy heat Harding wore his jacket, as always. He sat with his hands folded neatly on the blotter in front of him. The light bounced threateningly off his gold-rimmed spectacles, and his face wore that mean look of rejection which Gilchrist associated with his bank manager at home. People said Harding consciously modelled himself on the Head of the Service, but since Gilchrist had never seen Sir Richard Bryant that meant nothing to him.

'It's difficult enough to run the annexe, Gilchrist, without having my junior staff come in at all hours. No explanation to offer, hein?'

Harding always sounded German when he used this interrogative; but then perhaps he felt it went well with his status as Head of Geneva Section.

'No product either, I dare say. Hein?'

Gilchrist said nothing. For some reason he could not concentrate.

'It's very easy for word to get round a small organisation like this, you know. "Gilchrist doesn't toe the line and Harding doesn't seem to care." Hein?'

Gilchrist said nothing. He dimly registered that so far there had been no mention of the ominous 'procedures', but beyond that he was scarcely aware of Harding at all.

'It may not seem much to you. Taken by itself it may seem quite a little thing. But you see, Gilchrist, it goes on your quarterly register. It goes *against* you.'

The mysterious, seemingly unconnected thoughts which had been swirling around inside Gilchrist's head since his accident chose this moment to come together and form a conclusion. He looked up and saw that Harding's lips were parted, ready to speak.

'Could I look at the PB, do you think? Just for a moment.'

This request took Harding aback. He had been warming to the theme of office efficiency, long a favourite of his, and he did not expect to be interrupted. It was on the tip of his tongue to say so, but something kept the words unspoken. The 'PB' was the Portraits Book, a gallery of some thirty or forty photographs, numbered but otherwise unidentified, with which

12

everyone in the annexe was supposed to be familiar. Even junior staff like Gilchrist were meant to look at it once a week, to keep up with any changes. It was an office joke. Harding knew that. No one had ever asked to see the Geneva PB before, not in his time.

He deliberated a moment longer. Then he rose without a word, went to the safe in the corner of his office, unlocked it and took out the Portraits Book.

Gilchrist quickly scanned page one, turned over and almost at once gave an exclamation. Harding leaned forward in spite of himself.

'What is it?'

'Number Seven.' Gilchrist swivelled the book round for Harding's benefit. 'I saw him today. Twice.'

There was a moment of silence so profound that Gilchrist wondered if he had inadvertently said something shocking. For a frightful second he thought that perhaps Number Seven must have died years ago, and he had just made the most monumental fool of himself. . . Then Harding asked in a very low voice, 'You're sure?' And with a sensation of the most blissful exhilaration Gilchrist knew that it was all right, that it didn't matter any more if he was late, and Tilsen could look to his laurels. . .

'Quite sure.'

He rapidly explained what had happened, not omitting the quick glimpse he had had of the woman inside the car. Harding seemed troubled. He could not quite convince himself. Gilchrist looked down and saw his fingers toy with the thick pages of the PB, curling the top corners this way and that. He looked up again to find Harding's face very close to his own. There was doubt in his eyes, and something larger than doubt. Distrust, maybe. A reluctance to believe.

'You really are certain, Gerald?'

Gilchrist blinked at this unexpected, unprecedented use of his Christian name.

'Yes, sir.' The pointed ears, the hairstyle, the eyes, everything. . .'Yes, sir.'

It carried conviction. Harding recognised the truth. He shut the PB with a snap and returned it to the safe. 'That'll be all,' he said as he resumed his seat. 'Oh, one more thing. . .'

Gilchrist, already at the door, turned back into the room. His chief was sitting at the desk writing on the one-off pad, a hand shading his eyes and supporting his head at the same time.

'Don't be late again,' said Harding, but without rancour.

Gilchrist escaped, thinking, not unreasonably, that he had been lucky, and that he would hear no more of this afternoon's work. But it was not quite the end. He was dating Cheryl, the girl in charge of ciphers and cables on the floor below, and that evening, between mouthfuls of pizza and sips of red wine, she confided in him something which quite restored his sense of mission for the best part of a week: that just before tea time Harding had picked up the phone ('direct scrambler, no messing about') and asked for a priority Green line straight on to C's desk, routed through Crowborough ('Cheltenham not bloody good enough now'), and then spoken for a quarter of an hour.

But not even Cheryl knew what Harding had said to Sir Richard Bryant — which was that there had been a positive but so far uncorroborated sighting of PB/7 in Geneva, with a woman, apparently unsupervised; that according to Harding's most recent up-date key, PB/7 was General Stepan Ilyich Povin, Head of the KGB's First Main Directorate and Chief of Foreign Intelligence; and finally that as all the circumstances of the sighting suggested the most extraordinarily suspicious, urgent and dangerous come-on, would London kindly advise?

2

At the back of the darkened room a pin-point of light showed briefly and was extinguished; then the silence was broken by the harsh whisper of an electric fan. A beam lanced out, expanding, diversifying into many silver-white streaks until it reached the far wall where it formed a dull, smudgy rectangle. Shadows passed through the beam, severing its integral rays, and the smudginess slowly dissolved into high resolution colour.

Against the burr of the fan a voice spoke from the darkness.

'The Boeing E-3A Sentry, comrades. Known to the West as AWACS.'

The voice was quiet but it compelled attention. Every eye in the room was focused on the projected image of a large grey aeroplane with a curious round disc mounted on pylons towards its tail. The voice spoke again.

'Adapted from the commercial airliner called Boeing 707, the AWACS has a crew of seventeen and is powered by four Pratt & Whitney TF 33-100 A turbofans capable of developing a maximum airspeed of six hundred mph. The AWACS can remain on station at its normal operational height of forty thousand feet for twelve hours without re-fuelling, although it is equipped with in-flight refuelling facilities for use when necessary.'

The voice was speaking more quickly now, its owner evidently warming to his theme.

'You are looking at one of the most expensive aircraft ever to enter service. The United States Air Force want thirty-four of them. If they get them — and you may assume, comrades, that under the present Republican administration, they will get them — the United States will have the potential for constant saturation surveillance of Warsaw Pact forces throughout the world.'

The voice faded. In the pause which followed the low rasp of the projector's fan seemed unnaturally loud.

'The AWACS contains a jamming-resistent look-down surveillance command, control and communications system of unparalleled sophistication. It is capable of immediate data processing and can fly in all weathers. It can detect aircraft which are flying beneath a conventional radar net. The aircraft can defend itself, effortlessly, by first sensing the approach of any known make of missile and then turning it back to annihilate its own base. It is hard to put a convincing value on

15

this plane, comrades. When a crude prototype was used over Vietnam it multiplied the aircraft kill ratio *six times*.'

The voice spoke with quiet relish. By contrast the electric fan seemed somehow hostile, a sinister complement of the grey aircraft on the white wall.

'We in Russia have built a plane which superficially resembles the AWACS: the Moss-126. Compared with the AWACS technology, however, it is a crude child's toy. We have nothing to touch the AWACS for sheer strategic and tactical value. Left to our own devices, we never shall.'

The quiet voice dropped once more and allowed the men in the darkened room a few moments of freedom from its despairing, hypnotic message. When the voice spoke again its tone was cold, almost bored.

'Six months ago, comrades, American scientists at Maxwell Air Force Base achieved what to us is quite literally the unthinkable. They gave the AWACS a nil radar signature.'

Until that point the voice and the fan had held joint sway over the darkened room. Now for the first time they were challenged. A chair leg scraped on the floor. Someone muttered something inaudible and was instantly silent. The rustle of cloth on wood took longer to die away.

'They did this by coating the aircraft with a double skin, containing a honeycomb of low-visibility jelly substance, and painting the exterior with anti-radar paint. Such technology is not beyond us. What *is* beyond us is the way in which electrical impulses are used to activate this honeycomb. Until we have that knowledge, we can only reduce our aircrafts' signatures. The Americans can eradicate them. Comrades. . .'

The voice drifted into silence.

'That plane is magic.'

This time the pause was very long. But when the voice spoke again it reverberated with a confident, malevolent power which by its very unexpectedness was enough to jolt the hearers from their lethargy.

'Within a short time that aircraft — the very one you see there, on the wall in front of you — will have landed in Siberia. Intact. Fully operational. And then, comrades, we in the Soviet Union, we too. . .shall be magic.'

16

To Chief Marshal of Aviation Kutakhov the sound of his footsteps on the polished parquet flooring seemed like individual cracks of doom. With the aid of the projector's beam he made his way to the podium; as he reached it the lights went up and he blinked.

For a few moments the handful of other men in the room remained perfectly still while they considered their position. Engaged as they were in a treasonable conspiracy, they did not want, or indeed expect, to see among them a member of the Central Committee, a Hero of the Soviet Union, a member of the Main Operations Directorate and the Chief of *Voyenno vozdushnyye sily*, the Russian Air Force. The suspense engendered by his unexpected appearance was crippling. Then they began to notice details. The dark, wavy hair, usually brushed off the high forehead, was unkempt. The familiar chubby cheeks were sunken and the prominent smile-dimples had vanished. He was pale and clammy, and his fingers alternately tightened and loosened on the sides of the lectern. Kutakhov did not look like a fatal threat.

'Comrades. . .' The voice had lost its momentary vibrancy and was bored once more. 'Welcome the Commander of the Soviet Air Force. He has come to join us and he brings a message. Listen to him.'

Kutakhov stared into the room, his mind a blank. The palpable mixture of hostility and fear which rose from the audience threatened him like an ominously silent, creeping shadow. His tongue seemed to be glued to the roof of his mouth. Kazin had warned him of what this moment would be like. Kazin. . .the memory of that barbed interview spurred the old Marshal to a great effort.

'Comrades. . . I take my life and put it in your hands.'

The dozen or so officers seated below him stared back impassively. It was hardly an original thought. For years now most of them had been treading the twilight zone between life and death, security and discovery. They were used to it. Almost.

'I. . . I have to tell you. . .'

Kutakhov swallowed hard and tried again.

'I and Koldunov. . .we have been fighting a battle together.

17

With the Politburo.'

At mention of Colonel-General Koldunov, Deputy Chief of Staff of PVO Strany, the air defence forces, several of the officers exchanged swift glances. By speaking the name aloud Kutakhov had ensured that virtually the whole of the Soviet Air Force was now incriminated. If that was so, the balance of power was shifting. The possible consequences were stupendous, incalculable.

'Six months ago we went to them, together. We said, Give us an AWACS, the money, the resources, to build our own. Or. . .we shall lose the arms race.'

Kutakhov's voice was firming up. The passions which had carried him to this spot were triumphing over a lifetime of dedication to a great cause. A cause which had suddenly betrayed those who had done most to further its early advance.

'We must have the AWACS technology if we are to survive. Yes, it is as bad as that. Every bit as bad. I am talking about *survival*! For defence. For attack. Comrades, I am not blind, not a fool.' He spread his hands to embrace the room. 'You all know what is coming as well as I do. First, Afghanistan. Next, who knows? Poland? A warm-water port? Durrazzo, perhaps? Dubrovnik, even? Without a plane to match the AWACS these are dreams, unrealisable dreams. But. . .their answer was no. Detente, they told us. SALT. No, no, and again. . .no.'

The old man replaced his hands on the lectern. They were shaking.

'Such hypocrisy is sickening. We all know what the long-term strategic plans are. But because they're too mean to spend money on proper equipment they're prepared to sacrifice any number of troops, to overwhelm by sheer force of numbers. Comrades, I lived through the Great Patriotic War, like many of you. I won't be a party to that kind of cold slaughter ever again. What we need is machines. Technology. And so. . .here I am. You have a plan to steal this fabulous American plane. What I want to say is that I am. . .Koldunov and I are with you.' He drew a deep breath and seemed to be having trouble swallowing. 'Every one of us here in this room has taken the military oath. You know how it goes as well as I do. We have sworn unquestioningly to carry out the orders of our

18

superiors.' His voice rose. ' "If I should break this my solemn
oath then let me suffer the severe penalties of Soviet law and
the general detestation and contempt of all workers." ' He
paused, as if stricken dumb by his own incantation. The room
was stuffed to the very corners with leaden silence.

'You can have whatever you need. Planes. Men. Anything.
Only. . .' His head dropped on to his chest, so that his next
words were scarcely audible. 'If any of this comes out. . .we're
all dead. All of us.'

'Do not trouble yourself about that, Kutakhov.'

The old man raised his eyes very slowly, as if forced against
his will, to the far end of the room where the cold, bored voice
was speaking again.

'Whoever dies, it will not be you. With the Air Force on our
side, we are now invincible. And the Motherland is about to
change.'

From a common instinct nurtured by lifetimes spent in the
cold places of the world the two officers quickened their pace
as they emerged from the *dacha* and made for their car at the
foot of the steps. When the driver handed them into the back
seat the taller of the two men said, 'You are all right? They have
looked after you?' and the driver hesitated a moment before
replying, 'Yes. Thank you, comrade General.'

The taller man grunted and used the pause while the driver
went round to the front of the car to exchange an ominous
glance with his companion. It was warm in the back of the
Chaika, warm and well protected against the snowy February
night. For the first dozen miles of the journey back to Moscow
Kronkin and Mironov stared out of their respective windows,
each engrossed in his own thoughts.

No one could remember, or would own up to remembering,
who had first given them their defamatory nicknames, Little
Adolf and Fat Hermann. It would not have been during the
war, that at least was certain. Kronkin and Mironov fought
side by side in the defence of the capital and on the same
day received their five-pointed stars dangling from rectangles
of red silk. No, it was later, when these two Heroes of the
Soviet Union had found their double-niche in the GRU,

19

that the names had evolved and stuck. Kronkin: slim and short and abrasively gifted, always shouldering his way to the head of any queue. Mironov: tall and fat and jolly, his piggy eyes enveloped in folds of greasy flesh, following a step or two behind the leader, in a continual diplomatic attempt to smooth over the rough wake of his hurtling passage; rib-poking Mironov with his wet, throaty laugh. Little Adolf and Fat Hermann.

But now that they were both Lieutenant-Generals and Kronkin commanded the Military Intelligence Directorate, the nicknames, however appropriate, were not often heard. Anyone of any race who had fought the Germans in the Second World War would resent the imputations which those nick-names carried. But for Russians the insult went deeper, right down inside their souls. To them, the war and the Germans represented suffering on an unfathomable, unparalleled scale. A would-be suicide in search of a quick death could take cyanide. Or he might call Kronkin Little Adolf to his face. (With Mironov, the death would not be so quick.)

'Will you come and eat with us? After the funeral?'

Kronkin turned back to the interior of the comfortable car and lifted his hands a few inches from his knees. 'Thank you, Vladimir. But. . .no.'

He continued to sit bolt upright, hands soon replaced on his knees, which were neatly pressed together. His whole posture suggested a muted reproach for the heap that was Mironov.

'It must be hard, very hard. You should try to relax a little.'

Kronkin shook his head and smiled. 'Hard. . .yes. You love your mother, and. . .well. Even at ninety-seven.'

'A good age. Wonderful woman, *mon cher*, wonderful. I can see her now. Red scarf round her head. Rifle in her hands. She stood there, on top of that barricade, and they couldn't hit her. It was as if the bullets bounced off her dress. . .'

In spite of himself Kronkin's lips began a tired smile. He knew the occasion to which Mironov was referring; like his colleague he could recall it perfectly. His mother had been one of the first women to join the Party. During the war she had first organised the defence of Moscow, then gone out to the front to help put backbone in the Red Army. Even afterwards

20

she was always fighting, ever in the front line. Until three days ago, when the last enemy had finally slipped under her guard to deliver his merciful stroke. The one enemy against which not even the Party could prevail.

'You know, Vladimir, I don't think I could go through with this, not while she was alive. I owed it to her to wait. She wouldn't have understood.'

His solemn voice cracked, and he fell silent, suddenly engulfed by loneliness. He had never married. After his father was reported missing believed dead at the siege of Leningrad there had been just the two of them, his mother and himself, and of course there was the Party. Who needed a wife when the Party could provide father, brother, family and home? But now there was no one. Not even the Party.

Mironov, who was working up to his third divorce, tactfully stared out of the window, and said nothing. The silence lasted until they crossed the outer ring road. Then Kronkin reached across to tap Mironov's arm, and point a finger towards the driver's glass partition. Mironov nodded and leaned forward.

'You can drop us both off at General Kronkin's flat, Turasov.'

'Certainly, comrade General.'

A few minutes later the Chaika swung silently into Arbat, passed the Ministry of Foreign Trade, and drew up outside a discreetly superior apartment block set well back from the road. The two Generals got out and Kronkin dismissed Turasov until the next day. They stood on the pavement and watched the car's tail lights disappear, travelling north-east towards the city centre. It was sufficiently late for there to be very little other traffic. Kronkin waited until the big car was almost out of sight before he raised his arm. At once a black Zhiguli pulled away from its place by the kerb a few metres from where the two men were standing and drove off in pursuit of the Chaika.

'I still can't believe it,' muttered Mironov. 'A good man like that, it doesn't make sense. Fantastic driver, too. . .'

'Not tonight,' Kronkin said drily. 'He made several mistakes. And my source is perfectly sound. He assures me that Turasov has been spying on us, and tonight we took good care to see he had all the chances he needed. "Looked after" indeed! We know he refused to join the other drivers, we know he had no dinner. Where was he all that time, eh? I'll tell you: listening to Kutakhov come over to *us*! By tomorrow morning we'll know just how much he's managed to learn, and pass on. It can't be much. We've been careful enough.'

'Suppose it *is* true. . . I wonder who the customer will turn out to be,' Mironov said thoughtfully as he took his chief's arm and began to steer him towards the revolving door at the entrance to the flats. 'The most boring answers so often turn out to be right. Twenty roubles say it's the Americans.'

'No,' said Kronkin quietly. 'Not the Americans.'

Turasov had the heater turned up to full blast. His feet were like ice. His teeth were chattering, his clothes were soaked through with sweat that rapidly chilled against his skin. He was driving atrociously, and he knew it. What he needed, what he must have, was a drink. Vodka would help him, but it wasn't the cure. For Turasov's malady there was no cure.

Fear.

He had been afraid many times before. If you worked for the GRU that was only natural. But not like this. Never like this.

A strange sound forced itself between his lips. Turasov felt suddenly ashamed. He was whimpering. And he couldn't stop.

The car lurched against the kerb and he put on the hand-brake, forgetting to disengage gear. The engine stalled with a great expiring shudder. Turasov very badly needed to go to the lavatory but there was no time. He was already late. The burden of knowledge was slowly pressing him down into the mire. He felt that unless he could share it soon he would lose his reason.

He almost ran down the side street and rounded the corner into Sverdlova Ploschad. He did not see the two dark shapes which copied his every move as closely as if they were bound to him by invisible wires, always maintaining a steady twenty metres between them and their quarry. Turasov saw nothing as he pushed his way through the crowd of theatregoers leaving the Bolshoi. He had eyes for only one thing. . .and there it was. The Marx Monument.

Twenty metres behind him the two men watched Turasov. In the shadow of the monument they could just make out a second figure, crowned by a large fedora with an extravagant brim. For several moments Turasov and the man in the wide-brimmed hat spoke urgently; then they moved away into the pool of blue light thrown by a nearby standard, and one of the men from Kronkin's black Zhiguli raised a tiny camera.

The picture was interesting. It revealed Turasov's back to the camera, and the profile of a middle-aged man, his hand gripping the chauffeur's upper arm, talking animatedly. The expression on the middle-aged man's face beneath the fedora was curious. It registered sheer, stark terror.

As the GRU officer lowered his camera the man in the hat glanced sideways and for a second looked straight at him. Immediately the GRU men moved forward, shouldering their way through the tatters of the rapidly dispersing crowd. In the same instant the man cried out to Turasov as if in anguish and pushed him away; then he was running.

Without a word the GRU officers separated. The photographer moved smartly forward to slot his arm through the crook of Turasov's before the dumbfounded driver could realise what was happening. As he turned to face the black shadow which held him the second GRU officer raced past on his way after the man in the fedora.

Before he had gone many metres he realised that he was dealing with a professional.

The entrance to the Metro by the Central Lenin Museum serves not one station but three: Marx Prospekt, Sverdlova Square and Revolution Square. It is also a junction where three lines meet. As he caught a glimpse of the man in the fedora disappearing down the escalator it occurred to his pursuer that there could be few more suitable venues for a clandestine rendezvous than the one he had just witnessed. Besides affording good all-round visibility, Sverdlova Square gave on to this perfect bolt hole. He put on speed, thrusting aside the few late-night theatregoers who still obstructed the escalator. At the bottom he caught sight of the large hat, now revealed as dark grey, rounding a distant corner. The click of running footsteps bounced back at him from the ornate marble

23

columns which adorned the concourse. He had begun to sweat, and not only from exertion: the thought of going back to Kronkin without Turasov's contact was not a pleasant one. The GRU officer had been hand picked for this job because he was very good. The best, in fact. Failure was out of the question.

His quarry was making for the Arbatsko-Pokrouskaya line. As the officer pounded on to the north-bound platform he saw the fedora at its far end, the man's face turned towards him. Something about the expression was daunting in its effect, enough to make the pursuer hesitate for an instant before launching himself forward, one hand fumbling for his gun.

'*Odnu mjnutu!*'

The quarry grimaced in what might almost have been a smile, but he did not wait a minute. Instead, he jumped down between the rails, flashed a last look towards the GRU officer, who by now was halfway along the platform, and disappeared into the tunnel.

Without thinking the officer followed him. Only when the darkness of the tunnel had already swallowed him up did he realise that you cannot run in such conditions.

He came to a dead stop. Behind him the platform looked impossibly far away, as if viewed from the wrong end of a telescope. Suddenly he guessed that he must be silhouetted against the lights of the station. He wheeled round to face down the tunnel, peering blindly into the gloom. As he did so an insect seemed to rasp over his head with an angry hum.

Bullet.

The GRU man dropped to a crouch. His throat was suddenly very dry. He knew he must get down low but the third, live rail was within inches of his shoes. He shut his eyes and willed himself to think calmly.

It was growing colder in the tunnel.

The officer stumbled forward a few steps, trying to present as small a target as possible. The cold was becoming more intense. For a second he thought it was because he had moved further away from the warmth of the platform. Then it dawned.

A train was coming.

He stood upright and wheeled round, breaking into a run. Another bullet buzzed past his ear, this time to the left and low. But the rails at his feet were already alive and twanging with the rhythm of the oncoming train; the cold draught had become a gale; he could hear the rapid clank of the wheels. He shot a quick look over his shoulder and saw lights rushing towards him. In that split second it was impossible to gauge distances but the lights were close, far too close, and gaining rapidly.

The GRU officer began to sprint.

Now his head was filled with the roar of the train. The walls of the tunnel acted as a sounding board, siphoning the metallic rattle of the racing wheels nearer and nearer, amplifying their pulse beyond endurance. His head seemed ready to burst with blood. His heart was pumping dementedly. Steel on steel, the engine, lights. . .

He had nearly reached the platform. He cast another glance over his shoulder and shrieked, for the train was almost upon him and in the same flash of time the horn blared out to drown his terrified scream.

He heard the high-pitched screech of overtaxed brakes, faced the front once more, and bent for a last agonising effort. Every vein, every muscle fought to contain the impossible overload which his spent body demanded. Then his foot caught in a sleeper and he went flailing forwards with a squeal of terror, helplessly surrendering to death which he had not sought, the last outrage . . .

Even as he fell a militiaman and a porter, who had seen him coming and with instinctive presence of mind were kneeling on the platform, grabbed him and simultaneously threw their combined weights backwards. The GRU officer flew upwards and rolled over their prostrate bodies to lie motionless on the concrete apron, flecked by the light thrown from the windows of the train as it smashed into the station and ground to a halt halfway down the platform, its wheels locked.

The GRU officer lay on his back and gazed at the curved ceiling of Revolution Square station. With part of his brain he dimly acknowledged gratitude (he did not know to whom) at being alive. But as full consciousness returned another part of him began almost to wish that he had died back there in the tunnel. Because now he was going to have to return to Kronkin and report that as he fell forward on to the track he had, in what he believed to be the last split second of his life, noticed something: the rails were so arranged that a man — even a man wearing a fedora — might lie between them, without being electrocuted, and remain there unscathed while a train passed overhead, and might then get up, and dust himself down, and walk on up the tunnel. . .

But if you noticed these things (he could almost hear Kronkin say it), then please tell me this, comrade. . .why did you not do likewise?

3

Margaret Bryant consulted the map when they stopped for petrol in Besançon and decided to fork left for Pontarlier and Vallorbe rather than risk the more direct route through La Cure. It was February, there was snow even in England and reports as to the state of the pass conflicted. It was best to take no chances. She drove on without troubling to wake her husband, content to let him rest and having no use for his advice on the matter. She did not expect any trouble. They were travelling on passports which Sir Richard reserved for occasions such as this, when privacy was of the essence, and although the photographs were authentic the names were not. In northern Europe there is but minimal control over frontier traffic, and no one was interested in an elderly couple making for the Alps in a T registration Rover.

Only when they crossed into Switzerland at a little after nine at night did the policeman gently shake the slumbering passenger for long enough to examine his face in the direct light of a torch before waving them through. Bryant mumbled a gentle protest, but he was not surprised. With five of the world's most powerful Foreign Ministers and a Soviet Deputy Prime Minister conferring in Geneva their Swiss hosts could be excused a touch of uneasy zeal.

The beam revealed to the officer a pale, cheesy face of a smoothness unexpected in one whose passport proclaimed him to be sixty-seven years of age; blue eyes, neatly brushed grey-white hair, little else. The Englishman's expression was devoid of all content, and not merely from sleepiness: it was as if he had long ago been schooled to erase any trace of his innermost thoughts from the tell-tale screen of the face.

A slight deflection of the torch disclosed the taut, sharp-chinned profile of a woman of indeterminate age who looked into the light through hostile narrow eyes, defying the police-man to notice the downturned corners of her mouth where contempt and bored amusement bickered for supremacy.

An English male face and, perhaps, an archetypal female French one. The policeman consulted the second passport. Ah, no, Scottish.

Nothing suspicious there.

It was very late when Lady Bryant left the autoroute at Nyon and started the ascent to the Col de St Cergue. These roads were the worst they had encountered on the journey from London and now she was forced to keep her speed down. The Embassy instructions were short and precise. Right at the end she missed the turning up to the chalet, and had to reverse back round an awkward bend for the second attempt, but a few moments later she was pulling up outside the darkened house. She switched off the engine, relishing the feel of slackening muscles after eight solid hours behind the wheel. Her husband hated driving, whereas she loved it. When he told her that they were going to Switzerland for a few days, taking the car, she could hardly believe her luck. Until he added that it was on business.

Everything was silent. Even the sound of her husband's regular breathing hardly seemed to disturb the dark peace around her. She wound down the window and lit a cigarette, enjoying a short rest before the hassle of unpacking. Through the gap came the smell of hot oil and the squeaks of the cooling engine. She inhaled deeply and held down the smoke.

'Why have we stopped?'

Margaret Bryant sighed and threw her half-smoked cigarette to die with a fizzle in the snow outside. 'Because we're here. We've arrived.'

There was a second of silence, followed by a rustle as Bryant sat up and rubbed his eyes. 'Time?'

'Gone three.'

'You found it all right?'

'Of course. The notes were very good. I'm not a moron.'

She got out, taking nothing with her, and stared up at the façade. No chink of light showed anywhere.

'You'd better put the headlights on. I can't see a damn thing out here.'

The twin beams came on, illuminating the front door at the top of a short flight of steps. She heard the squeak of her husband's shoes on the hard, compacted snow and did not bother to turn round, knowing from the jingle of keys that soon she would be inside, wrapped round a large glass of duty free scotch.

'They've all gone to bed. I don't blame them.'

'No "they". Just us.'

She wheeled round in disbelief. 'Oh God, Richard, do you have to make jokes at times like this?'

Bryant inserted a key in the lock and after a moment the door swung open. He fiddled for the light, found it, and exclaimed with satisfaction.

'No joke,' he said, as he returned to the car for the bags. 'I told you this was business, Margaret, but you would come.'

It was not in the Bryants' nature to quarrel. He was a life-long Roman Catholic with strict views on the sanctity of marriage; Margaret Bryant (née McGregor) had the dour Presbyterian heritage bound into her as thoroughly as salt into an over-seasoned omelette. Such couples do not row. They have silences.

This silence lasted for the best part of two days.

Nothing had been overlooked by the Embassy. On the kitchen table was a long typewritten note covering everything

28

from the whereabouts of the made-up beds to the existence of half a litre of fresh milk in the refrigerator. At ten o'clock precisely (so ran the note) a maid would come in for two hours to tidy up and prepare meals for later in the day; at ten o'clock next morning a maid came in and did precisely that.

The Bryants did not go out, he because he could not risk being absent when the summons came, and she having no desire to quit the stuffy warmth indoors. Fortunately the chalet was large enough for them not to have to meet except at mealtimes, when both of them read. Lady Bryant steadily worked her way through Proust's *Remembrance of Things Past*; Sir Richard studied newspapers in four languages. When he was not eating or reading he walked up and down the long room at the front of the house, deep in thought.

There was one brief interlude: on the morning of the second day Harding, the local Section Chief, brought Gerald Gilchrist to meet Bryant. Sensing the young man's nervousness at his first encounter with C, the Head of the Service, Bryant sent Harding out and questioned Gilchrist minutely about his encounters with PB/7. Two hours of being forced to recall past events in one-second units gave Gilchrist a headache and incidentally recruited him to the ranks of those who thought that Harding set out to emulate Bryant. 'Like a robot,' he told Cheryl later, with feeling. 'China-blue baby doll eyes. And cold right through to the heart. . .'

After they had left, C declined lunch, preferring instead to lie down on his bed at the top of the house and try to convince himself that he wasn't lost on some wild goose chase, the purpose of which always eluded him.

By the end of the second day he was sick with the fatigue always engendered in a healthy man who is forced to remain indoors. But he dare not go out. He could not even risk going beyond the range of the telephone bell. At tea time he exchanged a few words with his wife and the atmosphere thawed sufficiently for them to spend the rest of the evening together by the log fire, engrossed in their reading matter. There was a television but neither of them cared for it. Likewise the radio.

After forty years of childless marriage it perhaps came down to this. They respected each other. They may even have

29

cherished each other. But they loved the silence.

At half past eleven Lady Bryant put aside *Swann's Way* and poured herself a nightcap for taking upstairs to bed. Bryant toyed with the idea of telling her that they were going home next day, and abandoned it. One more day. He would give Povin one more day. If it really was Povin, and if Povin really did want to see him, and if Povin knew where he was staying, and if Povin was not terminated by his own side, and if. . .

'One more day,' he said aloud, and his wife turned round in surprise.

The man on the hillside above the chalet felt comfortably at home in the snowbound landscape — the pines, with their feathery white burdens, the squeak of ice beneath his feet whenever he carefully changed position, the sharp-scented ethereal darkness around him, were all things which reminded him of Zhukovka. Even the little wooden house, with its solitary light shining from a downstairs window, somehow spoke of home. Only the river was missing, the silver-white curl under the moon which always told him that he was into the last mile, made him quicken his pace with thoughts of a fire, and whisky.

He had been standing in the shadow of a tree for over an hour now. It was in his nature to be cautious.

Somewhere close by a heavily laden branch divested itself of a day's snow with a 'swish', making the man start. He could not stay here for ever. Forward or back? Forward. . .

He moved silently down the slope until he was within thirty metres of the chalet. No one hindered him. Nothing stirred. Apart from the light sound of his own footfall, the woods remained silent.

The man took out a cigarette and, with the aid of a pin, fixed it to a branch of the nearest tree. Then, standing at arm's length, he lit it. He had been keeping it for just this purpose for some days; the dry tobacco sizzled and at once began to glow in the darkness. Immediately the man ducked away and to one side, waiting to see what would happen.

The wind moved the branch to and fro, so that anyone watching might think that the smoker was alert, engaged in some activity. The man waited. Nothing disturbed the peace of the night. At last he was satisfied. The Bryants were alone.

Cautiously, testing every step before he put his weight down, the man began the final descent to the rear of the house, keeping his hands in the pockets of his greatcoat. The left hand fumbled with a hank of cheesewire, twisted into a running noose so that a skilful user — the man was very skilful — could take off a sentry's head in less than a second.

The right hand clutched a crucifix.

Lady Bryant was on the bottom stair when she heard the soft scratching at the door behind her. At first she thought it was her imagination, or the wind, but the mysterious noise repeated itself at regular intervals, always in the same urgent rhythm. She turned round, irritated. It was on the tip of her tongue to call her husband, but then she shrugged and decided to see for herself.

She opened the door to reveal only a black, rectangular hole. No one was out there. It must have been the wind, then — a branch rustling against the eaves, something like that. Strange she had never heard it before.

She was in the process of closing the door, actually pushing it to, when a whirl of grey twisted round the right-hand side of the frame, coming to rest against the inside wall of the hallway. Lady Bryant gasped, blinked, and found herself staring at a tall man in his early sixties, with grey-white hair and prominent ears which stood out slightly from the side of his head; for a split second she thought herself face to face with some demon from Hieronymus Bosch. Surprise left her with a void in the pit of her stomach. Momentarily she fought for breath.

The man never took his eyes off her. With his right hand he reached out and closed the door very fast but very softly also. There was a smile on his face, the slightly impertinent smile of one who has pulled off a clever trick and is pleased.

As the shock wore off she was woman enough to notice that the smile was reflected in his eyes.

'Who the devil. . .?'

On hearing the Scottish outrage in her voice the intruder's smile widened, and he gently raised a forefinger to his lips.

31

Lady Bryant had the uneasy feeling that he was proposing a conspiracy to her: something clandestine and perhaps a shade improper. She was about to speak again when she saw the man's eyes suddenly narrow and fasten on something over her shoulder. She wheeled round to see her husband framed in the doorway of the living room at the front of the house.

For a long moment he did not appear to notice her at all. She had never seen him look so distant, so intent. Half unwillingly she turned back to the stranger, only to see her husband's expression mirrored on his own face. Between them, they obliterated her. She did not exist.

Then Bryant spoke, and she saw that he was in her world again.

'It's all right, Margaret. It's all right.'

He smiled at her, and it seemed that the tensions of the past few days had drained out of him, to be replaced by a sensation of almost unutterable relief, relief akin to serenity.

'Well then, I'll. . .'

She was reluctant to leave the two of them alone together. The look which she had seen pass between her husband and the stranger disturbed her deeply.

'You go to bed,' Bryant prompted her. 'Oh, and Margaret . . . I'll be late.' An echo of that earlier look. 'Very late, I'm afraid.'

Without looking at the intruder again she went quickly up the stairs to her bedroom.

For a few moments after she had gone the two men held their respective positions; then the stranger moved slowly forward until he was standing a few inches away from Bryant. There was a pause, while they continued to weigh each other up; the stranger reached out with a sudden movement to grasp Bryant's hands in his own; for a brief second they gripped; then the man pushed on past into the living room.

Bryant followed more slowly. His visitor was taking off his overcoat, kicking his boots against the hearth, casually making himself at home.

'May I offer you a drink, General Povin?'

The stranger looked up to see that Bryant was holding an unopened bottle of *petrovka*, and smiled. 'You do your homework.'

His English was excellent, Bryant noticed; the reports were true. 'If the British Secret Intelligence Service could not discover that the Head of the First Main Directorate was partial to a particular brand of vodka, it would not stay in business very long.'

'But what it seems the British Secret Intelligence Service could *not* discover is that I gave up *petrovka* four years ago.'

Povin had taken off his boots and socks, and was toasting his bare feet before the fire. He looked up quizzically, as if inviting a fellow Grandmaster to make his next move. Bryant did some quick mental arithmetic.

'After the Kyril affair?'

'As you say, Sir Richard. After the Kyril affair.'

Again that quizzical look, this time like a tutor who leads a bright student towards a connection. A moment's reflection was enough to give Bryant the answer.

'Ah. It was the price.'

Povin nodded. The tutor was pleased. 'Yes,' he said drily. 'The price of salvation. A life for a bottle of vodka. But there are limits. I would like a tumbler of Scotch whisky, please. Nothing in it.'

Bryant complied. The first exchange was a draw, he decided. But now he must concentrate on what was to come. He knew that down in the cellar the spools were slowly turning, recording for posterity one of the most remarkable conversations to which he had ever been a party. Analysis could wait.

Bryant sat down opposite the General and took a sip from his own glass. He found the sight of the Russian's bare feet incongruous, somehow out of all proportion to the seriousness of the meeting, and strove to concentrate. Povin looked fresh, he noted; fresh and unworried.

'We have not spoken, you and I, since the Kyril business. I was concerned for you.'

Povin shrugged. 'I went to ground. These last four years I have had to work so hard against you. Cover, you see. I am sorry, but. . .' He spread his hands and made a *moue* with his lips. 'It was little enough I did for you before, in any case.'

'It was enough.'

'You think so?' Povin sounded pleased. 'Well, maybe. But

33

when they shot Michaelov and promoted me to his place, I had no choice. Not everyone was fooled. To this day not everyone thinks he was the traitor.'

'Aach. . .' Bryant had not meant to betray his disappointment but the news, although expected, was bad. 'You are under suspicion? You are watched?'

'Oh, yes.' For the first time Povin showed signs of unease. He put down his glass on the table beside his chair and sat forward, clasping his hands in front of him. 'Friendly faces to the front. Saluting. Chauffeur-driven Chaika. Hot line to the Kremlin. But behind my back. . . It's the same for us all, of course. Hence this wretched Committee.'

'Ah, the interregnum. The KGB without a Chairman. Interesting, that.'

'For us, impossible. When Stanov resigned as Chairman. . . Hell, when Stanov was given the push. . .the boys in the Central Committee had had enough. No more Number One, just a board of the Heads of Directorates. Do you know, even the casting vote goes to someone different at each meeting? I tell you, we're getting more like a fat capitalist company every day.'

'It was always a little hard for some of us to tell the difference.'

Povin grinned, swallowed his drink, and held out the glass for more. 'So things are bad for us. Apart from the backbiting and the distrust, which were always there, people are starting to say we don't need the KGB any more. Detente. Who needs spies when you've got detente?'

Bryant returned from the sideboard with Povin's drink. 'Somehow I don't think you need worry about that.'

'You've seen the papers?' Povin waved his arm in the direction of the pile of newsprint round Bryant's chair. 'I don't have to tell you what they're saying. Why is everybody in Geneva, anyway? The Kremlin announces out of the blue a plan for limiting theatre nuclear weapons and schedules to it a timetable for reducing the number of missile silos in the Soviet Union. SALT 3 well on the way to signature. Geneva talks extended by two days to enable trade delegations to negotiate with direct access to the Foreign Ministers personally. Do you

34

believe it? Do you believe *any* of it?'

Bryant sensed that they were coming to the point. He was not yet ready for that. When they settled down to business it would be at a time of his own choosing.

'In the light of what you have said, your presence here, in this house, concerns me.'

Povin laughed contemptuously. 'It needn't. Officially, I'm here on a junket. I haven't had a holiday for years. They fitted me out with a woman and sent me off to stay at one of the best hotels on the lake. You want to know what's happening in my bedroom right now? Nataja, my "friend", is fast asleep — my God, how that woman can sleep! — and she won't wake up until gone ten tomorrow. During the day they watch my every move, but at night. . .that's another matter. Who's got the guts to walk through *my* bedroom door, eh?' He laughed again. 'No one's going to interrupt, Sir Richard. You're safe.'

During this explanation a look of profound distaste had percolated upwards through layer after layer of professional, studied indifference to find unwilling expression on Bryant's face. Povin noticed it and grimaced.

'You disapprove.'

'I neither approve nor disapprove. What you have been describing, though not in so many words, is what I would regard as a necessity of the service.'

Povin threw back his head and laughed. 'I shall remember that. How right that is! A necessity of the service. . .'

'But one which must have been particularly unpleasant for you.'

The irony was lost on the Russian. He merely shrugged and said, 'In the Soviet Union we regard these things differently. Even the most devout of us. We recognise them for what they are. Venial sins. You English call them venial and then do everything in your power to make them mortal. Not like us. . .' His voice drifted away. 'We who have real sins on our consciences. Real deaths. . . Aach! You hypocrites don't fool anyone.' Again the short, sharp laugh. 'Except maybe yourselves. What was that?'

Somewhere overhead they heard a loud noise. A few seconds' thought sufficed to reassure Bryant that some snow had slipped from the eaves, but Povin was suddenly nervous. He rose and hurried to the window, fingering aside the drapes.

'I should stay away from the windows, General.'

Bryant rose also; he went across to the door and extinguished all the lights. Povin flicked back the curtain, slowly returned to the fire, now the only source of illumination, and resumed his seat. For several moments there was silence.

'It was the snow, I think. It quite often does that. Another drink?'

The offer came out more pointedly than Bryant intended. Povin's refusal was correspondingly brusque.

Bryant was quite happy to allow the silence to continue. Any interview of this kind, conducted on such a rarefied plane, was bound to be a delicate mechanism much prone to minor breakdowns. There were no precedents. Perhaps once in ten years, no more, two men met like this, and spoke, and altered the fates of their respective worlds. The point would present itself, in due course.

'General. . .' Bryant sat forward to rest his elbows on his knees, rolling his glass between his cupped hands. There was a new note of diffidence in his voice which caused the Russian to look up sharply. 'I think this may be difficult for you, what I am about to say. If it is, you will tell me. But we may not meet again, and I cannot afford to lose this opportunity.'

'Go on.'

'What was it like, for you. . .four years ago?'

Bryant sat back so that his face could no longer be seen in the reflected firelight by the man opposite, and waited. For a long while all that could be heard in the darkened room was the crackling of the logs in the grate. Just when the silence was becoming a refusal to answer the question, Povin spoke.

'So difficult, so very difficult. Yes, you are right. It began on the day of the gala. I shall never forget it. You know, of course, that Stolyinovich and I are friends. There was a gala at the Bolshoi, and for the first time he was named leading artist. What a moment in his career it was! The supreme accomplishment. To lead at the Bolshoi. . .'

He tailed off. Bryant waited patiently, confident now that the rest would come.

36

'I had arranged a party afterwards. We had a box, one of the best. For days we had been going about like men holding our breath. And then, on the very morning of the gala performance. . .'

In the dim light Bryant could just see him raise his hands to his temples, as if striving to recapture the substance of the memory.

'Stanov had us all in. There was no reason to expect anything. Until we saw him. He'd had a stroke, of course, but we didn't know that then. He looked terrible. Half dead. Then he told us about Bucharensky. . .' Povin grunted. 'About Kyril.'

Not even Bryant's professional reserve was quite proof against the fateful name. He sat up abruptly. 'Yes? He told you. . .?'

'He told us that his trusted assistant had run off with half the contents of the blue safe, several thousand roubles, and the name of a top-ranking traitor in the Organs. And that he'd conveniently left behind a diary to prove it. We all had a look. It was in Bucharensky's handwriting. I recognised it and I imagine the rest did too. He gave us all the clues. . .but not the name.'

Povin stood up and began to roam about. Notwithstanding Bryant's earlier warning, the windows seemed to hold a special fascination for him. Bryant found himself uneasily wondering whether Povin was as alone as he claimed.

'I don't remember much else about that day. I suppose I went to the gala, the party even, I don't know. Oh, yes. . . I remember looking round the other faces in Stanov's room and thinking, My God, you all look as guilty as hell. When in fact it's me, I'm the one who's been giving away secrets all these years. . . And then I survived my first day without being arrested. Then another. A third. My brain began to work again. I examined the possibilities. There was never any doubt about what I must do, once I began to think properly. Michaelov had to go. Somehow Stanov had to be made to think that Michaelov was the traitor. After that it was easy.'

'Easy?'

More irony, also lost.

'I had much going for me. Everyone loathed Michaelov.

37

Round the Square people were openly saying that it was him, as little as two days after Stanov broke the news. Then once I'd got Michaelov thinking that Stanov himself might be the traitor he started to make mistakes. He sent an executioner after Kyril, and that was the breakthrough.'

'But what *was* Kyril?'

'A blind. A trap. Stanov sent him off because he knew that I — the traitor "I" — would have to stop him. If he was monitoring us all, he would have been bound to know of any attempt to interfere with Kyril. Bucharensky never knew anything. And Stanov lied to him. I'm convinced of that. It's why he failed at the end.'

'Ah, the end. But what was the end?'

'Kyril got the name. My name. I'm sure of that. But Royston tried to persuade him to share it. Kyril didn't trust Royston. He gave the wrong name — Michaelov's. And then Royston killed him. In cold blood.'

Now it was Povin's turn to enjoy the silence. Bryant looked up from the detail of the Russian's story, saw the monstrous tidal wave poised to crash down on him, and braced himself.

'It is one of the things I have come here to tell you, Richard.'

After all the hard talking that had gone before, Povin's voice sounded amazingly gentle.

'Royston's ours. Or rather, mine. I have been running the Head of your London Station for years.'

She awoke not knowing where she was, her brain teeming with undefined images. Darkness, a strange taste of iron in her mouth, cold. . . the duvet had fallen off the bed. She felt for it in vain, hesitated a moment, then sat up and switched on the bedside light. Not much of a risk, after all. General Stepan was a heavy sleeper and anyway, even if he did wake, he wasn't likely to be angry. Not like some.

Nataja caught sight of herself in the dressing-table mirror and instinctively raised a hand to push her hair back into some kind of shape. Not bad, said those instincts, not bad for. . .she consulted the travelling clock which Stepan had given her, a 'holiday present', he called it. . .for one-fifteen in the morning, with the weather freezing outside. Hair with plenty of body still, clear blue eyes, very wide and full, breasts. . .ah. Nataja drew in a deep breath, enjoying the reflection of the noble swell.

As always on first waking the whole of her attention was focused on herself, her body. She was alive, that was the main thing. Alive and in the West with a man who wasn't a pig. Her fleshy lips parted in a smile at the memory of their lovemaking. He had a lot of stamina for someone his age, and you didn't always expect his kind of consideration from a KGB General.

Nataja turned to inspect her second interest in life, the body of her current lover and meal ticket. And with a little pout of annoyance she realised that she was alone.

Her mouth was parched and she had a headache. But they hadn't drunk very much the night before, and she was off those funny tablets now. Odd. She wanted to go to the bathroom, for water and codeine. Nataja hoped the old boy wasn't going to spend all night over what he was doing in there. Somehow the older ones always seemed to be constipated. . .

She took a cigarette from the packet on the bedside table and lit it, watching her reflection carefully to see if she could capture that way of exhaling used by the heroine in the movie they had seen the day before. It looked effortless on the screen but turned out to be difficult in practice. She tried it several times and failed. Suddenly impatient, she swung her legs off the bed and went to stand by the bathroom door.

'Stepan?'

Her voice was low and coaxing. When she received no reply her hand dropped to the handle and she hesitated, suddenly frightened. Suppose he'd had a heart attack? Or cut his throat? Nataja shivered. You read about such terrible things these days.

She tried the handle and pushed. There was enough light from the bedroom to show her at once that the bathroom was empty.

For several minutes the absence of her protector made no impression on Nataja, whose thoughts never strayed very far from her own body and its requirements. She squatted on the lavatory and resumed her examination of the face in the mirror opposite, drank two glasses of water and swallowed a painkiller. Only then did it start to dawn on her, in a confused kind of way, that something might be wrong.

She wandered back into the bedroom, pulling on her dressing gown, and went to stand by the window. Below her, to the left, the lights of Versoix shimmered out across the lake. For several moments she stood there irresolutely, not knowing what to do. Then her instinct for self-preservation, never far below the surface, asserted itself. If nothing was wrong she would make a fool of herself, that was all; so be it. At least it would look as though she cared. But suppose somewhere, somehow, an irregularity *had* occurred. If she said nothing and the irregularity nevertheless came to light, her silence might be held against her. She could come under suspicion. The KGB would take her off the Special List. They would never let her come out to the West again.

That clinched the matter. Nataja began to sort out her clothes. She would report that an irregularity had occurred. She liked that word, 'irregularity'. As well as making her feel important, it was also neutral. It implied nothing. It accused no one.

A few minutes later she emerged quietly from the bedroom and looked to right and left. The corridor was empty. The third room along was occupied by the security officer. He would know what to do.

As she passed the door of the room next to theirs, however, she became aware that it was ajar. She stopped. Coming from inside were the sounds of low voices, with the occasional click of cards and clink of glasses. Nataja gnawed her lip. Stepan liked a game of cards, he had told her so. Wasn't she perhaps making too much of all this?

While she hesitated the door in front of her opened wider to reveal a corner of the vestibule, and she jumped back. The noises were louder now, coming through a crack in the door which led to the bedroom. Nataja craned to get a better look, but as she did so a dark shadow interposed itself between her and the lighted gap.

'Yes? What is it? You cannot sleep?'

She looked up uneasily, conscious that her heart was beating too fast for comfort. Without his habitual grey fedora Povin's henchman seemed almost naked, although he was dressed in a suit. The dim light of the corridor did strange things to the scar on his neck, making of it an open wound, a black orifice, liquid, obscene. . .

'Victor, I. . . General Stepan wasn't in his room. I thought . . .maybe. . .'

'He is relaxing. With some of his staff. The General likes to relax, you know that.'

She stared up at his unwinking eyes and there read an unmistakable command. As if to reinforce it the man called Victor slowly raised his arm to bar the doorway. But still Nataja hesitated.

Then she heard Stepan laugh, and in spite of herself she felt her body untense. She could picture him, now; it had all become real. He was sitting at a table, head thrown back in that splendid way of his, and he was laughing at the ceiling. Yes, that was General Stepan, the Stepan she had come to know so well these past few days.

The man in the doorway watched her as she turned and retraced her steps along the corridor, waiting until he heard the sound of her bedroom door closing. Only when he was satisfied that she was not coming back did he shut the door of his own room and retreat to his chair by the side of the tape recorder, which was about to embark on an argument over who had led the ace of clubs.

Povin searched his host's face for signs of a reaction to the news of Royston's treachery. Bryant said nothing. He was ruthlessly willing himself into a state of artificial calm.

'That's how I know what happened at the end. The first thing I did after I landed Michaelov's job was read Royston's report. Kyril gave him the name. Royston shot him and exchanged guns, so that it looked like suicide. Crude, but at the end of a crisis like that one, who's looking too closely? And anyway, he couldn't afford to see Kyril taken alive. He just might have talked. So Royston took a chance, and it paid off. Nothing to say?'

Bryant stirred. When he spoke his voice, to his irritation, cracked.

'You know very well what the possibilities are, General. Royston may conceivably be a traitor, but I shall have to make inquiries to ensure that no injustice is done through a KGB plot to discredit one of my senior officers. Or he may not be a traitor, in which case we have very successfully been fooling you these past few years.'

Povin laughed and shook his head. 'All this is true. Although if my motive was to discredit Michael Royston I think I might have found a simpler way. But there is another thing. . .'

The Russian rose and went over to his greatcoat. He fumbled in the pocket, and when he turned Bryant saw that he was carrying something in his hands, something that glittered in the firelight.

'I want to make a present to you. I want you to have this. Something that will remind you, whenever you see it, that we once met in this room, and talked face to face.'

He grasped Bryant's right hand and stuffed the glittering object into it, holding it there for a few seconds with a powerful squeeze. Then he stepped back, and Bryant saw that what he had been given was a crucifix. He looked up uncomprehendingly.

Povin shook his head and smiled. 'It is on that, the present which I give you, that I tell you. On the body of Our Lord Himself, Royston is working for the KGB.'

He sat down again. After a moment he reached out for his socks, lying in front of the fire, found that they were dry and began to put them on. There was a long silence.

'You said earlier, that was one of the things you had come to tell me. What else is there, General?'

Povin pulled up the last sock, wriggled his toes and grunted with satisfaction. Then he clapped his hands to his knees and turned to face Bryant.

'Down there in Geneva, they're gabbling about trade. Guns and butter, you understand, very commendable. I, too, wish to make a trade.'

Bryant raised his hands, palms outwards, like a bad priest recoiling from a sinner. 'I have no authority to negotiate, you must understand that. Also, money is in short supply at the moment.'

'Oh, I know all that. I don't expect an answer now, and money hardly enters into it.'

'I am prepared to listen.'

'Good. This, then, is the picture. You will know that relations between the KGB and the GRU are normally excellent. You even have a theory, or so I'm told, that the GRU is just another branch of the Organs, but I can assure you that the Chief Intelligence Directorate of the General Staff is completely separate from us. I have good contacts there. Or rather, I *had*.'

'Past tense.'

'Yes.' The buoyant enthusiasm of the past hour seemed to have yielded to a more sombre mood. 'A month ago, by chance, I discovered that Military Intelligence had been pushing something of their own, without any help from anybody. Very far advanced, it was. And. . .'

'Yes?'

'Astounding. Outrageous. They're even prepared to run the risk of a full-scale war. The end of detente, oh yes, but worse than that. What they are doing is to provide the means for the hardliners in the Kremlin to stage an irreversible comeback. And they were keeping it secret, not just from us, but even from the Politburo. It sounds crazy. It *is* crazy. But somebody's backing them, and whoever it is doesn't mind taking a chance or two. Which is why I'm here. The prime reason. I want to stop it.'

'What exactly is "it"?'

'I know only the bare outlines. I'm urgently trying to get more, but there's been a setback.'

He paused, and Bryant noticed uneasily that his face had set very hard.

'I had a man in there. Very close to the top, but shit-scared all the time. About a week ago he managed to overhear part of a critical planning session. Whatever they said, it was dynamite. When he met his control he was shivering so much he could hardly talk. Before he'd managed half a dozen words the control realised they were being watched, and he ditched the contact.' Povin grimaced. 'Just as well he did. A GRU *gaybist* tried to kill my control. As for the contact. . .'

Povin sat forward and rubbed his hands together, as if the gesture could cleanse his memory of something it preferred not to retain.

'They fished him out of the Moscow River next day. At first the militia thought it was suicide: there wasn't a mark on him. But we stepped in, discreetly, and ordered an autopsy.'

Povin half grunted, half laughed.

'Someone had shoved a high-pressure air hose up his arse and turned it on. A simple message. So simple it took me the best part of a day to decipher it.'

He paused. Bryant stared at him blankly.

'I'm sorry, I don't quite. . .'

Povin looked up sharply and after a moment's hesitation he smiled. 'You fuck us up. We'll fuck you up.'

Bryant's lips twitched; otherwise he betrayed no reaction.

Povin grunted again. 'All I've got is this. Before the end of the current talks an item of American hardware is going missing. A plane. After a few days the remains of it will be found, wrecked and useless, together with the bodies of the crew. In the meantime, we shall have had it, stripped it bare, let our top scientists swarm all over it. At a base near Irkutsk, that's the only other bit of hard information I've got. So far, it's very simple. An old-fashioned case of piracy.'

'What is this hardware?'

'Apart from the fact it's a plane, I don't know. Something up to date, that's my guess, something where we're known to be short of technology.'

'But isn't that rather going to point the finger at you?'

'That's precisely it. That's what they want. A message is actually going to be passed to the President of the United States, from a hitherto reliable source, that this hardware is in Russian hands. You know what that will mean?'

Bryant thought. 'He is a hawk, certainly. Not a man to shrug off insults.'

'Sir Richard, Sir Richard. . .have you any idea how much they all look the same to us, these Presidents? You can't tell black men apart. United States' Presidents give us the same problem. *Any* President is going to react the same way. Detente will explode. However much the Politburo protest,

44

the Americans will not believe them. Both sides will come under intense internal pressure to save face and act. There will be escalation. Unforgivable words will be spoken, irreversible things done. Then the plane will be found, the victim of an ordinary technical accident, or so it will be made to seem. The world will see that we were not to blame, after all. And the Soviet Union can consider at leisure how best to deal with the blind, unthinking aggression of the United States' imperialist war machine. Clever, is it not?'

Bryant found it not only clever, but frighteningly credible. His years of experience in intelligence had taught him many things, but no lesson had ever been more thoroughly learned than the sinister danger of a 'department within a department' — the agency which suddenly goes off on a frolic of its own. In his career he had known a Deputy Director-General of DI5 who wanted to assassinate a Labour Party Prime Minister, and he had personally been called on to deal with a militant group within one of his own departments which became enmeshed in an Army plot to take over the government. But if only it were as simple as that! Every intelligence agency which went off the rails had a powerful backer, somewhere. And in the Soviet Union there were so many backers, all struggling for power.

Povin was speaking again.

'I need your help. You are the only one I can ever trust in this matter. You must make me an introduction to someone in the CIA who can handle this. A man who will react in a sane, controlled manner, who carries enough weight to meet my price without haggling. Do you know of someone you would trust to negotiate this?'

Bryant hesitated. How to tell Povin that in Washington SIS's credit was nil, all because of the Russian himself?

Stall.

'I. . .may do. But forgive me, General, you have a certain reputation where the Americans are concerned. You dislike them. You distrust them. And yet now, if I have understood your proposal correctly, you want to protect them, do them a favour. Forgive me, as I say, but I was always under the impression that it was you and I who enjoyed the. . .special

45

relationship.' Bryant's wintery smile was reflected in the emphasis he placed on the word 'special'. 'And at such a time as this, with you under surveillance, the risk. . .! This GRU plan is a matter of high policy. It is well guarded. Its betrayal would lead to great danger for you. Have you considered these things?'

'Of course.' Povin sighed. 'The big decisions are never easy. That is why only a few people are ever allowed to make them. I am one. You are another. It was agreed long ago between us, I would not be your agent, but in time of gravest danger I would help. The danger, let me tell you, is grave. I believe that.'

Bryant found it impossible to doubt the sincerity in the Russian's voice. On eight separate occasions in all, Povin had proved himself. They were enemies in name, at times they had to fight each other hard, but when it mattered, really mattered, Povin had been true. He said there was danger. Bryant believed him.

'Who is behind this?' he asked. Who is big enough? Who has the nerve?'

Povin shrugged. 'There are so many candidates. For my guess. . .Kazin. Always Kazin. Beaten, never defeated. Disgraced, never destroyed. This side of the grave, Kazin.'

The one last pure Stalinite with a vestige of authority in the Soviet Union. Bryant could still not hear the name spoken aloud without being affected. Somehow it added authenticity to all that had gone before.

The Russian too was troubled. Bryant sensed it across the short distance which separated them. He had not yet spoken the whole of his mind.

'There is another reason why I am saying this to you. A personal one.'

Bryant waited. Povin seemed to be having trouble in finding the words.

'You remember I mentioned Stolyinovich earlier. Pyotr and I. . .well, we have known each other for many years. I cannot imagine a life in which he took no part.'

Another silence. Bryant wondered where on earth this was leading.

'They have recently refused him an exit visa. For the first

time. No explanation, of course. He was due to give a recital in
New York, but he had to cancel. I just couldn't reason it out.
Why lose so much goodwill, when detente is the fashion? Then
I saw why. It was because I am here. They are holding him, Sir
Richard. Holding him as security against my return.'

'Nothing like that has ever happened before?'

'Never. Admittedly, I rarely leave the Soviet Union, but there
has never been any difficulty. No, it is a sign. Something is
about to happen, is maybe already happening. That is what
decided me. I knew I had to talk to you, meet you after all these
years.' Smilingly he shook his head. 'I must confess to a small
disappointment. You give little away, Sir Richard. Perhaps I
hoped for too much. Perhaps I wanted to cross all barriers too
quickly, in my heart. . .to touch your heart also, I think. It does
not matter. What matters is that for reasons I cannot fathom I
am under suspicion once again, and this time I am too old, too
tired, to play the game any further. I am coming out, Sir
Richard. And I intend to bring Pyotr Stolyinovich with me.'

Of all the many strange things which Povin had said to
Bryant in the course of their long conversation, this was
the most astonishing. For a moment Bryant literally could
not speak. His mind went blank. When he recovered slightly
his first thought was one of gratitude for the unthinking
reflex which had made him extinguish the lights earlier, thus
reserving to himself the friendly protection of the darkness.

The supreme head of the Soviet foreign intelligence establishment was coming out. And he, Bryant, was expected to do
whatever might be necessary to ensure success.

'You wish. . .intend. . .to defect.'

'In exchange for whatever I can find out about the GRU's
crazy plan, as I still call it to myself, and operational information which will not actually endanger agents in the
field — aach, you know the old formula — I want two new
identities, two new lives. And a little peace. Peace not the
sword. . .which is why I must trade with the Americans I
despise so much. I cannot start again without Pyotr. He
represents the only real happiness I have ever known, outside
my religious faith. I am too old to go among strangers without
one friend by my side. I have made a study of these things, and I

47

know that only the Americans have the resources and the know-how to enable two such prominent figures as us to disappear. The arm of A2 is very long. It can embrace the whole world. You know this.'

'Oh, yes. I know about your assassination squad. But there are ways of "losing" people, even in England. I would not like to think of you, General, in some small American town, eating your heart out. And Stolyinovich. . .would he be content just to disappear, not play again in public, perhaps for years; to tie himself to some teaching job in a respectable but oh-so-dull minor university? Have you thought of that? Has he?'

'We have thought of these things. It is kind of you to raise it but, forgive me once more, what you describe could happen in England also, only with less security. No, Sir Richard. I am presented with a unique opportunity. It will never come again. The few remaining years of my life can be spent in constant fear, under the shadow of a repressive and bloody regime for which I now harbour only the profoundest hatred and contempt, or it can be spent with a measure of personal freedom, of rest. If you, a Catholic like myself, were to live in Russia, you would not find the choice difficult. Not if you had as much redeeming to do as I have, when time is short. For Pyotr it is harder, but his answer is the same.'

The vibrant note of pride rang in Bryant's ears long after the interview was over, crossing even the barrier of the tape which whirled in the cellar below.

'He said, "Wherever you go, and when, there I shall go also. Let us not talk about it any more." '

Povin stood up and began pulling on his boots. 'So you see, it is the Americans or nothing. I have never dealt with them before. They would be suspicious as all hell if I went to them direct. I need a good trade reference. . .you! And I know I need a really big price to buy what I want. . . I have that now. There will never be anything as big again in our lifetimes. But we must hurry.'

He stood fully upright and reached for his coat.

'The conference has been extended by two days to give the commercial delegations a chance. This piracy must therefore happen some time before next Tuesday. I will meet you, and

48

your contact man, in St Cergue this Saturday. That gives you three days; it will be enough. Ten o'clock by the nursery ski lift. Nataja and I are attending Gromyko's going-away party the night before; no one will expect me to be up and about before midday and I shall be back in my hotel long before then.'

'I can make no promises. I will try.'

Povin was already leading the way out into the hall. Having delivered his message, he seemed anxious to be off. Bryant repressed the hundred gnawing doubts which troubled him and concentrated on immediate practicalities.

'I cannot delay my return to Moscow for much longer. I am concerned for Pyotr. And Frolov, my deputy. . .' Povin grunted. 'A good man. A little sleek for one his age, perhaps, but competent. The more I leave him alone the greater the chance he'll get some clever idea into his head about having my job.'

In the total darkness of the hallway Bryant could not see his sudden grin.

'It seems to be an occupational hazard at the top of the First Main Directorate. Therefore I must trust you to act quickly, and with resource.'

They had reached the back door.

'So now. . .goodbye.'

Neither moved. They could not quite believe that the meeting had occurred, or that it was over. Suddenly, as if seized by the same emotion, both men reached out their hands and gripped, tightly; Povin stepped back, maintaining his grasp, the hands dropped. . .the door opened for scarcely long enough to admit a breath of cold night air, and Bryant once more stood alone in the empty hall, hearing only the wind in the trees.

He had just been offered the chance to bring off possibly the greatest coup in the history of twentieth-century espionage, and he had lacked the courage to tell Povin that it was hopeless. Hopeless, because Bryant was the only man alive who could negotiate the deal. . .and perhaps the last one to whom the Americans would ever listen.

Unless. . .

Bryant walked thoughtfully back to the living room and

poured himself a large whisky. As he sat down and raised his glass to his lips he realised with irritation, but without undue surprise, that his hand was shaking.

Downstairs in the cellar the tape recorders, having failed to register a human voice for three consecutive minutes, automatically switched themselves off.

4

When Senior Lieutenant Valyalin brought round the morning tea he found Colonel Frolov in his usual working position: legs crossed, resting on the desk, hands clasped behind his head, eyes closed. The room was fuggy with a mixture of Frolov's cigarettes, the fire, fighting for its life in the narrow grate, and the background heating. Despite this soporific atmosphere Valyalin prided himself on not being deceived by what he regarded as an elaborate pose. You did not become a Colonel in the KGB and First Deputy to the Chief of a Directorate by being indolent. No, it was a front designed to mislead enemies, those without the wit to get on for themselves.

Very quietly, so as not to disturb the profound thought processes of the recumbent figure by the enormous desk, the Senior Lieutenant cleared a tiny valley in the mountain of files and papers, and left a glass of steaming tea by the Colonel's right foot. He stepped back, careful not to make a noise with his boots on the polished wooden floor, saluted respectfully and withdrew.

Frolov, unaware of the high esteem in which he was held by his second secretary, slept peacefully on.

For the past week he had had to work much harder than he was accustomed to do. Povin had gone off to Geneva leaving him a great pile of matters to attend to in addition to his own work. Frolov rather resented this, because on inspection it emerged that everything left behind by Povin could have bided his return some ten days later. This spark of resentment, such a little thing in itself, at last prompted the good Colonel to take a step which had half attracted him (and of which he had been more than half afraid) for some time.

He was going to have a look at Povin's confidential dossier.

If it ever came out that Frolov had done this, it would mean trouble. Unfortunately, Frolov was not in a position to gauge whether 'trouble' meant a bollocking, or spending the rest of his life in a labour camp. So it must not come out. And that meant taking a few precautions.

In another, natural, valley among the mountains of paper, a wafer-thin electronic clock emitted a series of high-pitched bleeps. Frolov's eyes opened; he swung his legs off the desk and sat up, switching off the alarm as he did so. He had an appointment with the General Officer of the Day.

On his way out of the office he paused by the mantelpiece and slid his thumb over Mishka. Mishka was Frolov's mascot. His daughter had made the doll in school and presented it to him on his last birthday. The craftmanship was unexciting but Frolov cherished the tiny figure, keeping it in a place of honour over the fire. (His daughter was very anxious that Mishka should not catch cold.) Whenever Frolov was about to embark on something difficult or out of the ordinary, he stroked Mishka for luck. His subordinates noticed, as subordinates always do, and laughed — but very quietly.

Mercifully the Officer of the Day was Tsutskov, Head of the Second Main Directorate, who took no interest in First's affairs. Even so, as Frolov walked down the corridor he was sweating. He stood outside the General's door straightening his uniform for a full minute longer than necessary before he could summon up the courage to knock.

'In.'

Frolov entered. By way of sharp contrast to his own desk, General Tsutskov's was bare except for a glass of water. Well, it might have been water.

'What is it, Frolov?'

51

'I need an authority to inspect the Confidential Register, comrade General.'

'You've got a pink form?'

'Here, sir.'

As he laid the double sheet of pink paper on the desk in front of the General, Frolov had to fight down a desire to snatch it back. His contact in the 14th Department, Technical and Scientific Services, had assured him that it would work, that you could actually buy the stuff in some western shops, but Frolov was a layman and he didn't trust scientists. To him it was all a piece of mumbo-jumbo magic.

Tsutskov seemed to be scanning the pink form with more than usual attention. Frolov's forehead, wiped dry outside the General's office, was suddenly running with sweat.

In fact, as Frolov should have realised, the General was only doing what the regulations required of him. The Confidential Registry of the KGB was a sensitive area. It contained the dossier of anybody who was anybody in the Soviet Union, a kind of *Who's Who*, but with more interesting details. When a palace revolution occurred, as every few years it invariably did, this registry was the store from which they took the bricks to build tombs for the departed. The fewer eyes allowed to see it in times of stability the better. The General was merely reassuring himself that Frolov's request was in order.

The pink form was divided into two halves by a perforated line. On the left-hand side was the list of names against which a search was needed: single-spaced, numbered, typed in block capitals. Underneath the last name the requisitioning officer was obliged to rule off the page and place his initials opposite, so that names could not be added clandestinely after approval by a General Officer. On the opposite side the names appeared again, in the same order but in lower case, together with a short statement of the reason for the search. Once again, the requisitioning officer had to draw a line and initial it.

Without removing his eyes from the paper Tsutskov reached out slowly for the bell-button under the lip of his desk.

Frolov watched like a man hypnotised. His jaw dropped. He simply could not believe what was happening. A lifetime's service to the Organs, he stepped out of line just once, and

52

what happened? Disaster. What had given it away? What went wrong, for the love of Lenin? Think. He must try to think. An excuse. There was always a way out, given enough time. . .

The door behind the General's chair opened to admit his first secretary. Tsutskov reached out his hand.

'Have you had my pen fixed yet?'

Without a word the Captain placed a fountain pen in General Tsutskov's hand and withdrew, closing the door behind him.

From behind a kind of blur Frolov watched as the General signed both halves of the form, detached the right-hand page for his records, and handed the remainder back to him. Tsutskov looked up when the form was not taken from him immediately, saw Frolov's still-open mouth, and observed, with uncharacteristically dry humour, 'Be careful you don't swallow it, Colonel.'

Back in his own office Frolov threw himself on to the cupboard where he and Povin kept the drink. It was no time for half-measures; he found a tumbler and filled it. Fortunately, before he had taken more than a couple of gulps he remembered that under the self-same regulations which had caused Tsutskov to scan the pink form so closely, he was obliged to execute his search in the Confidential Registry within two hours.

He pulled his chair up to the desk, swept papers on to the floor right and left, and brought his anglepoise desk lamp down to within a few inches of the pink form. His contact in the 14th Department had taught him exactly what to do. With the point of a penknife he carefully began to scrape away at the edge of the last typewritten name. Almost immediately a tiny corner of paperlike substance showed itself proud from the form. He scraped a little more, then with his fingernails he peeled back a long thin strip. The last name authorised by General Tsutskov had gone, to be replaced by that of General Stepan Ilyich Povin.

Frolov drew a deep breath and expelled it in a long sigh before hastily swigging at the tumbler by his side. Then he burned the thin pink strip, which had served its purpose. The only thing which could upset his plans now was the possibility of a comparison being made between the two halves of the form. But in practice that never happened. No one down in the Confidential Registry was going to challenge General Tsutskov's signature, especially when presented by the Acting Head of the First Main Directorate.

Under the pressure of constant expansion, many of the KGB's departments have been hived out to various locations in and around Moscow, but the Confidential Registry remains where it has always been ever since December 1918: in the basement of the headquarters building alongside Dzerzhinsky Square. It took Frolov less than half an hour to gain admittance to the heavily guarded Registry section and obtain possession of the six files which he had requisitioned. Five of them he promptly dumped on the floor. The sixth he took over to a table at the end of the narrow passage between two stacks.

The atmosphere in the basement was stuffy and cold, but Frolov didn't notice. Povin's file was very thick. He looked first at the end. There had been no entry since his last promotion to Chief of Directorate. He began to work slowly backwards. Everything glowed with honourable achievement. Frolov had rarely come across such a 'clean' file, at any level of Soviet society. He began to sense disappointment. As he went back the pages travelling under his hands started to yellow, a sign of their age. Whatever defects might have existed there, Povin would long ago have lived them down.

He had almost reached the front of the file and his mind was no longer on the job. It had been an interesting exercise, that's all. Frolov never seriously expected to find a black mark. If it ever existed, it would have effectively prevented Povin from achieving his present high station. It was getting late. He had a logjam of work to tackle back in the office. Nothing more to. . .

Frolov's hand stopped moving. He turned back a page, then another. For a second he couldn't take in the significance of what he had found. When he did, his first action was to change seats, so that his body was between the passageway and Povin's file.

He was shaking with excitement. He took out his handkerchief and mopped his forehead several times before wiping

54

off his palms. But what to do? He could not stay here long, they would be checking on him soon, he would never get another chance to come back. He forced himself to be rational, and think.

Frolov knew only certain basic facts about Registry files: for him, records were tools to be used in time of need and then promptly forgotten. He knew, for example, that although computerisation was making giant strides in the Square, it had not yet reached this basement; none of the files stored down here would be on microfilm or tape elsewhere, and none of them would be duplicated. He was looking at a unique record, compiled in a unique way, a way still current in many of the departments upstairs. Every time an entry was made, an officer took a fresh sheet of thick, parchment-like paper and, with needle and thread, literally sewed the new facts into the file. It was preposterously archaic, but so far the hidebound traditions of the bosses, coupled with the astronomical cost of replacing the system, had ensured its survival.

Such a system necessarily involved that it was impossible to remove an entry without leaving signs of tampering. What Frolov had found was a thin strip of paper, running the length of the file, between two full pages. Someone had taken a sharp blade and cut out one whole page of Povin's dossier.

Frolov swallowed, and looked carefully over his shoulder to see if he was being observed. The long passage stretched away into obscurity, beyond the range of the single yellow bulb which burned above his head.

It had taken all his courage to sneak a look at this file. The thought of tampering with it never crossed his mind. The penalties would be unimaginable. Frolov could not conceive of any punishment savage enough for the perpetrator of such a crime. The thought made him go hot then cold. He swallowed again.

On the thin strip remaining someone had written a date, in pencil — 29.4.81 — and a tiny emblem, which looked like a human hand. Frolov turned forward to the end of the file. 'Eighty-one. Before Povin's final promotion, but not much before. Whoever had made the final entry had presumably not bothered to check back. What did the hand mean? Could it be

55

a sign that the mutilator of the record was possessed of some high authority undreamed of by Frolov? Suppose someone had come from the Kremlin, from the Kommandant itself. . .?

Frolov slammed the file shut. By now he was sweating with sheer terror. He knew he should never have gone through with this. He must get the dossier back at once, go away and never come back, never think again about what he had found today. . .

But his curiosity was stronger. He re-opened the file at the missing page. He had to know what Povin was doing at the time. His troubled eyes ran hastily down the left-hand page. Entries made by a certain Major Oblensky. Povin new from KGB training school, No. 372. Good reports. Frolov did some quick calculations. Just post-war. Oblensky was almost certainly dead, quite probably purged. Povin would have been too junior to have been embroiled in all that. But such data was easily assembled elsewhere, from personnel records. Then on the next page. . . Still Oblensky, one year later. Frolov frowned. For some reason Oblensky had made a great many more entries than one would normally expect to find in connection with such a junior officer. Something about Povin had intrigued him. What could that have been?

Frolov had seen enough. This file could tell him nothing more. But he had a lead to follow. If he wanted to.

As he slowly made his way back upstairs, past the sentries who checked his papers on each floor, Frolov had plenty of time to reflect on whether he wanted to. He had been given a scare. Finding further information would be no easier. But there was more to it than that. Much more.

When Frolov was chosen as Povin's first deputy he ought to have been promoted to at least Major-General. That was his right — in his opinion. There were precedents. But here he was, four years on, still nothing but a grey Colonel among all the other grey Colonels, indistinguishable from the herd. It rankled. It rankled particularly because the more Frolov saw of Povin's job, and the way Povin went about it, the easier it seemed. It was a job that he, Frolov, could do. Damn it, while Povin was away in Geneva, Frolov *was* doing the job, and well enough, too.

If there was one thing Frolov would have liked to be more than a Major-General, it was a Colonel-General. And if there was something he wanted to be more than Povin's deputy it was. . .

Frolov put these thoughts out of his mind. There was a long way to go yet. First thing — clear the decks for action. Cancel everything in the diary. Povin would be out of the country for some days yet, and Frolov was capable of summoning great energy when required.

He arrived back in his own office and sat down, drumming his fingers on the desk. Suddenly he caught sight of Mishka, and without a pause his hand reached out for the telephone.

'Get my home, will you.'

Senior Lieutenant Valyalin would have been slightly awed to see the way in which his boss's profile softened as he waited for the call to be put through. Boris Frolov had married late in life, after giving up hope of ever finding the right woman. His marriage, to a graceful blonde nearly twenty years younger, was idyllically happy. So it caused him real distress to tell her that he would have to work late that night; and when he asked her to kiss their two little babies for him it was as well that the Senior Lieutenant was not present, for the tear in one eye would have needed some explaining away.

5

Gerald Gilchrist had mixed feelings about the Austin Allegro. It didn't go with his new-found station in life. In the space of a few days he had risen far and fast, leaving the wretched Tilsen nowhere. Take this morning, for instance: Harding had assigned him to drive 'The Chief' wherever he wanted to go. Even his boss stood a little in awe of him now. 'Be careful,' he had said, but in a friendly, half-joking way. Gilchrist was on the way up, all right. No doubt about it. But if he was going to drive 'The Chief', surely he ought to have been given, well, a Mercedes?

'Money,' he'd said bitterly to Cheryl the night before. 'It's all they think about. That, and "Buy bloody British".'

Yet there were advantages, Gilchrist had to admit that. His father ran an Allegro, so he knew where the controls were and what the car could do. He didn't want to make any mistakes while Sir Richard Bryant was riding in the back seat. In his heart of hearts, Gerald was glad they hadn't given him a Merc. And when Bryant told him just how tight the morning's schedule was he felt positive relief.

They ended up meeting Kirk Binderhaven's plane at Genève-Cointrin in time for a hurried dash to the little ski resort of St Cergue along roads still treacherous from the previous night's snow. To Gilchrist's intense disappointment Bryant kept the soundproof glass partition firmly closed during the drive. In view of his recent high-speed progress through the ranks of the Service he felt he had a right to know what was going on. He wasn't just the book-keeper now, he told Cheryl, whose silence was doubtless meant to signify agreement.

As it was, in the course of the journey Bryant, oblivious to his driver's aspirations, gave the American a highly selective account of what Povin had told him two days previously. Then he sat back, keeping his head turned so as to study his visitor's reaction.

Bryant had faith in this man. They first met when Binderhaven was still working for the CIA, in circumstances where Bryant judged it wise to run a check on his background. To read the reports was to enter a different world. One day Binderhaven was at Harvard doing post-doctoral research into minor German poets of the early nineteenth century; the next he was on secondment from a Navy SEAL, running spike teams for SOG into Cambodia at a time when the United States had no official presence there. One particular death trap on the border was known as 'Hotel-9', and that became Binderhaven's speciality. It was there that he won his Medal of Honour, unpublished and unpublicisable, like a Cardinal's

58

breve destined to remain for ever *in pectore*. Bryant once mentioned Hotel-9 to the Military Attaché in Grosvenor Square and, on seeing his lips turn white, understood much.

Then came the years in the CIA, the reproofs for over-zealousness, the increasingly acrimonious service reports on a man for whom Cambodia had been just the beginning of a war which never ceased, but who was relegated by his age to a lowly role in what he contemptuously saw as the rearguard. The ways parted, with expressions of regret on both sides. Since then Binderhaven had never settled for very long in one place. For a time Bryant kept up with him, motivated by forces which he could not explain even to himself. The two men had last met in a grey African dawn on a deserted airstrip for long enough to exchange heavy blue serge sacks, each sealed with wax and lead, and a long expressionless look; then Bryant had gone back to London with the makings of the new Zimbabwe on the seat beside him, and Binderhaven went into the bush once more, on his way to rejoin Wandel and his Grey Scouts in the never-ending search for 'terrs'.

Externally, there was not a lot to show for so much experience. He was in his mid-forties but looked younger, especially when, as now, he was dressed informally, as though for *le sport*. A small detail but Bryant approved of it; the meeting was, after all, to be held on the ski slopes. His close-cropped fair hair had kept its colour, the weather-beaten cheeks suggested only good health and, perhaps, an outdoor occupation. The flesh of his face and, for that matter, the rest of his body, was still remarkably firm. Only the mouth and eyes occasionally told another story. Binderhaven's mouth was a downturned circumflex, remote and austere in repose, as if his lips were clamped very tightly together. His teeth were strong and even, but blunt, worn down by constant grinding in his sleep, the only outward manifestation of a tension which stretched back into Cambodia, and Hotel-9.

His eyes were very large and open, their irises a deep brown. When Binderhaven wanted to he could throw himself, all of him, his whole past and present, into those eyes, and at such times he looked exactly what he was: a resolute, daunting and exceedingly dangerous man.

'Why me? Why this way?'

Bryant was jolted uncomfortably out of his reflections to find the wide eyes full upon him and for a moment was confused. 'This way?'

'Not through channels. The official intelligence establishment.' The white teeth were still sharp enough to cut off the final word with a terminal snap.

Bryant sighed. 'Do you really have to ask that question?'

'I'd like to hear your version.'

Bryant hesitated. 'Have you been in Washington lately?'

'I asked around a little. You wouldn't win a popularity contest right now.'

'Exactly. I've kept Povin to myself for years. In the end, your former employers found out and they couldn't take it. I don't blame them. For years I'd been preaching the virtues of shared intelligence; of course, the weaker ally always does. Now it has rather caught up with me. In Washington they simply wouldn't believe any of this. I have no credit left, you see. No credibility. I'm sorry, that's the "in" word, isn't it? So it has to be this way. Your way, with as much unofficial support as you can get.'

'Is that all?'

'All?'

'Seems to me, this Russian General isn't the only one who wants to trade.'

Bryant said nothing.

'He sees a way out to the West. You see a way of getting back inside Langley. Or am I wrong?'

'Do my motives really enter into this?'

Binderhaven shook his head and smiled. 'I guess not.'

'If you come in, your funds will be guaranteed. Can we not leave it at that?'

Binderhaven shrugged, unaffected by the snub. 'Surely. Is there anything in what he said about Royston, by the way?'

'Oh yes. We've had two days in which to construct a map. Frightfully obvious when you see it, like all these things. It was Royston, incidentally, who told the CIA about Source Nidus. We're leaving him in place for a while, but he's harmless now. There's been a good deal of unpleasantness in London which I won't trouble you with. Grosvenor Square have not been

60

exactly helpful. Apologies are, as usual, in order and will be tendered.'

Binderhaven made a face. 'It'll need a damn heck of a lot more than apologies. Let me tell you what the scuttlebutt is in Washington right now, how they see it. You were right, I didn't really have to ask. Anything that concerns Povin, your "Source Nidus", comes under the heading of bad news. You never let them in on that one. They don't expect to be let in on everything. But on something that big. . . Well, I'm telling you what you know already, I guess. It rankled. It still does. You claim to have had no contact with Nidus for four years. Some of them believe you. As I do. But some of them don't.'

Not for the first time, Bryant experienced the frustrating sensation of dealing with a nurseryful of spoiled children.

'General Povin had a prejudice against Americans which I could not overcome,' he said. 'We had something in common, our religion, that was all. I don't have to tell you about these things, Kirk. Recruitment is as strange as falling in love. But a slight thing can suddenly overcome years of resistance.'

'I understand that. In fact, quite a lot of folk at Langley would go along with you. But why has the good General suddenly overcome this aversion?' He raised a hand before Bryant could speak. 'Oh, I know what he says, and that's fine. As a story. But on your own say-so, you haven't dealt with him for four years. What's to say he hasn't been turned? That's what they'd be asking in Washington.'

'The Russians don't turn spies. They shoot them.'

'With respect, only the most stupid intelligence director would voluntarily rid himself of an operative at that level of experience and capability, while there was still some alternative. There are always pressures. . .'

'Povin is a bachelor and has no relatives living.'

'But there's this pianist.' Binderhaven grimaced. 'Sir Richard, you know, don't you, that in the grand old country of the free we have this class of citizen designated "the faggot"? Well, the fag is either worshipped as almighty god returned to earth, or he's mutilated to death in a back alley, and there just doesn't seem to be anything in between. You know how Washington stands on that right now.' He closed his eyes and allowed his head to rest for a moment against the padded seat. 'If you were to tell them about the pianist back in Langley . . . Wow!'

'There is not the slightest suggestion that General Povin and Stolyinovich are engaged in that kind of relationship.' The idea made Bryant feel hot and angry.

It showed in his voice. Binderhaven opened his eyes and smiled. 'Wouldn't need suggestion in Washington, Sir Richard. Everyone'd be way, way ahead of you.'

Bryant pursed his lips and looked out of the window. He had foreseen many problems, but not this one. The injustice of it got under his skin.

'Suppose I did go through with this. . .proposal. Suppose I put it up to them in Langley, with a recommendation. What do *you* think they'd do?'

'They'd say to check it out. But only as a compliment to your own very impressive track record and history of co-operation with the Company, Sir Richard. Basically they'd think it was an elaborate trap and they ain't falling for it, no siree. What I call the lip-smacking, hillbilly element are enjoying a good time right now. Everyone smart as a whip and not ashamed to say so.' He shook his head very slowly. 'I tell you, sometimes that place has to be seen to be believed. Anyway. The buzz-word is "self-fulfilling prophecy".'

'What?'

'Self-fulfilling prophecy. Some of them must have been reading *Time* magazine, I guess, the language is getting awful fancy. The idea's simple enough, though, and it's beginning to dominate everybody's thinking out there. Let me try to explain how it'd work in this case. A man comes out of Russia, looking over his shoulder the whole time, and says, "The Soviets are going to highjack the Big Apple, or something, get yourselves prepared." The President straps on his old six-shooter and strides out on the porch. Next, the Big Apple disappears. Who can've done it? Answer, why, the Russians did it! Didn't you hear what the Commie said? He came out of Russia, looking over his shoulder . . .'

Bryant laughed. He couldn't help it. 'In other words, Povin would be seen as the first step in a major KGB conspiracy against the West.'

'That's what they'd think back in Langley, yes.'

'And what do you think?'

'I think it's always wise to preserve an open mind. Is this St Cergue?'

Bryant picked up the phone by his side and spoke softly into it. For a second Gilchrist panicked while he tried to remember which button on the handset he was supposed to press, and the car swerved dangerously, causing him to flush with embarrassment.

'Is this St Cergue?'

They were breasting a rise. Ahead of them Gilchrist could see the usual Swiss mountain scene laid out in the sunshine: chairlifts, multi-coloured specks on white slopes, a church spire, attractive yellow-walled houses. It ought to have been St Cergue, the map said it was, but, oh Christ, suppose it wasn't . . .

A road sign. St Cergue.

'Yes, sir.'

Gilchrist heard the American say, 'Pretty. But is it safe?' and Bryant replied, 'I've had men here since last night. They say it's clean. We'll know for certain in a moment.' Then the intercom went dead and he knew no more, but it was enough to make his heart race.

Bryant slid back the partition. 'Pull in by that café over there.'

Gilchrist did so, executing the simple manoeuvre with what he liked to think was unobtrusive efficiency. Bryant wound down the window. Almost immediately a woman came out of the café, looked straight at him, did a convincing double-take, and walked over to the car.

'Hello,' she said, bending low to Bryant's level. 'Did you enjoy the party last night?'

'Wonderful, wasn't it? Did the Johnsons get back all right?'

'Oh, yes. We took them as far as Nyon.'

Bryant smiled and waved goodbye. Binderhaven looked at him inquiringly, and was met with an embarrassed half smile.

'All secure. As long as the wretched Johnsons got home, everything is well. Silly, isn't it?'

Binderhaven shook his head. 'I don't think so.'

Bryant tapped Gilchrist's shoulder. 'You're coming with us. I want a witness, so keep awake, will you.'

Gilchrist was as awake as he'd ever been. He'd just over-heard a genuine piece of trade-craft, expertly done for real. It was his first time, and like all other first times the experience brought with it a premonitory twinge of nerves.

The three men got out of the car and began to walk in the direction of the nursery slopes, indistinguishable from the scores of other skiers who thronged the little main street on a Saturday morning. As they came up to the chairlift the church clock chimed the hour, and Gilchrist exhaled a gasp of surprise as he saw that Povin was waiting for them.

The Russian bent down to loosen his grips, stood his skis upright in the snow and removed a pair of goggles. As he did so he tossed Gilchrist a quick, appreciative grin. The young man was too overcome with admiration to respond. Povin wore a blue and red anorak over elasticated black trousers, black and gold mittens, knitted woollen hat: to Gilchrist he looked like just another elderly but fit European reassuring himself that not all the muscle tone had gone. He gave each man a firm handclasp, and pointed in the direction of the main street down which they had already come. The group began to saunter, Gilchrist a step or two behind the others, but straining every muscle, every nerve, to hear what was said.

'Anything new?'

'Only a deduction on my part. The date. February twenty-third, is Soviet Army Day. A holiday. It would be highly appropriate, no? Can you ground everything on the twenty-third?'

Binderhaven did not allow his smile to waver for a moment. 'Not on your say-so, I'm afraid. They'd be bound to take it as a trap.'

'Richard has told you of the conspiracy?'

'Yes.'

'What do they say about it in Langley?'

'They don't know anything about it.'

'What?'

'I'm not CIA, General. Sir Richard says this thing has got to be handled unofficially. Or not at all. I agree with him.'

For a moment there was silence, while the men continued their stroll down the street. Then, in a low voice, Povin began to argue. Like many Europeans, he gesticulated fiercely during the outburst, illustrating his points with ample gestures. Bryant walked with his hands behind his back, an expression of mild interest on his face; Binderhaven continually looked about him; only Gilchrist, with his tense, pale face and stumbling, anxious walk, seemed out of place.

At the end Povin stopped and turned to face Bryant. 'You are insane,' he said very quietly.

Bryant shook his head. 'Not insane, General. Just facing up to realities, ten years too late, that's all. There is only one course open to us. To destroy the plane on the ground, at Irkutsk, before your specialists can get near it. For that a covert operation is required, with US facilities offered strictly under the table. Which, in turn, means Binderhaven. He's kept up his contacts and has almost infinite goodwill with the people who matter. I've used him before in just this way. I know.'

Povin drew his breath in sharply. 'You want to see me killed?' he asked savagely. 'What kind of a deal is that? You want to debrief a corpse?'

'Those are the only proposals.' Binderhaven's voice had taken on the stony indifference of an official. 'I've nothing to add at this moment in time.'

There was a long silence. Povin seemed to be wrestling with indecision. It was not until they had almost reached Bryant's car that he spoke.

'You leave me no choice.'

There was bitterness in his voice; bitterness and despair.

'I'm afraid not, General. It means danger for all of us, but especially you, I realise that. Can we rely on you, though? Without your full co-operation, we cannot hope to succeed.'

Povin suddenly seemed to give up the struggle. 'All right,' he said wearily. 'You can have anything within my power to give you.'

Binderhaven spoke crisply. 'I shall infiltrate the men and their weapons by different routes, General. You can help there.'

Povin raised his head and Bryant saw that his face was

haggard. 'If you believe that, you don't know much about the Soviet Union.'

'More than you realise, perhaps. Don't give up on me before we start, General, I've got problems enough. Sir Richard'll let you have a shopping list and you'd better start filling it.'

Binderhaven's voice was hard. Povin stared at him for a long moment, then nodded briefly. 'I've already said, I'll do what I can.'

He gave the American a curt handshake, reserving such warmth as he could muster for Bryant. His eyes softened as they lighted on the elderly Englishman who had tried to help him, and failed. 'Goodbye, Sir Richard. Something tells me we shall not meet again. Too bad.'

'You're over pessimistic. This is not the end.'

'Maybe. Goodbye.'

They shook, and Povin turned away. Before he had gone more than a few steps, however, he stopped.

'They told me last night that you and your wife are seen to be enjoying a holiday at Round Hill in Jamaica. Very clever, that. I should have liked to discuss it with you.'

On the last word his gaze deflected to Gerald Gilchrist. Neither spoke; but as he looked into the young man's scared eyes Povin was suddenly afflicted by the memory of another straight-standing, eager young man on the threshold of a career, and his lips curved in a rueful, sympathetic smile. To Gilchrist it seemed as though the Russian understood all too well what he had learned over the past half hour: the inevitable price of advancement is awareness of some things which it is better not to know.

A final wave of his hand and he left them, making towards the station. Binderhaven and Bryant walked back to the car. Bryant waited until they were well on the way to Nyon before he spoke again.

'What did you think of him?'

'Impressive. Seeing him, hearing him talk, made everything kind of real to me. It's a plot well into the mainstream of Soviet policy. All my years in strategic studies, all my instincts, yell at me that, yes, this is it, what they've been waiting for, the big one. As a scenario it has excellent values. But. . .'

66

Bryant sighed. 'But. Exactly. Back to the self-fulfilling prophecy.' He treated Binderhaven to a sharp scrutiny. 'And there are the considerations which we have not so far discussed, aren't there?'

Binderhaven was genuinely surprised. 'What are those?'

'Well let's start with this one. Suppose the Company did get into direct contact with Source Nidus. Through you.'

'Yes.'

'Source Nidus wants to defect.'

'So he'd have us believe.'

'Let's assume it's true. What would the Company prefer? To spend a lot of money on housing Nidus and friend in Kansas, or keep him in place in Moscow for another ten years?'

Binderhaven wriggled himself a little more comfortably into the car's soft upholstery. 'I confess I hadn't thought of that one.'

'No one thinks of everything. Not even me. You caught me out earlier with this silly homosexual angle.'

'Even if the angle exists, it's very insignificant compared with the possibility that some of this just might be true. And if it's true, I need to start infiltrating men into Irkutsk *now*, not in the middle of next week.'

'Ah. So you were genuinely impressed.'

'Enough to stop resenting your dragging me over. Enough to make me want to make a few calls on a very, very secure line indeed.'

Bryant raised one eyebrow. 'What, you mean before you take the evening flight home?'

Binderhaven turned his head and gave Bryant a suspicious look which, after a few seconds, slowly dissolved into silent laughter. 'I did just happen to bring a toothbrush.'

'Ah. One capable of being dismantled, I see.'

'Say again?'

'The two suitcases which my driver loaded into the boot. One for the brush and one for the handle.'

Binderhaven's laughter exploded, but Bryant merely smiled his usual wintery smile.

'Stay, why don't you? Stay until Soviet Army Day, and we can celebrate it together.'

6

Colonel Frolov parked his unobstrusive grey car along with several hundred others in one of the approach roads to the Dynamo Stadium and lit a cigarette. On either side of him animated groups of pedestrians made their way towards whatever it was that happened in the stadium on February nights. Frolov naturally approved of anything that kept the *narod*, the proles, quiet but he was not a sporting man himself and it irritated him to have to wait while the crowd dispersed. He had no intention of attracting attention while representatives of the Fifth Main Directorate were on the streets to monitor the various accesses to the stadium, as they invariably were on such occasions.

At last the road where he had parked the car was empty. Frolov nevertheless hesitated, the memory of his morning in the Confidential Registry still fresh and troublesome in his mind.

He had covered a lot of ground since then. Major Oblensky, Povin's first boss, disappeared in one of Stalin's purges, leaving a widow who could not be traced anywhere, and a daughter who lived in Piscovaja Ulicia, two blocks from where Frolov was sitting. If events had taken their usual turn the daughter should have ended up in a labour camp. Something, however, either inefficiency or a powerful family connection, had sufficed to preserve the girl for higher education, and that was her saving, for notwithstanding her disgraced name she was somehow permitted to meet and marry one of Russia's unacknowledged elite — a hydraulics engineer. True, he was no genius. . .but compared to what normally awaited persons in Raya Oblensky's position, life with him must have represented heaven on earth. And that was not all. Although Fedor Timofeevich Klimov, her husband, had not enjoyed the kind of career engineers yearn for (something to do with his choice of bride, perhaps?) he still had enough dangling between his legs to fill his wife's belly a couple of times. Frolov smiled at the almost embarrassing richness of choice before him. Smiled. . .and hesitated.

This business was not getting any easier. He was leaving traces all over the place, and had begun to understand the mentality of the gambler who seeks to recover escalating losses by yet another throw of the dice. At the end of the road there had to be what all agents long for: a product. There had to be. Or else.

Frolov got out of the car, locked it, and began walking. Ten minutes later he was on the third floor of a not particularly good apartment building, searching the corridor for the Klimov's flat. At last he found it and pressed the bell. His heart was beating with unaccustomed speed, the result of too much excitement on top of too many years spent in an office. He shook himself angrily. KGB men had nothing to fear.

The woman who opened the door, on the other hand, knew what fear was. It had engrained itself in her lined face, so that although Frolov knew her to be in her late forties, she seemed more like sixty. Excellent. If he had been wearing the winter everyday uniform of a Colonel in the KGB, with its dreaded royal blue shoulder boards, fear would have been natural. But he wore a civilian suit, and the smile on his face was kind, so the only possible conclusion was that her fear came from within.

The woman in front of him was very tiny, the product of years of childhood malnutrition, and her face was pasty for want of fresh air. She wore a black dress over thick grey woollen stockings which matched the colour of her dull, dirty hair. Frolov waved her gently aside, like a master declining the services of his lackey, and stepped into the tiny apartment. Raya Klimov, née Oblensky, being used to authority in all its many guises, made no attempt to stop him.

It was the smallest self-contained flat Frolov had ever seen.

69

One room doubled as sitting room and bedroom. A curtain drawn across the corner probably concealed their cooking facilities, and the only other door, half open, revealed a wash basin. Klimov's years of study and service had brought him just one luxury to set him apart from his fellow citizens: a bathroom, integrated into his living quarters. Frolov looked around him with genuine interest, trying to picture how he and Ilinichna and the babies would exist in such a place.

He had plenty of time for these reflections. No one spoke to him. Raya Klimov stood with her back to the door, staring at her own feet. Her husband, sitting in one corner of the cramped room, had put aside his newspaper and was looking at her. Frolov realised that neither of them had the slightest need to ask who he was or by what right he broke into their tiny world. He felt relieved. In all the circumstances he preferred not to have to show his card unless it was absolutely necessary.

There was no third chair for him, but that fitted in with his plans very well. He took the seat vacated by Raya when she got up to answer the door and, after a long, gloomy pause, brought out a flask of vodka.

'Raya Klimov, daughter of Oblensky, KGB Major, traitor, shot. . . I want to discuss old times. Bring glasses.'

She raised her hands to her face and he could hear her crying. Then, as suddenly as she began, she stopped. She went behind the curtain and came out with one glass, which she placed before Frolov, and two cups. Frolov poured. When he had finished he raised the glass and said, 'To the health and long life of General Stepan Povin.' Klimov merely looked puzzled; after a second he shrugged and downed his vodka. But his wife's eyes strayed to Frolov's face for the first time, and he read there something which pleased him, a kind of wild hope, as if she suddenly saw a road through the poison thicket which enveloped her.

Frolov poured again. This time the woman was the first to drink. He poured a third time, then recorked the flask and put it back in his pocket.

'If anyone asks about this meeting, it never took place. Understand that. But you needn't fear, no one will ask. Not if you're sensible and do as you're told.'

He allowed the message time to sink in. At last Klimov, the engineer, spoke.

'We know nothing, comrade. We have nothing. We are good, loyal citizens of the Soviet Union. Tell us how we can help. We will do whatever we can.'

It was a brave little speech in all the circumstances, but Frolov repaid it with a long look of disdain. After a while the woman could stand it no longer; she broke in, 'No, Fedor, no. It's me he wants.' She appealed to Frolov. 'That's right, isn't it? Because I'm my father's daughter. . .' She was weeping again. 'All these years we've got by, Fedor and me. We've lived it down. We've moved about, in case it got known. Don't ruin us now, I implore you, comrade. On my knees. . .' She was actually kneeling in front of him, her hands clasped in front of her face.

Frolov looked down on her with growing interest. 'Do they teach you to clasp your hands like that when you pray, Raya? In the church. Where you go. Sometimes.'

The expression of despair which came down over her face as she heard these words made Frolov wonder whether it was worth dragging in the children. Better get it over with.

'And your daughters. . .did you teach them to pray too, perhaps? One of them is in Leningrad, I think. The other in Kiev. They tell me interesting things about the one in Kiev. How she consorts with Jews, Raya. A Jewish lover, some even talk of that.' Frolov shook his head very slowly. 'It upsets me to hear such talk.'

For a moment Raya Klimov stayed on her knees in front of him, her face lowered. Then, as if convinced that she had nothing to hope for and nothing more to lose, she rose painfully to her feet and stood in front of him, waiting.

Frolov smiled. It was time.

'I told you, I want to discuss the past. Once. Tonight. Then you will never see me again. There will be no consequences. Your daughters will not suffer, your husband will keep his job, this apartment will continue to be yours. There is just one condition. Only one. That to all my questions you answer truthfully, completely, quickly. Do you understand?'

71

The woman nodded once. 'Yes.'

'Good. It will not take long. First. Where were you living in 1948?'

'Kirov. Ulicia Lenina.'

'Number eighty-three. Your father lived there with the rest of the family?'

'Yes. He was billeted at home.'

Frolov continued to ask her questions which were designed to test whether she was lying. He already knew the answers to all of them. On each occasion she answered honestly and rapidly. He saw that, like many mothers the world over, she was primarily concerned with dates. Her children's birthdays, the day she last saw her father alive, these were burned permanently into her brain. But in between. . .nothing, or all but nothing, remained. At last Frolov judged it was time to move on.

'Did your father ever discuss work at home?'

'I was only a girl, comrade. I would not have known. I cannot remember.'

'You recall nothing? Nothing at all?'

'Well. . .'

'Think carefully, Mother Raya. The toast I proposed at the beginning. Who was it to?'

No answer.

'The name. What was the name?'

'Povin.' It came out in a rush, the second syllable barely distinguishable from the first.

'Yes, Povin. Who is General Povin?'

The woman shook her head violently.

'And yet you knew his name. Don't try to pretend otherwise.'

Again she was mute. Frolov deliberately poured himself another tot of vodka, leaving the cups empty.

'Your father mentioned that name.'

'No!'

Frolov was puzzled. It sounded like the truth.

'I warned you what would happen if you tried to play games with me.'

He tossed down his drink and made as if to get up. The

72

woman shot a sudden look at her husband. Beneath lowered lids Frolov followed her glance and saw Klimov join his hands together, as if pleading with his wife not to be a fool. Frolov started towards the door.

'Wait, comrade. Wait. . .please! I have something to show you. Only. . .'

'Only?'

The woman had her back to the wall, literally and metaphorically. Inside, Frolov checked himself. People in that situation do irrational things. He said nothing more, but waited.

'Only. . .no one has ever seen it. Ever. Except Fedor here. And if it were to become known that I had kept it. . .after all these years. . .'

Frolov sat down again. 'I have already promised you that your secrets are safe. I am not going back on that, you know. Come, what is it that you want me to see?'

Raya shared another long, despairing look with her husband, who nodded; then she disappeared into the bathroom. Frolov heard creaks and grunts. When she re-emerged a few moments later she was holding three dusty old exercise books.

Frolov could no longer contain himself. He snatched them from her and opened the first one at random. At the top of the page was a date, followed by small, neat handwriting. He looked up wonderingly.

'A diary.'

'Yes. My father's.'

For an instant the room seemed to shudder before Frolov's eyes; then it steadied again. Quickly he began to leaf through the dusty old books. The earliest went back a long way, to Oblensky's time at officer training school; it was full of romantic mush about various girls he had known, and undigested Party dogma lovingly transcribed wholesale into the cadet's notebook. Frolov wasted no time on it. The second covered a later period, but the dates were still too early. He grabbed the third, and as he saw the magic year, 1947, his heart gave a great thump. He upturned the open book, so as to keep the place, and fumbled for a cigarette.

While the Klimovs watched from their respective corners of

the tiny room, Colonel Frolov sat under the single yellow light bulb, twin to that in the Confidential Registry, and read page after page, impervious to the steady stream of ash which sank gently down from the tip of his smouldering *papyrosi* to land on the cracked linoleum under the table.

When he had finished the last page of the last volume he closed the book, gathered it up with the other two, and sat in silence for a long moment while Raya closed her eyes and prayed.

'Here.'

Raya opened her eyes and could scarcely believe what she saw. The man in the brown suit was offering her the books. For a second she wavered, sensing a trap; then she reached out to grab them and hold them to her breast.

'If you'll take my advice, you'll burn them. They have no literary merit and are ideologically unsound. If he went around saying that kind of thing, no wonder they shot him and good riddance. You're a fool to hang on to them. Today it's me. I don't give a lump of cold dogshit. Tomorrow. . .who knows who it'll be tomorrow night, eh? Or the night after that. Tell me, have you ever slept easily one night in your life, knowing that puke's under the floorboards?'

Raya was crying again. 'I thought. . .perhaps, one day, the diaries might help to clear his name. . .'

Frolov laughed out loud. 'They'd condemn him a hundred times over.'

He stood up and walked to the door. On his way out he stopped to take a last look at this extraordinary residence and its miserable occupants. He wanted to be able to describe it to Ilinichna while it was still fresh in his mind. His eye lighted on Raya's tired, lined face, and he smiled at her.

'You needn't fear, comrade. We shall never meet again. If only all my. . .clients. . .answered so well, there'd be a lot less pain in the world.'

On his way down the dingy stairs a single sentence from the last volume kept up its monotonous rhythm inside his brain. There was only one sentence which concerned Frolov. It came in the middle of a short paragraph dealing with Oblensky's lieutenants.

'*Most of them are idiots,*' it began. '*But whenever I complain they tell me I must make do. Now the best of them, Povin, is becoming a Christian. What should I do? Report him, I suppose. If I don't someone else will, and they'll wonder why I didn't. If I do, I lose my only competent junior. I'm starting to hate this place.*'

Frolov knew just how he felt.

7

Joe Faber had a theory that in every mission you needed a lucky break. Just one. It didn't matter when or how it happened, as long as you were ready to grab it with both hands; given a lucky break you could win. Without it, no dice.

This time the lucky break came right at the start, as he and Frank Mannheim approached the second immigration desk from the left in the European Arrivals Building at Moscow's Sheremetyevo Airport. It took the form (if that word applied to anything so gross and shapeless) of Leonid Ivanovich Premkin.

Premkin weighed 300 pounds. If it is true that a man is what he eats, he was a pile of fried potatoes and chicken fat shored up around a liquid inner core of vodka and cheap calorific beer. He was in his mid-fifties and neither his doctor nor his wife expected him to outlast the decade, or, indeed, particularly wanted him to. His cholesterol count was abnormally high, he suffered from periodic shooting pains in his chest, his back hurt more or less continuously; as a result of these cumulative misfortunes his temper was short. And today, as he sat in his usual place behind number two immigration desk, he had toothache.

A lucky break. Just one. And Joe Faber was looking right at it.

He didn't know that, of course. He saw the grey, puffy face with drops of sweat chasing each other down the rolls of flesh squeezed out by the tight uniform collar, and groaned aloud. Too late to shift sideways into another queue; that would attract attention. Besides, the guard's eyes were firmly fixed on him and the sten gun was pointing at the floor right next to Faber's shoes.

At last he was almost at the head of the line, and the vibrations had become very bad indeed. He could see that the guy was in pain, and that his only relief seemed to lie in harassing the passengers who stood helplessly before him. Moscow immigration was always hell, but this. . . Faber took a closer look. In the same instant, without any conscious command from his brain, the American's body smoothly began to put its self-preservation system into operation. The muscles tensed, the skin on his face contracted, adrenalin flooded through him. Faber felt all these things happen and couldn't understand why. Then he looked again, and suddenly he knew. Something told him that the immigration officer was in a critical condition, and hence was an incalculably dangerous man.

'Come forward. You expect me to get over there and carry you? Eh?'

Premkin knew some English but today he felt disinclined to use it. He could not be expected to know that Faber spoke and understood Russian. The passport lying on the desk was a perfectly genuine American travel document.

'Sorry.' Faber tried to make his voice sound casual. He saw the officer's eyes narrow to milky slits and fumbled for his handkerchief to wipe away the sweat on his palms.

'You speak Russian?'

'Some, yes.'

Premkin flipped open the passport. 'Name.'

'Faber.'

'*Full* name.'

'Joseph Daniel Faber.'

'Joseph . . . Daniel. Jewish?'

76

'No.'

'You have any relations in the Soviet Union?'

'No.'

'No *Jewish* relations, Joseph Daniel Faber?'

Faber's hands were shaking. He pulled out his handkerchief and wiped his nose in an attempt to cover his anxiety. He felt Mannheim stiffen and looked to one side to see that a senior officer was slowly working his way down the line of desks, placing a sheet of paper on top of each.

Something was wrong. The Soviets were expecting them. *No! Don't act dumb.*

Faber forced himself to stay calm and think. The documents were in order. He and Mannheim were travelling on their own passports, Binderhaven had stressed the importance of that, and they each had letters of introduction issued by the Ministry of Foreign Trade. They could talk their way out of this. They could survive it. They could survive anything.

Except a full body search.

Premkin read through Faber's passport very slowly, subjecting even the blank pages to a minute examination. The officer with the sheets of paper reached No. 2 desk and laid one of them on its soiled chipboard surface. Premkin squinted briefly at it and pushed it aside.

'What is the purpose of your visit?'

'Business.'

Premkin sneered. 'And what exactly is your business?'

'I'm in furs. This here is my partner, Frank Mannheim.'

Premkin scowled at the other man. 'Later,' he said. Mannheim shrugged and bent down to place his suitcase against the front of the desk, next to Faber. He so arranged the movement that for a few seconds his face was within centimetres of the sheet of paper which Premkin had pushed aside.

Faber was handing over his letter of introduction. Premkin first squinted at it, then held it up to the light. All around them passengers came and went, the loudspeakers emitted harsh, unintelligible sounds, men pushed huge trolleys of luggage this way and that. Faber was aware of none of it, which was strange, because over the past few minutes his sight and hearing had both become abnormally acute. He and Premkin were alone, locked into their own little bubble of silence, where everything that the man opposite said or did seemed magnified a hundred times.

'I shall verify this. Don't move.'

Premkin put out a hand to lever himself out of his seat. Faber licked his lips. He tried to say something and failed. Beside him he could sense the forcefield of Mannheim's tension suddenly swell out to engulf them both, and his whole body chilled. Faber knew that his face was white.

'Uugg-gh. . .'

Faber stared. The fat human hillock behind the desk was holding a hand to his face, obviously undergoing an extraordinary spasm of pain. Faber swallowed, unable to comprehend what he saw. Then Mannheim was elbowing him roughly aside.

'You have toothache, yes?'

Premkin mumbled something indeterminate.

'I, too, suffer from it. Look. . .'

Mannheim opened his mouth and removed a soggy wet pad of cotton wool from his cheek.

'My dentist gave me this stuff before I left New York. I have an abscess but he said it'd hold me until after my trip. It works. You want to try some?'

Mannheim pushed a phial of liquid under Premkin's suspicious eyes, and for a terrible moment Faber actually knew what it meant for the heart to stop beating.

'Here, let me show you. Take a few drops on the pad. . .there you go.' Mannheim demonstrated by shaking the phial on to the grey blob in the palm of his hand and reinserting it in his mouth. The Russian hesitated a few seconds more. . .and took the phial. He had no cotton wool so he threw back his head and allowed four or five drops to fall on to the throbbing tooth. Faber felt the blood rush into his face.

For a moment Premkin's expression remained unchanged. Then he smiled. A look of amazement mingled with relief spread its stodgy way across his features.

'It works!'

His smile faded.

'It is difficult, sometimes, to obtain such things in the Soviet Union.'

Faber became aware of a small commotion a few desks up from where he was standing. He turned his head to see a group of passengers being led away under the watchful eyes of a guard. They looked distressed.

'Keep it. I've got two more.'

Faber was jolted back to an awareness of Premkin's face, which now wore a look of cunning desire.

'In the Soviet Union medicines are superior. It is acknowledged everywhere. Only. . .occasionally it is difficult.' Something of the former jeer was back in his voice. 'We are compelled to rely on capitalist-fascist states to import necessary raw materials.'

'All the more reason why I would ask you to accept this small gift. To cement the goodwill which is always on the increase between our peoples.'

Mannheim's voice was sincere, even a touch humble. Faber was dumb with admiration.

For a few seconds longer the Russian appeared to hesitate. Then, 'You have a passport?'

Mannheim handed it over. Premkin treated it to a cursory glance before returning it, together with Faber's letter of introduction.

'Go through, please. May you enjoy your stay in this, our beautiful country.'

As they went through the gate Faber threw a last look over his shoulder to see the Russian still staring dreamily at the little phial clasped between his podgy fingers.

A lucky break. Just one.

'Jesus! That was close.'

They were standing on the tarmac apron, waiting for the next cab in line.

'Too damn right it was close. Did you see what was on that sheet of paper?'

Faber quickly turned to face his friend, alarmed by the worried tone of his voice.

'Priority one notification: all US citizens entering to be subjected to maximum security procedures. Those guys you saw. . .they were being taken off for the treatment.'

Faber exhaled a long breath through his teeth. As the cab drew up alongside them Mannheim said, 'Kirk was right, buddy boy. The barrier's coming down and we scraped underneath it. Let's get the hell out of here before that lump of lard changes his mind.'

The taxi driver set Faber down at the Rossiya Hotel in Razina Street, and took Mannheim on to Yaroslavlsky Station. It was the middle of the afternoon and the concourse was relatively empty. There was nobody else in the men's room. Mannheim locked himself into a cubicle and humped his suitcase on to the seat. His fingers were agile and he worked quickly.

First, he removed the two sodden pads from his mouth and sucked hard to get the saliva flowing again. He did not have an abscess; the pads were there to fill out his cheeks and make them correspond to the picture inside his passport. Mannheim, however, was never less than well prepared: he had guarded against the possibility of a cursory search by equipping himself with the prescription-only mouth treatment which he had given to Premkin. Next, he removed the toupé which covered his bald crown and combed out his hair. From the open suitcase he took cold cream and more cotton wool, with which he removed the layer of complexion colouring with which he had entered the country. A few minutes with the portable electric razor sufficed to take off his moustache and shorten his sideburns.

Then Mannheim took out his passport and with minute care unpeeled the wafer-thin photograph which he had earlier superimposed over the original one. It came away cleanly with a soft, sucking rasp. He propped the passport open on top of the suitcase, squatted down and compared the first photograph with the reflection of his face in the tiny hand mirror that went with the razor. Only one detail remained. Mannheim extracted a pair of photochromatic glasses and put them on. The prescription was very mild, just enough to avoid any suspicion which might attach to unground lenses but with no perceptible effect on his eyesight. The overall transformation was considerable. Mannheim slipped out of his jacket and shirt

80

and rapidly exchanged them for other clothes in the suitcase. The whole exercise took less than ten minutes.

He flushed the cotton wool pads and the shreds of the surrogate photograph down the lavatory, emptying the tank twice to ensure that everything was taken well down into the sewer, then quickly packed up the rest of his equipment. He was ready to go, but for a moment he hesitated with his hand on the bolt.

He had crossed the Russian border on innumerable occasions, in many different guises. This time it was different. He had no weapon, no alias, not even a proper plan. Inside the lavatory cubicle there was an illusion of security, of peace before the coming storm, and Mannheim was somehow reluctant to leave it.

It will be all right, he told himself. As long as they don't stand you in front of the immigration officer and say, 'Is this the man you admitted?' it will be all right.

Mannheim drew back the bolt and stepped out of the cubicle, feeling in his pocket for the roubles he would need to buy a one-way rail ticket to Irkutsk.

8

Lieutenant-Colonel Mitch Kruger awoke to find broad beams of sunlight flooding into his quarters. He sat up in bed, rubbing the sleep from his eyes. The first thing he saw was a hand-painted sign on the wall. 'Remember,' it enjoined him, 'Today Is the First Day of the Rest of Your Life.'

Kruger smiled. The sign was a present from the local high school to the men of the gallant 552nd Airborne Warning and Control Wing stationed at Tinker Air Force Base. Each room

81

in senior officers' quarters had one. There were five basic messages: 'It's not the size of the man in the fight, it's the size of the fight in the man', 'My country, 'tis for thee'; Kruger couldn't remember the others. A lot of people sneered at them. Not Kruger. Not this of all mornings. Because this really was the first day of the rest of his life.

He dressed quickly, paying special attention to the soles of his flying boots. They looked fine but Kruger was nervous about them. Control had told him not to worry, because who was going to look at the soles of his boots, for Christ's sake, but Control wasn't going to fly the damn aircraft.

The last thing Kruger did before he left the room was pick up the photograph of his wife which stood on the dressing table and examine it. His feelings about Helen were mixed. Although he'd always known that this day would come, even when he married her thirteen years before, it was strange to think they would never meet again. They had parted the previous night, because he was required to sleep on base before any important flight; although they had done this many times Helen seemed to know something was wrong. She kept telling him to be careful. . .

The memory stirred Kruger to inspect the soles of his boots yet again.

His walk to breakfast took him outside, into the bright early-morning Oklahoma sun. It was one of those clear days which you sometimes get in mid-February, with more than a touch of warmth in it. The light frost which Weather had predicted the day before was already dissolving into the ground.

Kruger made an unusually good breakfast for him: steak and eggs and two full glasses of milk. The flyer's breakfast. Between mouthfuls he studied the weather display beamed electronically on to the screen at the far end of the mess hall. Low winds, some CAT at 50,000 feet and above — that wouldn't worry him — and rain and low level cloud spreading from the west later, with hail an outside chance. Kruger lit a cigarette and drew down a lungful of smoke. The last item interested him.

He asked about it in Flight Dispatch but there was no further word. Here he was joined by his co-pilot and first officer, Captain Peter Everest.

Everest saluted formally. As senior AWACS pilot on the base Kruger was entitled to a lot of respect, but that wasn't the only reason for the formality. Kruger had a reputation for handing out tough discipline on officers and enlisted men alike. Today, however, Everest noted with relief that his mood seemed mellow. Kruger put an arm round his shoulder.

'You ready for a trip to Alaska?'

'Sure thing, sir. Weather looks OK.'

Kruger nodded. 'What about fuel?'

They laid out maps and graphs on the counter while the Master Sergeant waited for his signed indent. Everest wanted to keep the load light but Kruger overrode him. 'Just a hunch, is all. Full tanks.'

Everest raised an eyebrow. Nearly 23,000 US gallons was a lot of fuel.

The two men picked up their flight bags and went outside to where the jeep was waiting for them. On the short journey to the steps of their aircraft Everest was thinking what a swell day it was for flying. Kruger's attention was all taken up with the huge grey smudge which increasingly filled his vision as they approached.

The sight of 11415 never left him totally unmoved. He could have told you anything you wanted to know about the aircraft's capabilities, including some that weren't in the book. He knew, for example, that the Westinghouse AN/APY-1 radar, scanning through a radius of 360 degrees, returned high PRF signals to the plane's IBM System 4-Pi CC-1 central computer and data processor, thus enabling the monitors to scan ground and air for over 250 miles. He knew that its radar could track 600 targets simultaneously, free from ground clutter, and that the computer could identify and fully interpret 240 targets at one time, measuring the dimensions of each, computing its altitude, speed and directional bearing. Kruger could fill a book with the technical details of the AWACS he flew day in, day out, through the year. But he could also see the wood for the trees. He knew that the military implications of the aircraft were enormous, that while the AWACS continued to enjoy supremacy the Russians could never claim to have drawn level in the arms race. It was like having the tank while your enemy was still dependent on the horse.

The Russians had something similar, a Tupolov Moss-126. Compared to the AWACS, it was crap. For one thing, it had no look-down facility, and so did nothing to solve Soviet low altitude tracking problems, which were immense. For another, there were only ten of them, and at least a hundred would have been needed to patrol even the major sectors efficiently.

But compared to 11415, Kruger's aircraft, the Moss was a junkyard. For Kruger's plane had recently received special treatment, something to set it apart from the rest of the AWACS fleet.

11415 was now a total stealth aircraft. It had been given an outer skin of low-visibility material, and as a result it was very nearly invisible on a radar screen. Nearly. . .but not quite. Not, that is, until today.

Today Lieutenant-Colonel Kruger, senior AWACS pilot in the United States Air Force, was scheduled to fly 11415 up to its new home in Alaska, where it would operate on the front line with the Soviet Union — an invisible but all-seeing, all-knowing Eye with sufficient intelligence gathering potential to split the Russian's eastern defences wide open. Somewhere along the route Kruger was going to throw a switch. And the AWACS was going to disappear completely.

At the foot of the steps he waved Everest on. 'I'm going back to take a look. Start the pre-flight rundown.'

Kruger walked to the tail and climbed the rear steps.

The plane was originally adapted from the commercial Boeing 707-320-C, but its interior now bore no relation to the cabin of a passenger plane. He made his way slowly forward, stopping to look at every bank of instruments, every console. Immediately to his right as he came in was the spare survival equipment, and beyond that, the toilet. Kruger walked through the galley and into the rest area, then continued on to the communications sector, past the radar receiver and signal processor, the Duty Officer's Station, the multi-purpose consoles; past the data processor on his left and the computer console on his right, and so to the flight deck.

Normally the plane carried a crew of seventeen. Today, however, on what was officially designated a test flight, there were just eight men on board: Kruger; Everest; Frank Oxford, the senior technician; an orderly; and four technical staff to monitor the sophisticated equipment.

Everything seemed in order. Kruger retraced his steps, slowly walking down the thickly carpeted aisle which ran nearly the length of the port side of the plane. Oxford was already sitting at the Westinghouse console, earphones in place, while his four technicians went through the pre-flight equipment check. Now only the orderly was unaccounted for. Kruger reached the galley and drew aside the curtain.

'Good morning, Colonel. Coffee freshly brewed, if you want it.'

'Thanks, I'll have a cup. Hey, take one through to Captain Everest, will you?'

As the man left Kruger looked down at his name label. Chase. Was there a Mrs Chase, he wondered? Baby Chases?

Kruger raised his right leg and rested it against his crooked left knee so that he could remove the sole of his boot. He twisted, pulled, and the sole came away to reveal a small metal cylinder attached to its inner surface. Kruger released the tube from the spring-clip which retained it in place and weighed it thoughtfully in his hand.

Opposite him, just above eye level, was the aircraft's air-conditioning unit. He had a clear understanding of how it worked, Control had seen to that. High-pressure air was bled from the engines and cooled in a heat exchanger before being fed to the cabin, with any excess expelled through one-way valves set in the hull. The aircraft supply passed through a humidifier before flowing through the cabin at a controlled rate of 6,000 cubic feet a minute to give a complete change of air every three minutes.

Kruger raised his hand and lifted the flap in front of him. He was looking for the inlet vent which permitted the crew to bleed pure oxygen into the system.

'Everything all right, sir?'

Chase returned from the cockpit to find Lieutenant-Colonel Kruger casually buttoning the top pocket of his flying jacket.

'Sure, everything's fine. Get ready for take-off now.'

Kruger proceeded on his way to the cockpit where he found that Everest had just completed the pre-flight checklist. He eased himself into the left-hand seat and put on his headphones.

'Hello GMC, hello GMC. Permission to start up requested by eleven-four-one-five, Lieutenant-Colonel Kruger piloting as flight captain.'

There came the familiar crackle of static.

'This is Ground Mission Control Tinker Field, Central Air Force Region. Permission granted, eleven-four-one-five.'

Everest reached for his microphone and spoke to the air-craftmen on the ground. The four engines fired in quick succession and gradually ran up to full before dying away to provide minimum thrust for taxiing. More static.

'Eleven-four-one-five, you are cleared to Elmendorf Field, Alaska and have taxi clearance. Taxi to runway left via the outer.'

Kruger eased the throttles forward and took his feet off the brakes. The plane began to roll.

'Eleven-four-one-five, hold short of the runway. Your fighter escort precedes.'

Kruger lined the plane up at the far end of the runway and watched while two F-15s roared off into the wind, their after-burners glowing red against the clear blue sky.

'Eleven-four-one-five, you are clear to line up and take off, wind two-sixty at eight. *Shoot, boy!*'

Kruger grinned. This send-off, strictly unofficial, was the hallmark of a Tinker Field controller. He pushed the throttles forward and said, 'Trim all.' Everest obediently set the pressure ratios for the four engines. Power built up to maximum. Kruger hesitated another second, released the brakes, and spoke again into his microphone. 'Eleven-four-one-five rolling.'

The one thing Kruger could never make himself like was take-off. The huge radome made everything feel top heavy. He was so used to grappling with the misplaced extra weight that he doubted whether he could have flown a conventional Boeing without retraining.

The plane gathered momentum down the runway.

'Eighty knots.'

'Confirm. I have the stick.'

'One hundred. . .one hundred ten. . .velocity one!'

'Rotate.'

The flashing white marks of the runway disappeared to be replaced by pale blue horizon. There was a bump, the familiar dip in the base of Kruger's stomach, and they were airborne.

'Velocity two. Positive rate of climb, and we have lift-off.'

The radio crackled. 'Eleven-four-one-five, now climb to 22,000 and hold for rdv with fighter escort. Do not, I say do not, leave 22,000 without permission.'

'Acknowledged.'

Kruger kept the stick hard back. Everything was going well.

'Gear up. . .flaps twenty. . .retract flaps.'

Suddenly the fighters were with them, one on each side. Kruger gave the thumbs up, and was acknowledged by the port Eagle. Shortly afterwards he received permission to climb to his operational height of 40,000 feet, and proceed towards Fairchild AFB in the far north-west of mainland America at an undemanding 510 miles an hour. He and Everest removed their headsets more or less simultaneously.

'Do you really think that thing'll work?'

Kruger followed the direction of Everest's pointing finger. Behind the navigator's seat stood a black box, three feet by four feet by two feet. In the manifest it was barely described as 'ECM', which stood for Electronic Counter Measure. Scientists had been working to put it together for upwards of ten years now, and in the course of the next few hours Kruger was going to test it for the first time in flight. On the ground it worked perfectly.

'If it functions down there, I guess it'll be OK up here.'

Everest shook his head. 'I just can't figure it out. To make a plane just . . . just disappear like that.'

'Only on radar. If you could make it really disappear, so no one could see it at all, now that'd really be something else.'

'Maybe that will come, sir. When the Second World War started, no one had heard of radar. Then came low visibility materials. Who knows what'll happen next?'

Kruger smiled. In fact he knew exactly what was going to happen next. He stood up and took off his jacket, loosening his tie at the same time, and sat down again.

'Kind of hot in here.'

He turned to look out of the window. His watered-down reflection in the perspex told him nothing. He saw a bronzed face topped by ultra-short hair, fierce little brown eyes, a thin mouth. The face was sweating a little. Control had told him to take each minute as it came, but he couldn't help looking ahead and worrying. The makers of the gas in his little cylinder had warned that in one case out of a thousand there was sometimes unpleasantness at the end. He was praying for that not to happen. Everest was okay. None of this was his fault.

All his life since military academy Kruger had been preparing for this day, knowing that it might never come. In that time he had made a niche for himself in the Air Force, acquired a wife and a home. No children, thank Christ. But when Control crooked his finger, seventeen years on, he didn't hesitate. The original indoctrination had been too thorough ever to be worn down by the constant dripping of domestic comfort. The fear ran too deep.

Kruger put the plane on to automatic pilot, and went aft to the galley, where he ordered two cups of coffee from Chase.

'Hi, Frank.'

The senior technician looked up with a friendly smile as Kruger handed him the second cup. 'Morning, sir. Why thank you. Everything going just fine our end. Let me know when you're ready to test the new baby.'

'I'll do that. I've just taken a look at the sealed orders. We're aiming for a pair of co-ordinates a couple of hours away. That gives maximum saturation coverage to Alaskan Air Command as well as SAC West. When we get a couple of miles short. . .'

Kruger continued to talk for a few minutes while he scanned Oxford's face for signs of trouble. There were none. He moved forward again, pausing to exchange a few friendly words with the technicians bent before their illuminated screens. Everything was fine, they all agreed, just fine.

Back in his seat he sorted through his orders once more. He noticed that the fighters kept their distance, and was relieved.

The orders were explicit. In something just over two hours the test would begin. He would be far out to sea, over international waters, at the maximum point of distance from the North American coastline. It would take Alaskan Air Command a long time to scramble enough fighters to find out what was going wrong. The composite Wing consisted of a combat support group and thirteen aircraft warning squadrons, but everything was directed towards the coast of the Soviet Union and the Arctic wastes beyond. The only thing he had to watch for was Shemya AFB in the Aleutian Islands, but Control had told him not to worry about that. They had a plan. They had a plan for everything. . .

Time passed uneventfully. About an hour later he linked into SAC Joint Area Command. As he did so he allowed himself the brief luxury of contemplating the arrangements which, at that very moment, were being made to welcome him home. The First Deputy Commander-in-Chief of PVO Strany, Marshal Koldunov himself, was in the headquarters of National Air Defence Command, watching his progress across the north Pacific. In Siberia the Commander of Fighter Aviation, Lieutenant-General Borovykh, was raising a mighty bow of aircraft from the Laptev Sea in the north to the River Amur in the south: Flagons, Fishpots, Firebars, Fiddlers, Foxbats. . .the whole range of Soviet fighters, deployed for him.

And somewhere, tucked beneath the wings of an Aeroflot Ilyushin bound from Tokyo to Vancouver, two MiG-27s, fully armed with 23mm Gatling guns and AA-8 Aphid dogfight missiles, proceeded undetected towards contact . . .

The radio crackled. 'Eleven-four-one-five, this is SAC West. Do you read me? Come in please.'

'I read loud and clear.'

'General Avis here, Kruger.'

'Yes, sir.'

'Any problems so far?'

'None, sir.'

'Now hear me, Colonel. We're going to start the countdown in about ten minutes. You're dead on course and thirty seconds ahead of schedule.'

'Confirm.'

'Remember, keep talking. Whatever happens, keep talking until contact is resumed. Your escort is going to maintain visual contact at all times. . .'

Kruger grinned. They were not quite stupid. It had dawned on them that an aircraft which disappeared from a radar screen in mid-flight might, conceivably, get lost. Hence the fighters.

'And don't worry, Colonel. We expect things to go wrong on this flight. Now, I'll leave you and your crew to make final preparations. Roger and out.'

Kruger removed his headset. He was pleased to hear that the General expected malfunctions, because he wasn't going to be disappointed.

'Guess I'll take a leak,' he said as he stood up. Everest nodded. Kruger made his way aft, stopping to speak to Oxford on his walk to the galley.

'Shut down everything, Frank. Strict radio silence from now on, down at this end. No emissions of any kind.'

'Acknowledged, sir.'

Oxford reached for his microphone and started to put his orders into effect. Kruger watched for a moment before proceeding on down to the galley.

Chase, the orderly, was stretched out asleep on one of the bunks. Kruger passed quietly by and stood before the air-conditioning unit. He looked at his watch. Two minutes exactly, Control had said: the timer on the seal will give you two minutes. Be ready. . .

Kruger waited for the second hand to reach the top of the dial. 55. . .56. . .57. . .

He inserted the little cylinder in the valve and held it steady. . . .59. . .60.

Kruger twisted. The tube locked on to the valve and stayed in position when he took away his hand. For a few seconds he looked at it, his face expressionless; then he backed out of the little galley and began to rummage in the survival kit locker next door.

When Kruger re-entered the cockpit half a minute later Everest looked up to see with surprise that he was carrying a small cylinder of air and oxygen attached to a face mask.

'I reckon this thing has a gremlin.' Kruger held the mask to

90

his face, twiddled the outlet control and shook his head. 'Would you believe it, they send us up with junk like that. . .'

Kruger strapped the mask on to his face, opened the valve and looked at his watch. Suddenly he didn't want to see anything, and turned to stare out of the window.

Beside him Everest made what sounded like an enormous, loud hiccup. Kruger turned round, very slowly, half dreading what he might see.

Everest sat slumped in his seat, head thrown back, eyes closed. On his lips were the beginnings of a smile. Kruger found that he had been holding his breath. He released it in a deep sigh, part gratitude, part overwhelming relief.

His heart was beating unnaturally fast. He made himself stand up and once more went aft. Everything in the main cabin was quiet, all the electronic gadgetry had been shut down pursuant to his own orders. Kruger checked the five bodies of the technicians, feeling for signs of life. There were none. He stood up from the last one and made his way back to the galley. Chase must have woken up before he died: he was slumped against a stores locker, motionless, a crumpled paper cup near his right hand. The water had spilled, leaving a long dark stain which spread almost to Kruger's foot.

He stepped back and drew the curtain to, knowing that he was alone in the aircraft.

On his return to the flight deck he sat down with a final glance at his watch. The air would be clean again now but he hesitated for a few seconds longer, suddenly afraid.

What if they had tricked him? Suppose Control was lying about the gas in the cylinder. . .

The radio call light flickered. Kruger wrenched the mask from his face and drew a deep breath.

'Eleven-four-one-five, this is SAC West, do you read?'

'Loud and clear, General.'

'Giving you a count of ten. Ten. . .nine. . .eight. . .'

Kruger stood up and went over to the black box behind the navigator's chair.

'Four. . .three. . .'

Kruger placed his finger against the master switch.

'Zero!'

Kruger pressed.

As he made his way back to his seat he could hear the confused sound of cheering in his headphones. General Avis came on the air again.

'Guess you know what that means, Colonel. The damn thing works.'

'You can't see me at *all*?'

'Nope. You were pretty faint before, of course, but now you're gone. Completely. Not even a shadow. Tell me, Colonel, what's it like to be the world's first invisible man?'

Kruger swallowed. He could think of nothing to say. Not even Control had been able to foresee the mystique which would surround this moment. Kruger slung his headphones around his neck and looked at his watch. His pulse was throbbing, he could feel the blood thumping through the big artery in his neck. Any second now. . .

'Colonel Kruger!'

More confusion in the 'phones. This time it wasn't cheering. There were cries of alarm, orders immediately counter-manded, shouting.

'Colonel Kruger, you're about to have company. Two air-craft we can't identify. They're emitting the correct IFF code of the day but won't respond to radio contact. Bearing one-ten out of nowhere. They may not see you until it's too late for them to evade. Make due east and give her all the power you can, Colonel. Colonel? Eleven-four-one-five, do you read me? *Colonel Kru. . .*'

Kruger switched off his radio. By now he had strapped himself in, the autopilot was cancelled and he was ready for action. A last look to either side — the fighters had not changed station — then he put the Boeing into a sharp dive and gave her full throttle. His airspeed soon reached 600 mph, the maximum. When he was little more than a thousand feet above the ocean he levelled out and set a course north-west by north. The fighters were still beside him; Kruger could see their pilots try to attract his attention, first by visual signs, then by calling up his emergency code on the radio. His forehead broke into a sweat. Where the hell were those MiGs? He was flying the United States' most priceless military asset straight towards

92

Soviet Russia, ignoring all signals to stop. Sooner or later those Eagles were going to get orders to blast him out of the sky. What was Borovykh playing at?

Suddenly a flash of silver rippled across the Boeing's nose, followed almost at once by another. Two fighters in US livery; Kruger knew they were both emitting Code 6, the code of the day, from their Identify Friend and Foe equipment. They seemed almost to brush the aircraft's outer skin, and Kruger instinctively pressed back against his seat. Ahead of him the sky was empty. He darted a look to either side. The F-15s had gone.

Kruger did not see the dogfight, such as it was. The MiGs came out of the setting sun in classic style, and homed in on the portside Eagle. While the first Russian jet executed a high pass across the F-15's starboard wing, to draw fire, the second went into a tight, flat turn, wing-tip high, and came back underneath. Its first Aphid homed rapidly on the Eagle's APG-63 radar beam, found target and exploded on impact, sending burning wreckage and one charred human body plunging into the icy sea.

The first pilot never had a chance. He saw two 'friendlies' racing towards him at high speed; next second he was under attack. But the second Eagle was prepared. The pilot cut his radar with a sideways slash of the hand and climbed almost vertically, gaining height until the less powerful MiGs were forced to give way. At the pinnacle of his climb the pilot looped over and dived beneath the still-climbing Russians before they could respond.

Kruger, by now a good fifty miles away, saw none of this. Ahead of him the dark ocean stretched away to a cloudy horizon. It was empty.

He began to tune the radio. We shall transmit the morse letter O every five seconds, Control had said. That way you'll be able to find us on frequency *before* you need us. Don't neglect it.

Three longs. There they were. Kruger twisted the dial a fraction and listened. Dash-dash-dash. Pause. Dash-dash-dash. Pause. . . He was tuned in to Russia. All he had to do was follow the fragile beam stretching out towards him from infinity, and he was home.

Kruger's hands were clammy. He wiped the hair from his forehead and with his free hand reached for the water flask. Only a sip, now.

They had warned him about this part.

You'll be quite alone, said Control, and heading into empty space. You know we're there, on the radio, but you mustn't break silence until you're well inside Soviet territorial airspace. We'll tell you when you are. Don't try to be smart and guess. Remember, too, that we can't see you any more than the Americans. You're invisible. We'll have to estimate your position as best we can. If we think you're in real danger, only then will we contact you over the ocean. . .

Kruger's eyes strayed to the radio. Apart from the intermittent three longs, it stayed silent. He swallowed. His throat was parched.

A hundred miles behind him the battle was nearly over. As the Eagle pilot completed his loop the still climbing MiGs split into two arms of a V. The F-15 pilot followed the left-hand branch, loosing off one of his AIM-9 infra-red Sidewinders. Seconds later a purple and orange ball of flame marked the demise of the first Russian casualty. The pilot threw his F-15 into its incredible fourteen-degrees-per-second turn and regained Mach 2.5 speed, feeling the blood drain away to his feet. The head-up display simultaneously warned him of an approaching missile. Instinctively he corrected the turn and went into a corkscrew dive away from the white streak of the Aphid, which plunged harmlessly towards the sea.

A thousand feet above him the MiG pilot's finger curled round the trigger of his six-barrel Gatling. In the split second while the Eagle hung between the final twist of the corkscrew and its next manoeuvre, he fired. The two planes began to climb together, the F-15 rapidly gaining height on the Russian before suddenly it seemed to slow, falter, level out. A thin white vapour trail fled backwards from its starboard wing. The Russian brought the nose of his MiG-27 up a fraction, held her steady, and fired again. The Eagle had lost all power. Before he was aware of it the MiG pilot was on top of his enemy. As he began the evasive climb something seemed to erupt beneath him; his helmet was thrown against the toughened perspex hood, the stick juddered in his hands, for a hateful second he was out of control. . .then he gained height with the funeral pyre of his victim glinting dully through his anti-ray visor.

The MiG pilot flew north-west for just long enough to mark Kruger's AWACS on course for St Matthew Island before breaking away northwards for the safety of the Chukchi Sea.

Kruger flew steadily on. Everything was normal. He had more fuel than he needed, the radio stayed silent, sea and sky were empty to the horizon. He began to repeat to himself Control's words of comfort.

It will seem a long time. You will feel very lonely, very exposed. Such feelings are normal, but they are also misplaced.

For you must consider how little the Americans can do. Their land forces are useless in such an emergency. In the air they can do nothing. You have no radar signature, your radio is silent. The most natural assumption is that you have ditched. When they check it out they will find one of our spyships steaming in a circle right underneath the scene of your last recorded contact. They are going to waste a lot of time over that, Mitch.

Will they fire a missile after you? Hardly. They won't know in which direction you're flying and the risks of launching a heat-seeking missile so close to Soviet territory are stupendous. Suppose it overshot. . .

The AWACS had dropped below 500 feet. Kruger jerked on the stick, his heart pounding violently, and felt the heavy aircraft respond with protesting slowness. *Concentrate!'*

And no hot pursuit, Mitch. Control's smooth voice murmured quietly on inside Kruger's brain like a hypnotist's recording. To cover all the sectors where you might be they'd have to scramble planes from all over the States and send them towards Siberia at Mach 2. The Kremlin would read that in only one way: a declaration of war. No dice.

That leaves you with just one problem: the US Navy. If a cruiser happened to be in the right place at the right time, it could shoot you down. Their electronics would be bound to pick you up, even on a cloudy day. So before you even begin to highjack that AWACS, Mitch, we'll divert the cruiser. We'll

95

arrange for the captain to have something a little more exciting to chase. A Charlie-class submarine on the surface, complete with missiles. And if ever you're tempted to underrate the importance of your mission to us. . .just remember, Mitch, that's how far we're prepared to go to save it.

Kruger repeated the last words to himself over and over again. Still the silent sea stretched out ahead of him, dark grey steel under the low sub-Arctic sky. What were they doing at SAC West? *For the love of God, what?*

They were losing valuable time, squandering it like water.

For the best part of an hour before the MiGs started their run-in the attention of just about everyone in SAC West had been concentrated on the AWACS' progress. Routine low intensity surveillance of the Command's airspace continued, but there was nothing unusual in the pattern of traffic, civil and military, which criss-crossed the screens. The crisis, when it came, was all the worse for being totally unexpected.

The first to recover from the shock was Colonel James Andrews, the mission ground-controller. He ordered an immediate read-out of all aircraft movements within 500 square miles of Kruger's last reported position, then got on the phone to the headquarters of the Defence Satellite Communications System in Washington. Within minutes the first photographs were beaming down from the Ferret satellites stationed over Alaska and being sent along the wire to Elmendorf Base.

This took six minutes from their last radio contact with Kruger.

Very little time was wasted over the Soviet spyship. That problem was rapidly delegated to the Navy with a shrug.

The radar photographs provided by the satellites were of poor definition, made worse by the low level cloud and freezing rain which had started to drift down from the Pole. At about the same time conventional radar began to show up an enormous flight of hostiles on the US-Soviet border in the Bering Sea and an unnatural amount of interference. Andrews swore and banged the console in front of him with his clenched fist. Confetti. The bastards were trying to jam his electronics with confetti.

Ten minutes since last radio contact.

Andrews reached out for the red phone and in less than the seventeen seconds' tolerance permitted under the rules had connected himself to the National Military Command System in the Pentagon. Twelve minutes after Kruger broke off contact the order was given by the Chairman of the Joint Chiefs of Staff to go to Defence Level Four.

It was then that somebody first produced a fuzzy multi-spectral photograph of what might have been the AWACS, flying approximately north-east towards Eilson Field. Precious minutes were wasted while civil and military flights were eliminated one by one.

Seventeen minutes after Kruger's last recorded message Andrews decided that the grey smudge in the photograph was more probably than not the missing aircraft and he ordered up two squadrons of F-16s to intercept, one from Eilson and one from Elmendorf. Within seconds of taking off the Eilson squadron leader announced that the unidentified aircraft was not giving off an IFF code, which threw everyone into panic again until General Avis remembered that the AWACS' own IFF transmitter had been switched off in order to make the test flight more realistic.

Twenty-one minutes after the breaking of radio contact the Elmendorf squadron commander reported visual contact with a Boeing-707 civilian cargo plane in the approximate position indicated by the multi-spectral photograph. Andrews cursed again, swung his planes back through 180 degrees, put up everything he had and sent them all hurtling towards their fail-safe points on the US-Soviet frontier.

Three minutes later the President of the United States, speaking via the Automatic Secure Voice Network, personally ordered Andrews to hold his aircraft short of fail-safe and concentrate all his energies on conventional electronic saturation surveillance.

But by that time Kruger and his AWACS were far away.

The radio suddenly crackled and immediately went silent.

Kruger leaned forward, his face tense with excitement. Had it been his imagination? Or was it. . .?

97

'Good afternoon, Colonel Kruger.'

He closed his eyes with relief. He had made it. He had crossed the ocean. He was safe.

'Do *not* acknowledge this communication, please. In a moment you will receive instructions to alter course and height. Obey promptly. Maintain your present speed.'

Kruger listened attentively while the details of his new bearing were read out, and immediately executed the necessary changes. It was beginning to grow dark, and the cloudbank on the horizon was gaining greater substance. Suddenly he saw lights ahead, slightly to port. Was that land? Surely not. Then he saw that the light came from what seemed like little more than an outcrop of rock hardly breaking the surface of the wide sea. Cape Nawarin. The outermost limits of Soviet jurisdiction. . . He took his hands off the stick for long enough to clasp them before his eyes in a gesture of gratitude before settling down to steer the AWACS into the gathering dusk.

He had to change course several times in the next two hours, on each occasion gaining height to rise above the worsening Siberian weather. His instruments told him that he was flying over difficult, hilly terrain while the outside air temperature dropped steadily. Kruger was growing tired. The water in his flask was almost gone, and still there came no sign of the welcome landing strip they had promised.

Lights. Far away to starboard, illuminating hillocks of snow. A settlement, maybe. . .

The radio came to life.

'Please prepare for landing, Colonel Kruger. You have been warned already about the surface. Be ready with maximum reverse thrust immediately on touch-down. Visbility is down to fifty metres and you will have a left-to-right crosswind of six knots. The flares will be extinguished as soon as you land; do not be alarmed by this.'

The voice gave him calm, precise directions for the approach. Kruger concentrated all his waning attention on the voice and the strip of white flares growing ever larger through the front windshield. The snow seemed to be coming straight for him in white streaks of tracer. Too low, damn them, surely they were bringing him in too low. Was that a clump of trees on the left? Oh, God, God. . .inner marker! Gear. *Gear!*

His landing wheels came down just in time. Moments later they hit the runway, travelling at well over a hundred knots. As soon as the bump transmitted itself through the muscles of his arm Kruger reversed all the throttles and raised the spoilers.

Nothing happened.

He was travelling at nearly a hundred miles an hour along a sheet of ice and there wasn't a damn thing he could do about it. He twitched the rudder, and the nose responded. He touched the brakes. He was undoubtedly slowing. Eighty miles an hour. . .seventy. . .sixty. . . A moment later there was no doubt. He had control.

But the line of flares had almost run out. Ahead of him was only darkness. His jaw dropped and he pressed harder on the brakes. Forty miles an hour.

Skid.

The line of flares suddenly turned askew, the nose wheel simultaneously went soft on him, he heard high-pitched voices shouting outside. By now the plane was travelling at less than twenty miles an hour. He felt the nose wheel sink, lurch . . and then the plane came to a shuddering stop.

Outside everything was black. The flares had been extinguished. With a shaking hand Kruger shut down all systems. For a moment he couldn't move. Then he struggled up, not quite understanding his difficulty. The plane had embedded itself in soft snow at an angle. He had to climb uphill to get to the pilot's door.

As he swung it open a dozen torch beams converged on his face, and he raised an arm to ward them off. More shouting, in a language he didn't understand. Then a ladder was pushed up to the plane and held at the necessary awkward angle while he clambered down it.

The cold pierced his flying jacket from the first second. His ears were numb before he reached the ground. At the bottom they wrapped him up at once in a padded coat, put a fur hat on his head, and half supported, half carried him across to where the Mil-Mi-8 helicopter was standing. Strong hands pulled him up. As his head cleared the level of the floor he heard a voice. A familiar voice.

'You see, Mitch,' said Control, 'I told you it would work.'

Kruger lay on the deck and stared up at him, incredulous. 'But you. . .you're. . .'

Control crouched down beside him. 'I'm here, Mitch. I'm real. Feel.'

He offered Kruger his arm. The American took it.

'Simon. . .how. . .why?'

Control laughed. 'Not Simon. Not here. That was in the old days, in America. Here my name is Nikita Vasilevich Butenko. And I am here to welcome you home. *Your* home. Drink this. It'll make you feel better.'

Butenko's sharp eyes had seen something as yet unperceived by Kruger himself: reaction was setting in. The man needed rest. He looked over his shoulder and beckoned discreetly to the military doctor, who nodded and began to prepare a syringe.

Suddenly Kruger's glazed vision registered something strange by the open door of the helicopter. A moon. No: a round smiling face, barely visible above floor level. And next to it a taller man, with a red star plainly visible on the front of his fur hat, who did not smile.

'This, then, is the one?'

It was the jolly moon that spoke. Kruger heard Control reply with an unaccustomed note of respect in his voice.

'Yes, General Mironov. This is the one.'

As Kruger continued to stare the moon waned, so that only the tall man beside it remained visible. Then he, too, disappeared. Kruger swallowed.

'What happens. . .now?'

Control laughed good-naturedly. 'I never let you ask that question, did I?' He laughed again. 'Nothing. For the moment, we all go away. The men. Their equipment. Us. Everything.'

It took several seconds for the full meaning of this to penetrate Kruger's exhaustion.

'You mean you. . .you're going to *leave* it. . .out here?'

'With the wolves for company.'

'But that's crazy!'

'Is it, Mitch? Sit up a moment. Look.'

Through the helicopter's open door Kruger saw the snowflakes falling, and beyond that the outline of his plane. Already it had lost its sharpness under several inches of white powder. He looked up at Control with incomprehension in his eyes.

'Where does a wise man hide a leaf?' he heard the soothing voice ask him from somewhere infinitely distant; and in the same kind he answered, as so often before. 'In a forest.'

'And where does a wise man hide something from a heat sensor?'

Then, just before he slept, Kruger saw it. The whole thing. The beauty of it. The grandeur.

It was going to work after all, just like they said.

From far, far away he heard himself answer Control, like a child who suddenly, after long effort, perceives.

'Under a blanket of snow.'

Control gathered his limp body into his arms and hugged him tightly to his breast.

'Welcome home,' he whispered. 'Welcome home.'

9

No trace of the relaxed atmosphere which attended Bryant's first meeting with Povin now remained. The General had been met while he was still fifty metres from the chalet and brought down in a circle of thick, protective bodies to where C and Kirk Binderhaven stood waiting. Once inside the mood was tense but brisk.

'I am sorry about the date.' Povin sounded dispirited. He held an untouched drink to his chest, placed a hand on the mantelpiece and stared into the fire.

'It doesn't matter. You got so much else right.'

'The question is. . .' Bryant moved away from his position

by the window and lowered himself primly into an armchair. 'The question is whether you have anything more to tell us.'

For a moment there was silence while Povin continued to study the pattern in the grate. Then he straightened up. He seemed to slough off his weariness before their eyes, and for the hundredth time Bryant tried in vain to imagine what reserves of energy, of resilience, Povin must have needed over the years.

'Yes. Plenty. Success makes for exultation, and exulted people talk loudest of all. They're talking in a way which means they know they've won already. And I don't like it. You — ' Povin extended his glass towards Binderhaven — 'I can't afford to wait any longer. I need some answers of my own. You know the deal I want?'

'It's been explained to me. I'm certain there's nothing that can't be negotiated. So long as between us we can deliver.'

Povin grunted. 'That we can do. I believe that, now. What happens to my information once it's left me is up to you. I can't guarantee the recovery or destruction of the plane, Binderhaven. But you'll do everything in your power to see I get my two tickets no matter what happens, right?'

Binderhaven was angry.

'General, we are talking about trying to save the world from Armageddon and all you can talk about is your price? What kind of man are you? I was led to believe that you operated out of some kind of higher idealism, inspired by your religion.'

'Aah, shit. Don't you understand what I'm going through? Eh? Is it so dark where you're standing? Come over here by the fire, feel the heat, feel it burn you, scorch your hands! Go sit in the Square, back in Moscow, sit there for ten years, waiting for the sound of boots in the corridor outside, then come back to me and preach.'

Povin angrily hurled his glass into the grate and watched the resulting grey cloud of ash rise and dissipate. There was silence.

'I think,' said Bryant from the depths of his armchair, 'that this is all rather far from the point. General, would you be so good as to sit down and tell us what you know. And you, Kirk. . .may I suggest that you sit down also? That's right. Now, General. . .?'

102

Bryant turned to the Russian like the chairman of a brains trust consulting his most cherished but prickly expert. Povin ignored the invitation for a moment; when he did begin he spoke haltingly, still labouring under his sense of insult.

'The pilot of the AWACS was a GRU sleeper. He neutralised the rest of the crew shortly before the MiGs went in, then flew to Siberia, the far north-east. There are hundreds, thousands, of temporary landing strips there. They opened up one for just long enough to take the plane, then abandoned it again. By now it's covered with snow. That's so that your heat sensors in the satellites won't pick it up. Then everyone upped and left.'

Binderhaven leaned forward excitedly. 'You mean it's unguarded?'

'Oh, completely. They know you'll be scanning every square inch of the Soviet Union and they don't want you to see any unusual activity, any unnatural concentration of troops. No one's to go near it for ninety hours. After that time they'll dust it off, de-ice it, and fly it somewhere they can go over it properly.'

Binderhaven frowned. 'Risky. At that stage it'd be wide open for our satellites to pick up.'

'They have foreseen that. They are preparing decoy planes, Moss surveillance aircraft with jet engines. Several have just entered service. They will say that your satellites have detected one of their new aircraft, and you will not be able to prove the contrary.'

Binderhaven was silent. Povin took advantage of it to ask, 'What is happening in Washington?'

Binderhaven eyed him sourly. 'You really expect me to tell you that, General? Even if I knew. Which I don't.'

Povin shrugged. 'I was interested to see your reaction. After all, we're going to be comrades from now on. Fellow citizens shortly, I hope. But since you're still disinclined to trust me, let me tell you. Everyone's going crazy. The radios of the two F-15s which were escorting Colonel Kruger and his plane were jammed. As a result you have no idea what happened, none at all. The captain of the Aeroflot plane, which was nearest at the time, reported what may have been a mid-air collision between two unidentifiable aircraft of military type, but hardly anybody believes that.

'Your ferrets were confused by confetti, which we scattered, but you've checked with your sources in Moscow and you know that a big exercise in the Bering Sea had been planned months ago, so you can't make anything of that. And you never did manage to track down Kruger after you lost him. By shutting down all the electronics he ensured there were no emissions which could be traced.'

Povin grinned, his inherent national pride not quite proof against the skill with which the operation had been put together.

'And there were "ghosts", too, weren't there? That Boeing cargo plane. . .Oh, don't look so surprised, you know what I'm talking about. Way off the filed flight path, right? I should investigate the pilot, if I were you. How much time did that lose, I wonder? And then the Moss-126 that we floated out over Komandorskie Island. . . Did the radio scanners wet their pants when they saw that, eh?'

Povin's smile faded a little. 'But your biggest problem at the moment is keeping this whole thing under wraps. The President is due to make some kind of decision later tomorrow.'

Povin laughed, his good humour suddenly restored. 'If you like, I can get you a six page single-spaced report on the nutritional content, history and psychological value of the jellybean. What do you say?'

For a second Binderhaven melted. 'I'd swap it for the CIA's but that's twelve pages and it'd leave me up. And you've made your point. You have as much idea of what's going on in Washington right now as we do.'

'So, then. Let us get on. In three or four days' time Colonel Kruger will be taken back to his plane and told to fly it somewhere more accessible. It will be an air base north-west of Irkutsk, near Lake Baikal. Kruger will not know where he is going until he is actually airborne. The base has no name, only a number; it is far from any human settlement. I will give you the co-ordinates. You want to write them down?'

It was Bryant who replied. 'Repeat them several times,

please. We shall remember them.' And the tapes will if we don't, he was thinking.

Povin obliged. He repeated the numbers four times in all, until the others were satisfied that they had them accurately engraved on their memories.

'The scientists will be waiting. Scientists and technicians. They will take tens of thousands of photographs. They will construct laser holograms of some of the most important components which interest them. . .particularly the anti-radar system. Then, the Air Force are going to break it up, carefully, in such a way as to make it look as though the plane crashed into the sea and exploded on impact. The wreckage will be airlifted on to the *Kiev*, which will dump it out at sea, not too far from where Kruger began to divert. The last step is simple. We arrange for a disinterested third party — say Canada — to find traces of the wreckage. Probably we shall float some of it into the path of one of her submarines. And there you are — an ordinary accident, the sort of thing that can bedevil the best prepared pilot. The sealed flight recorder will tell whatever tale we wish.'

Povin sat back, knowing what Binderhaven's next question would be.

'And do you have any ideas on how this might be prevented, General?'

Povin smiled. 'I know what your President's first reaction will be, if that's any use. The GRU's games computer has produced all the likely scenarios. First comes a low level, high speed raid to blast the AWACS on the ground.' Povin shrugged. 'It's not impossible. You know how our air defences are. Out of a thousand planes, one might get through — probably would, in fact. If he could get permission to overfly China, come in from the south, the odds in his favour would increase. That's not impossible either, of course. Lake Baikal is close to the border. But in Moscow they're betting he won't get permission, and won't dare take it regardless. An airstrike is what they're hoping for because it means they've won straight away. You've blundered into the trap. But the GRU think it won't happen. The AWACS is the single most vital link in your defences, but if it comes to the crunch there are thought to be enough sane men close to the President to guarantee that the USA doesn't go to war with the Soviet Union over its loss. So the second scenario is the one they're expecting: recall of ambassadors, total severance of all contact at every level, no grain exports, immediate military aid to China . . . And once that happens, we can forget about detente for the rest of our lives.'

The three men sat sunk in gloom. After a while Bryant stood up and went round filling their glasses.

'But there is another way. The way we have already chosen.'

Binderhaven looked up to see that Povin's face wore a troubled look.

'We are going for EST. As far as I can see, they're not expecting that. They just don't think it's possible.'

'EST?'

Binderhaven turned to Bryant. 'Emergency Service Team. The sort of thing usually done by your SAS. In the US Army we call it a Special Force Group, in the Navy it's SEAL.'

'And in the Air Force,' said Povin, looking at the ceiling, unable even at this critical moment to resist a demonstration of how much he knew, 'Special Operations Wing.' He lowered his eyes to Bryant's face. 'Opa Locka Field, Florida. The base from which they flew support missions for the Bay of Pigs.' The smile to which he treated Binderhaven was glacially polite.

The American took no notice.

'We put in a team. . .two teams, in fact. A ground-to-air missile attack. . .they could take the AWACS as it's coming in to land. . .'

His veneer of caution dropped. He stood up and began to pace backwards and forwards.

'It'll work. I expect it to work. But we'll be taking almighty risks. And we'll never get out alive.'

'You might,' said Povin. 'Remember who you're talking to. I still pack a punch. I've been thinking it over since we last met. I could help get the men in, you were right about that. I could maybe even smooth their passage to the target. Afterwards they could perhaps lie low for a few months, then we'd get them out. I could help arrange that also.'

106

Binderhaven stopped in mid-stride and faced the Russian. 'I've been thinking about it, too. The less you have to do with all this the better, General. What you don't know you can't tell. We'll handle this alone. You're practically inviting us to invade the Soviet Union with a clandestine force. You know what that would mean if we were caught, specially if we had missiles in our grips.' Binderhaven shook his head. His smile was arch. 'You sure don't make it any easier to trust you, General. I never heard such a proposal.'

'But you yourself said it would work. . .'

'So it might. But if a General in the KGB knew it was on the cards. . .oh, come on.'

The Russian sighed. 'Very well. As I said before, what you do with my information is up to you. Let me at least finish all I have to say. I have arranged to be told very shortly after Kruger takes off. I have a good contact, he owes me a lot. Now that the lid is coming off, he's bursting to talk. As soon as the news reaches me, I will forward it. I do not know how, but I will find a way. The days of our leisurely relationship are over, Sir Richard. A brief period of all out war, and then I am finished in the Square. From now on I sleep in my boots and work how I can.'

He stood up, and the other men rose also.

'I must go now. I am recalled to Moscow for the day after tomorrow. That is quite normal; there have been no sudden changes of plan. I want an answer, Binderhaven. A definite proposal, with dates, times and places. You understand me?'

'I understand. I'll go the rounds in Washington, do what I can.'

Povin nodded abruptly. 'I hope so. Good night.'

Bryant escorted him to the back door, where the sentries were waiting. As he returned to the living room Bryant was suddenly assailed by tiredness. Binderhaven noticed, and reacted with sympathy.

'We work long hours.'

Bryant yawned and nodded. He was secretly worried about losing his grip. So many days away from his London head-quarters made him feel forlorn and isolated.

'Povin's right about one thing,' said Binderhaven.

'I still happen to think that Povin is right about most things. But go on.'

'Those were the only two options. Washington has gone to pieces, by all accounts, but everyone's agreed on one thing: the AWACS is the best form of defence we have. We simply can't allow that particular aircraft to be examined by Russian scientists. It puts us ahead in the arms race by at least ten years. Unless the Soviets get to see inside it, they'll just never catch up.'

'You really think the President would argue for the kind of raid that Povin outlined? You've probably no idea how astonishing that sounds to English ears.'

'Oh, he's just the man to do it — and enjoy doing it.'

'So it's this EST thing. As I thought it would be, all along.'

Binderhaven stretched out his legs and examined his shoes. 'I don't like it. It scares me, Richard. The President would never buy it, that's the first thing. We'll have to keep it secret from him, from the State Department, the Pentagon. . . Suppose the Russians rounded up a bunch of guys in Siberia, American citizens, armed with missiles. If they'd already succeeded, OK. The Russians would never dare make any of it public. But suppose they're waiting for them already. Suppose the KGB *expect* these guys? What then?'

Bryant said nothing.

'Anyway, I guess we'll soon know.'

It took several moments for the implications behind this remark to penetrate Bryant's tired brain. When he looked up he found Binderhaven's eyes watching him closely.

'I assume we're being recorded right now?'

'Yes.'

'Who gets to hear the tape?'

'Myself. Possibly the Prime Minister, but by no means certainly.'

'Well. . . I seem to be holding the ball and I guess it's me who decides who runs with it.' He hesitated. 'I have a man on the Trans-Siberian right now, travelling east from Moscow. Another's due to follow him in a few hours. And a third's flying to Siberia tomorrow night. They're due to meet up in Irkutsk. And I'll be there, too.'

'Good God!'

'I didn't reckon the General ought to know about that. The fewer the better.'

'These men are armed?'

'No. It was judged too risky. We'll need help from Povin there, that I grant you. No, these men just happen to be heading towards more or less the right area. It's the one thing we have going for us. Irkutsk is on the shore of Lake Baikal.'

'What do they do once they get there?'

'Wait for me to catch up. They're being met by an Emily. The local Intourist girl.'

For all his concern, Bryant was impressed and even slightly reassured by this news. An 'Emily' is a particular kind of agent: a national of the target country who makes a mistake — just one — and is thereafter under the control of the CIA. Given long enough, they often become the most reliable of all possible contacts.

'But can you do it in time?'

'I think so. The Trans-Siberian Express is usually on schedule. If all that Povin says is true, we have another three, nearly four days before the AWACS is dug out and moved. If I go in and join the train at Novosibirsk, which is what I plan to do, we'll have between twenty-four and forty-eight hours to stake out the target. If we can't do it in that time. . .' He shrugged.

'You're not going to like this, Kirk, but I think you should tell Povin. He could help you.'

Binderhaven chopped the air with the cutting edge of his right hand. 'No way! Sorry, Richard, but that's how it is and that's how it stays.'

'I think you're wrong.'

'Maybe I am. But this guy comes out of the blue, says he wants to exchange being top KGB General for life in the Mid-West, together with boyfriend, and by the way, would we care to send a bunch of armed troops into Siberia? None of it hangs together. No, we'll wait and see how good his information is. So far he's doing OK. I've made soundings, like I told him. This deal he wants to make. . . It's possible. But I tell you, Richard. . .'

Binderhaven stood up and went to stand by Bryant's chair. He spoke the next words very quietly.

'If one of us gets killed, just one, however much like an accident it may look. . . General Povin is going to stay right where he is. In Moscow. For keeps.'

10

Senior Lieutenant Valyalin was becoming a little concerned about Colonel Frolov's behaviour. The night before his chief had kept them all until after nine o'clock, running to and fro between the office and the Registry, carrying great bundles of files, making précis of individual case histories. When Valyalin reported for duty this morning, rubbing the sleep from his eyes, he found Frolov still at his desk, musing over files. On the wall behind him, however, was something new: a huge chart showing a pyramid of names, hundreds of them.

The Senior Lieutenant decided to take a chance, and peered closer. The very top name, in red ink and underlined, was simply 'Mishka'. He blinked, then it dawned. A case name, inspired by Frolov's lucky doll which sat, grinning blankly, on the mantelpiece.

Immediately underneath the same Mishka, also in red but not underlined, was a name he knew. Stolyinovich. A lot of Valyalin's waking hours had been filled with that name recently. He felt he was becoming quite intimately acquainted with the famous concert pianist. Interesting, too: plenty of meat. He wondered, not for the first time, how Stolyinovich had managed to escape the attentions of the Second and Fifth Main Directorates for so long, since he travelled frequently abroad and had some friends who were, to put it mildly, anti-Soviet.

All the other names in the pyramid were entered in black.

Some of them he recognised from recent researches, others meant nothing to him.

'Come over here, Valyalin. Sit down.'

Valyalin pulled his chair close up beside the Colonel's. If Frolov was exhausted by eighteen hours on the go, his voice showed no sign of it. For a wild moment Valyalin wondered if his boss was 'high' on something, then discarded the notion as very probably treasonable.

'Here, you want one of these things?'

Frolov held out a packet of Novostj. His second secretary thought longingly of the Winstons in his own top pocket, and accepted.

'Now listen. You've worked hard these past few days, you and the boys, and I'm grateful. Let them know that. But this Stolyinovich thing is now officially closed. Get me?'

Valyalin nodded.

'I don't have to tell you how hush-hush it has to be kept. Top pianist, stayed with Old Eyebrows himself, Lenin Prize, you name it. Hot shit, eh?'

Valyalin nodded again.

'We had a rumour that he was a carrier. Nothing specific, just enough to make us want to check up on him. Well, we've done that now, and he's clean. Clean as a whistle.'

Valyalin raised an eyebrow.

'I know what you're thinking. He's a sodomite. So are plenty of others I could mention. But there's no scandal and he leaves the kids alone.' Frolov spoke a couple of names. One of them belonged to a candidate member of the Politburo. 'I don't have to stress that we are hardly going to put these men on trial because they have unusual sexual tastes.'

'No, sir.' Valyalin risked a small joke. 'We'd need another floor in the Butyrki to hold them all.'

Frolov guffawed loudly and slapped Valyalin on the back.

'Good boy. Realistic. I like that. Now listen. I want you to take all these files back yourself, *yourself*, you hear? Spread the word. The investigation's over, it never happened. No matter *who* asks. Got that?'

'Yes, Colonel.'

'Get on with it, then. Oh, leave the chart. I'll dispose of that.'

'Yes, sir. Who is Mishka, sir?'

Frolov looked up with a scowl, saw the innocent look on Valyalin's face and thought better of what he had been about to say. 'Whoever he was carrying for. If he was carrying. Which, as it turned out, he wasn't. Now on your way.'

Frolov waited until Valyalin had gathered up the files and departed before putting his legs on the desk and folding his arms behind his neck. Not even his tiredness could quite overcome the excitement he felt daily growing within him.

Povin and Stolyinovich were friends. It went way back. Stolyinovich was homosexual. That they could overlook. But emerging was a pattern which could not be ignored quite so easily. Nearly three quarters of Stolyinovich's known friends and associates were Christians, open or secret. That proportion was high. Frolov regarded it as statistically significant. What was more, there was evidence to suggest that Stolyinovich himself was a believer.

Frolov wished he wasn't so tired, because he knew that there was a choice facing him and he couldn't duck it any longer. He could pull back now, and the chances were that would be the end of it. No repercussions, no complications later. Or he could go on. But if he went on, he had to identify a goal: something precise and definite at which to aim. It was no good looking for vague dirt to hang on Povin: at his level that was sometimes possible but it led nowhere, because the people you reported it to had their own sordid secrets to hide, as well as a vested interest in keeping their fellow moguls in power.

Only if you happened to grab the swing in the moments before a palace revolution, only then did the opportunities for placing a knife in an unwanted back become boundless.

He must define his suspicions. Until now he had been putting it off. Was there a charge he could bring home to Povin, or not?

Not everyone was pleased when Povin landed the job of Head of Foreign Intelligence. There were people who said — very quietly — that although Michaelov was a bastard, the traitor was someone else. Such people never so much as hinted at a possible candidate, but you didn't have to be Einstein to make the connection. And if it could ever be proved. . .

Frolov glanced up at the calendar. He still had a few days before Povin was expected back from Geneva. Maybe he needn't decide just yet, after all. If he could only talk to someone who was close to the ins and outs of the Kyril affair. Someone who was now neutral, on the sidelines, with no axe to grind. Someone like. . .

Stanov.

He picked up the phone. As he did so he chanced to catch sight of the doll's beady eyes glinting down at him from above the fire. Mishka. . . Frolov licked his lips.

'Valyalin. . . I'm taking a quick trip. Arrange a flight to Tbilisi. I'll be coming back the same night. And Valyalin. . . if anyone asks, I'm at home with influenza and not to be disturbed by anyone. Do you understand? Not by *anyone*.'

As he replaced the receiver it seemed to him that there was something at the back of the doll's glassy eyes which he didn't much like.

11

It was a day for surprises. First the Director of the Central Intelligence Agency steered Binderhaven away from the black Lincoln waiting on the Langley forecourt and pointed him in the direction of a grubby green Ford Mustang parked discreetly out of sight behind a belt of trees. Then the Director took the wheel himself. Lastly, instead of taking the freeway for Washington he turned west, and within half an hour had Binderhaven thoroughly lost in a maze of pine-skirted dirt roads.

Binderhaven asked no questions. When this kind of thing happened it boded no good, and he preferred to wait for his trouble to catch up with him rather than go to meet it. But he was not unduly surprised to detect the Director's reluctance to be seen with him in public.

It was the kind of grey winter's day which shades all colour from the landscape. Under a sky of low cloud they climbed steadily through the wooded hills until at last they emerged from the treeline on the side of a bare hillside bounded by a tall perimeter wire fence. Binderhaven found it all infinitely depressing. Lumberjacks had been at work and the black soil was littered with mutilated tree stumps. Towards the top of the hill a gang was still attacking one of the last standing pines, their bright over-jackets the only touch of colour as far as his eyes could see, the 'clunk' of their axes echoing through the cold air of late afternoon.

The car drew up outside a gate in the fence. Binderhaven looked out and recognised two of the Director's 'mob', as they were known within the Company — the mafiosi who guarded the *capo di tuti capi*. They were unmistakable in their neat Saks overcoats, sunglasses worn to protect them against a non-existent sun, and hard, downturned faces. Binderhaven smiled without humour. He had always found the theatricality hard to live with. He never got used to it. At the end of his four years with the CIA he still found it just as irksome as the day he joined.

Between the gate and the crown of the hill where the lumber gang were working stood a tumbledown shack. It consisted of old planks, much discoloured by wind and rain, complemented by sheets of corrugated iron and metal stakes. Through the Mustang's tinted glass window Binderhaven could hear the high-pitched groan of a power saw.

'I suggest you put these on, Kirk.'

The Director was holding out a pair of long rubber boots; Binderhaven noted that the chief's feet were already similarly shod.

'Your size. I checked records.'

Binderhaven grinned and bent awkwardly to take off his shoes. By the time he had finished the Director was standing up to his ankles in thick mud, surveying the scene. As Binderhaven came up behind him he turned and smiled, pipe in hand. Binderhaven looked to see which it was and saw with relief

114

that he had chosen an old favourite, a briar with a bowl carved into the likeness of a human face. That was OK. It meant this windswept dump was unlikely to be the scene of his termination with maximum prejudice. The smooth meerschaum which the Director was rumoured to keep for hatchet jobs had been left at home.

As Binderhaven joined him the Director turned and began to trudge up the hill, fiddling with his pipe the while. It struck Binderhaven that they made a pretty incongruous pair: the Director in his knee-length suede overcoat and trilby hat, himself in mohair coat over ridiculous gum boots. He felt exposed, and very cold. The wind was sharp enough to take off the outer layer of skin.

'Dick Helms told me about this place, of all the damned people. Reckoned to use it about once every ten years. 'Course, Directors tend not to last that long.'

Binderhaven remained silent and conserved energy for the climb. The Director, a sprightly 67-year-old, talked on.

'This outfit's owned by an ex-employee of ours. Employee, hell. . .used to run the Pacific Seaboard Desk. Nice and quiet. Exposed, too. All those guys — ' the Director gestured with his pipe stem in the direction of the lumber gang — 'are told to look out for strangers.'

They were approaching the shack. The noise of the saw was louder now, so much so that Binderhaven found difficulty in concentrating.

'And the racket means we can't be bugged.'

As if to prove it he pushed open the door of the shack and ducked inside. Binderhaven held his hands to his ears. The shriek of metal on hardwood was almost deafening. As they entered, a third man appeared out of the gloom beyond the mechanical saw, surveyed the Director for a moment, and nodded. The Director raised his pipe in greeting with a smile. As if satisfied, the newcomer reached out a hand to the power console and the noise subsided to a tolerable level. Binderhaven lowered his hands.

'Can you leave it like that, Mike?'

The third man nodded and went out. The Director watched him descend the hill towards the fence in silence. His hands were busy with a box of matches, the ritual of filling now complete.

'Once every so often, Kirk, it becomes necessary for a Director of Intelligence to have a conversation which is impossible. Just literally that. A conversation which cannot conceivably have taken place — and so did not. You follow me?'

Binderhaven was aware of a new source of cold. It seemed to radiate from within his body, in time to the beating of his heart. He was scarcely conscious of the cheek-burning wind, which penetrated the gaps in the walls of the ramshackle hut, or of the noisy saw behind him. All his energies were focused on the Director.

'In a couple of hours' time I'm due at the White House. The President's going to listen to me — and others — then make up his mind. What's he going to do, Kirk?'

Binderhaven said nothing. Every instinct told him that the slightest movement, the simplest word, could one day be used against him. In silence and stillness lay his only chance of safety.

'Well, let me make a few suggestions.'

In spite of the draughts the Director's pipe was glowing, a skill perfected on the deck of many a ship in his previous Service incarnations. If he was aware of Binderhaven's growing tension he gave no sign of it.

'Basically they're the same as Nidus outlined, according to your account. The President could do nothing. That way the Soviets get to see inside of our aircraft, they break the secret of anti-radar. . .'

'But is that really so?' Binderhaven was uneasily aware of a new note of desperation in his voice. 'Can we be sure that they have the expertise to understand the technology? Maybe we're overrating the Russians.'

The Director smiled patiently. 'They'll understand it, Kirk. Remember, they'll be looking over a fully operational, working model. The real thing, set, primed, ready to go. There's no doubt about it: the Russians will be able to analyse the technology and then copy it.'

Binderhaven said nothing. The Director's lips twitched in a

116

half smile, but apart from that he betrayed no reaction.

'Like I was saying, the President could do nothing. No war, no risk of war. But as we both know, the President isn't going to favour that option. So what's next? Well, he's aware that it might be theoretically possible to infiltrate some men into central Siberia. Trouble is, they're unarmed — just in case they're caught. There's limits to what they could achieve with their bare hands. And, of course, there'd be no question of enlisting General Povin's help. None whatsoever. You still with me, Kirk?'

Binderhaven forced himself to look the Director in the eye. He had heard that this was a good man to work for. You did not dissemble with such men.

'To be frank, Mr Director. . .I'm not sure I want to be anywhere with you right now.'

He had put in a plea for some strictly unofficial help. Now, he was getting his answer. And for the first time, he felt unsure.

The Director grinned. For a few moments he smoked his pipe in silence.

'That's understandable. But why not see where we get to anyway? I've dealt with two options. Now for a third. The President can order the Joint Chiefs of Staff to prepare a military solution — nothing less than a full air strike on Soviet territory with the aim of destroying the AWACS on the ground. And you know something, Kirk? That's exactly what the President's going to want to do.'

'That's what I was afraid of.'

The Director looked sideways at Binderhaven and his eyes were suddenly hard. 'There's no doubt about it, Kirk. You want to take some time and think about that?'

Binderhaven turned away and went to the door whence he could see out across the hillside. The Director had merely spoken aloud what he had been inwardly dreading for days now. It was an impossible, incredible nightmare. It also happened to be coming true. He clenched his hands in the pockets of his overcoat and closed his eyes.

'Come over here, Kirk. Want to show you something.'

He turned back to see the Director disappear into the gloomy recesses of the hut. A moment later a light flickered on and he registered a workbench fixed to the rear wall. The Director was standing next to it. On the bench beside him stood what looked like three executive briefcases.

Binderhaven came closer. As he approached he saw that the cases varied in size a little, and were of different colours, but were otherwise indistinguishable from one another and from thousands of similar objects that appeared each day on the streets of Washington.

'Open one. Any one.'

Binderhaven chose the nearest. His first impression was one of clutter. Then he examined it more closely and saw that it had been packed with immense care, so that every inch of space was fully used. There were two lengths of tubing, a hank of thick black wire, what looked like a rifle's telescopic sight, and a long, round solid object resembling an outsize bullet. The rest of the case was taken up with bits and pieces which Binderhaven couldn't identify. He looked up to find the Director's eyes fixed firmly on his own, and smilingly shook his head.

'It's a General Dynamics XFIM-92A Stinger. Shoulder-fired, surface-to-air missile launcher. That. . .' He indicated the bullet. 'That's a smooth-case, fragmenting missile. Only one, no room for more. Whole thing measures sixty by two-and-three-quarters by five-and-a-half inches when assembled, weighs thirty-one pounds complete, can be set up and launched by one man. It has a range of three miles and it's accurate: I mean, wholly accurate. It's got something called passive infra-red homing, which latches on to a vapour trail rather than afterburn. All you've got to do is point it up and in the vague direction of whatever it is you want to hit.'

The Director closed the lid of the case with obvious care.

'You see these combination locks? Be careful with them. If you set all the nines, right across, you prime the auto-destruct. Unless, of course, you've pre-set the safety device. When this thing goes up, it takes everything within a radius of a hundred yards with it. There's nothing left for a hostile to analyse. So like I say, be careful how you handle them. And don't try to unpack them before you need to: you'll never get 'em back in the cases.'

Binderhaven knew the time had come to take care of an

obvious point. 'I'm assuming you're going to let me handle these?'

The Director paid no attention. 'Officially, those weapons don't exist. They're not on any Service inventory. They've been stripped of any identification marks they ever had. I went to considerable lengths to get them, Kirk, but they're clean. No way can they be traced back to me. The question is — do you want them?'

Binderhaven stared him in the eyes for a long moment before replying. 'I want them, yes. But there's one thing puzzles me. Why are you letting me have them? I mean, why *me*? I didn't exactly qualify for my long-service gold watch, remember.'

'But you're all I've got, Kirk. You've met Nidus. No one from the Company, myself included, is voluntarily going to come within a thousand miles of him. Nidus is the only man who can get these weapons to your emergency team in Siberia. And you're the only man who can get to Nidus. You also happen not to be connected in any way with the US Government or any of its intelligence agencies.'

He hesitated, as if reluctant to go on.

'There's something else, at that. I said earlier, I checked out your record. You're an idealist, Kirk. That was part of the problem when you worked for us. Well, maybe now we need an idealist.' He blew out his cheeks and smiled. 'Simple, isn't it?'

The Director turned to rest his back against the workbench. Binderhaven did not follow suit. Instead, he placed his hands on the wood and allowed his head to sink forward on to his chest. Suddenly he felt very tired.

'In the unlikely event of the President going ahead with his preferred plan, as I know and as you know he will want to do, there is going to be a war.' Now it was the Director's turn to sound unconcerned, matter-of-fact. 'A global conflict. I needn't enter into a debate with you over that, Kirk. Let's just say that I'd prefer for there not to be a war. Maybe there's only an outside chance of one — but I'm still going to do everything in my power to stack the odds against it. Let's suppose I have the chance to try for the destruction of that damn plane before the Eagles go in. What am I to do, Kirk? Pass it up?'

'Are you sure you have even that chance?'

'How d'you mean?'

'Suppose Nidus doesn't deliver. . .has no intention of even trying?'

'Oh, but he will. I've talked to C, long and seriously.' Seeing the surprise in Binderhaven's look he smiled, and tapped out his pipe on the workbench. 'He's convincing, Kirk. Although he did once let us down very badly. But even if I'm wrong about Nidus. . . I'd rather take my chance. Anything's better than the alternative, even a no-hoper. Because you see. . .at least I'd have tried.'

Binderhaven raised his head.

'I'd have done what I could.'

'And if we're caught? Caught with those things in our possession?' Binderhaven was surprised at the bitterness in his voice.

The Director allowed the pause to develop for rather too long. 'You won't be,' he said gently. 'Remember what I said about the auto-destruct mechanism. I told you I needed an idealist.'

'And if we don't have time to use it?'

'Then here in Washington we can talk our way out. We don't know the men, the weapons look like ours but we have no manufacturing records for them. It's not so far from the truth. This is a mercenary operation, with C paying your expenses, courtesy of the British taxpayer. Kirk. . .' The Director took Binderhaven by the shoulders and made him look into his own eyes. 'I can see it. Believe me, I can. All kinds of things could go wrong. Nidus could be a double agent, just waiting for me to do what I'm doing right now. The guys who go may get caught. Any one of a hundred things might happen, and blow us all to hell. But right now, all I need is the answer to one simple question. Are you prepared to take the risk that the President might just conceivably order a strike?'

Binderhaven moved away to the door. Behind him the Director struck another match and re-lit his pipe as unconcernedly as if he had just offered the Company's former employee the chance of buying into a sweepstake.

From where Binderhaven was standing he had a perfect

view, not of lumberjacks or the still-frosty hillside, but of a hopeless future. Whatever happened, his life was going sky-high. Besides, what was the point of reviewing a decision irrevocably made? 'I'm way. . .way. . .ahead of you.'

The Director came to stand by his side. 'What?'

'I'm booked on tonight's plane. The other three are already on the inside.'

For a moment the Director said nothing; then Binderhaven heard a chuckle at his shoulder, and turned to see his companion shake his head.

'McDonnell, I suppose.'

A sudden vision came to Binderhaven, as the hillside beneath him dissolved away. Darkness all around, the lapping of water. Snap of a concealed sniper's bullet. Groan, rigorously suppressed, the world turned upside down, white fire crackers dancing along the river bank, two men falling, falling. . .

'McDonnell, yes, he's one.'

As the Director heard the name force its way softly through Binderhaven's clenched teeth he knew a momentary chill which had nothing to do with the frost outside.

'No second thoughts?' he said quietly, after a pause.

'None.'

The single word was spoken softly to the outside world, somewhere beyond the treeline, but the Director's ears were sharp that day. 'Good,' he said. 'Then let's get the hell out of here.'

12

Father Michael's last act of the day before leaving the tiny church of St Nicholas was to replenish the earthenware pot of grain which stood on a table by the door. It was there that the faithful said prayers for the departed, standing just as Fr

Michael stood now, remembering those of his flock who had passed over. So many, too many, the old man thought sadly to himself, as his hand fumbled for the light switch. A last look round: the heavy screen, rich with icons and candles, the altar table, font and Book, everything in its appointed place, untouched by the woes of the world outside. The door creaked as the old priest let himself out into the biting cold; then the church was once more given up to stillness, and a darkness made more dense by the solitary red eye of the Saviour's burning grace.

As he fumbled with the key the old man's mind turned, as so often before, to the days of Father Dudko. While blessed Father Dimitri had remained among them it had seemed almost as if a new resurrection was nigh. That couldn't last, of course. They, the Organs, were like death, coming for everyone in the end. Even for poor Fr Dudko.

Father Michael eased his weary bones into the front seat of the tiny Zaporozhets-968 parked by the kerb outside the church and heaved a sigh of relief. The car was very old and very frail and therefore had a lot in common with its owner, who was passionately fond of it. The car was all that stood between him and compulsory retirement by the church authorities, since without it he could no longer have managed his daily round. No one was quite sure where the car had come from, and Fr Michael took care not to ask any potentially embarrassing questions. One day it was just somehow 'there', that's all anybody needed to know, and who said miracles belonged to the Testaments?

Fr Michael inserted the key in the ignition and breathed a short prayer. Sometimes the Zap started, sometimes it didn't. When he first owned it, a good few years ago now, there had been incidents with the militia, always asking him to move along and making endless trouble when he couldn't, because a piston had failed, or the plugs were wet. But recently there had been a thaw; not much of one, but a distinct and very welcome tinge of warmth none the less. The militiaman was now as likely to give him a friendly push as ask him to move on. At least under Brezhnev (God rest the old brute's soul) the Church knew where it was, like everyone else. . .

'Don't be alarmed,' said a quiet voice very close to his ear. 'Start the engine and drive off as usual. Don't turn round.'

For a moment there was silence while Fr Michael strove to steady his hands and ignore the ugly palpitations of his heart. His heart was like the engine of the Zap: living on borrowed time. Or so the doctor and the mechanic told him.

'God has come for me at last,' he said, his voice heavy with ironic amusement. 'About time, I say.'

'Not the other gentleman?' said the quiet voice pleasantly.

'The Devil work for the Organs?' Fr Michael sounded very shocked. 'How could you suggest such a thing, my son?'

Povin laughed softly. 'Start the car,' he said.

In the priest's one-room apartment it was very cold even with the single bar of the electric fire glowing away in the corner. The two men sat without light, enjoying the peace of each other's company. Old friends, these, with not much call for words. . .

Povin could just make out the angular black shape of the priest's body, and the two dull eyes which stared at him from within his thick, bushy beard. It was very far from being the first time that he had sat in this chilly room with Fr Michael. What troubled him was the knowledge that this might be the last.

'Do you want some tea?'

'No thank you, Father.' Povin dug into his overcoat pocket and pulled out a flask. 'Will you have some of this?'

'You know I never touch it,' said the priest, after a long pause. Povin smiled but did not reply. 'A taste, then. Enough to moisten a finger's end.'

And soak your beard six times over, thought Povin with compassion. He passed the flask across and watched the old man take quick, nervous swigs before handing back the flask with unmistakable reluctance. Povin took it, but continued to lean forward as if striving to discern Fr Michael's features. At last he sat back, but with the air of one who is not yet satisfied.

'Do you want to confess?'

'Not tonight.'

'Why not tonight? It is as good as any other time.'

'There's nothing new.'

'There's always something new.'

Silence fell once more. The exchange had to be repeated for form's sake, both men knew that. It was not as if either of them expected a different outcome.

'Do you remember telling me once. . .?' Povin began, only to tail off indecisively. The priest folded his hands in his lap and looked at the fire. Povin tried again.

'Do you remember saying, we should always have our bags packed, always be ready to depart at a moment's notice?'

'Indeed. My bags have been packed and in the hallway for a great many years now, only somehow the cab never seems to arrive.' It was as though irony distilled itself somewhere deep inside the priest's soul, so intricate a part of him had it become. 'Russian-made cab, I daresay. Always breaking down. . . Why? You going somewhere?'

Povin said nothing, but took another long pull from the flask while Fr Michael averted his eyes. When Povin handed it across to him he took it without looking, as if his hand were guided by instinct.

'Not going anywhere,' said Povin at last. 'Just thinking about the future, that's all. About when I'm dead.'

The priest looked up sharply. 'That's a strange thought, coming from you.'

'Why? You think I'm exempt, perhaps? Because I'm a General in the Organs I've somehow been endowed with eternal life? Maybe you're right at that.' Povin's voice was bitter. 'What other damnation would be sufficient, after all? To live for ever. . .'

Povin slumped in his chair, and for a moment Fr Michael thought he was about to drain the flask to its very dregs. But instead, after a long pause, the General corked it with steady, meticulous care, and replaced it in his pocket.

'Why this concern?' For the first time the old man's voice contained a note of what might have been anger. 'You chose your path. In the beginning, when you first sat in that chair, we would agonise together through the night and I did what I could to dissuade you but still you chose. *You*, Stepan Ilyich. No one else. *You*.'

124

'What choice? You make it sound so easy. For someone in my position . . .'

Fr Michael sighed loudly enough to check the rising whine in Povin's voice, and for a moment there was silence.

'We've talked of this before,' Povin said wearily. 'Many times.'

'Indeed, yes. Somehow it has never been resolved to the satisfaction of me or you. Or, I suppose, God.'

'Or my mother. Suppose they had never taken her away. What if I had prevented that in the first place?'

Fr Michael sighed again. 'There was nothing you could do for her. If you had tried, they would have shot you both.' Now it was the priest's turn to sound weary. 'Of course, you were not called upon to make that sacrifice. Besides, it made no difference. She was not the stuff of which martyrs are made. I forgave you long ago. God forgave you long ago. So tell me, Stepan Ilyich . . .' The old man leaned forward to rest his arms on his knees. 'Why can you not forgive yourself?'

Povin hung his head. Here was a question he could not answer. The silence following the priest's words stretched out to the far horizon which represented his death and whatever lay beyond that.

He rose abruptly and began to stride up and down the narrow room, hands clenched to his forehead.

'What would you have done in my place?' he muttered.

For a long time the priest sat in silence, trying to put himself in the place of an ambitious young Lieutenant at the start of a career who suddenly discovered that his mother had secretly embraced the Christian faith and was in danger of being betrayed to the authorities by her own husband. Fr Michael had performed this mental exercise many, many times before; the answer was always the same. The ambitious young Lieutenant was powerless to prevent his mother's arrest, just as when, two days later, she was returned to her home in the middle of the night, wandering in her mind, half naked, bloody, bruised, there was nothing he could do to prevent her renouncing Christianity for ever. Nothing.

But a fuse had been lit.

The old man shook his head slowly from side to side, and

remained silent. After a while Povin removed his hands from his forehead and heaved a long, deep sigh which tore at Fr Michael's heart.

'I want you to have something.' Povin rummaged in one of his pockets and pulled out a thick envelope sealed with wax. 'Here.'

'What is it?'

'Nothing dangerous, I guarantee that.'

'Ah! Money, then. Money is always dangerous.'

'I promise that it is not dangerous, not in any physical sense.'

The priest shrugged. 'You think I care about that any more? At my age? Let them come.'

Povin had recovered his composure. When he spoke it was in his usual tone of quiet reasonableness. 'You should not talk like that, Father. It's a foolish thing to say.'

'Is it?' Fr Michael chuckled softly to himself. 'All they can do is kill me, Stepan Ilyich. My body, I mean. When I was a boy I used to hear the old men say that — they can only kill me — and I'd shudder, but now I know it's true, you see. And it would make such a change, wouldn't it . . . doing the right thing for once, doing it all the way. . . But there, my son, this too is a well-trodden path for us. . .'

'The packet,' Povin said dully. 'Keep it. When you have not seen me or heard from me for two consecutive months, then you will know the time has come to open it. You will see what has to be done. Yes, there is money. And. . .and my testament. Not much to leave, but what there is. . .well, you will see when you read it. You will know what I want done, and how.'

There was a long silence, broken only when the General stood up and took the old priest's hand.

'You never saw her again afterwards?'

Povin always asked that question. The answer was always the same. Fr Michael shook his head without speaking. Povin gently withdrew his hand, squared his shoulders, and walked stiffly to the door. There he paused, as if seeking some more appropriate, final word with which to take his leave. Fr Michael looked up at him, at this man possessed of secular power to a degree almost beyond his understanding, and instead saw only a tortured youth, his face white and tear-streaked, rocking endlessly to and fro in the chair opposite, the fuse burning very close now. . .'What could I do?' the young man was crying. 'What could I do, *what could I do?*'

For a long, long moment Povin stood framed in the doorway, a doorway of Time, and to the old priest it seemed that nothing had changed or would ever change, seemed also that this was the last time. . .then the doorways were empty, the room was silent, and there was only a package sealed with wax to remind him of a life's beginning, and its likely end.

13

Kirk Binderhaven stared into rather than through the doubleglazed window of his compartment on the Trans-Siberian Express. Like Colonel Kruger a few days earlier he was trying to read his own expression, but the flat, snow-covered tundra on the other side of the glass made his task difficult.

The knuckles of the hand gripping the frame were white. His whole body felt clammy. He was not used to being afraid, so he had no defence against it. He could be rational about his fear: for an hour or so during the afternoon he had discussed the feeling with Nat McDonnell, his number two, and they had concluded that the claustrophobia was to blame. Give Binderhaven an automatic and an impossible position to storm single-handed and he'd laugh out loud with sheer joy. Lock him into a stuffy, overheated train for two days, surrounded by Russians to whom he must always present a smiling face, and he was useless. Worse than useless. Afraid.

Binderhaven had flown straight from his meeting with the Director of the CIA to join the train halfway along its seemingly endless journey to Nakhodka on the Pacific. Already he felt that another hour on the so-called express would kill him.

127

It affected McDonnell differently. He had been on the train when it left Moscow, and so had had more time to twist and wrench under the strain. With each moment that passed he became more silent, more tightly wound up, until he added to Binderhaven's worries the fear that his companion might crack.

Binderhaven lowered the window a fraction and took the biting Siberian cold full on his sweaty face. It brought momentary relief which faded as soon as the icy wind began to penetrate his parched skin. He raised the window and latched it, reducing the monotonous clanking rhythm of the wheels to a quiet background beat.

He had grown to hate this train.

It was nothing to do with the compartment. The rolling-stock had been manufactured in East Germany and was a model of long-distance comfort: the seats in the two-berth 'soft' class compartment were well upholstered during the day and at night they folded down to make wide, soft beds. The *provodnik* lady was assiduous with clean sheets and cups of tea from her coal-fired samovar. The worst things Binderhaven and McDonnell had to endure were the icy blasts of air between carriages when they walked to the dining car, and the lousy food once they got there. Black bread, tinned sardines and watery Zhigulovsky beer, which comprised lunch that day, was a far cry from their normal peacetime diet.

Then there was the enforced, mind-rotting boredom.

They couldn't exercise. Binderhaven wanted to do 200 push-ups but there wasn't room in the compartment and the corridor was too public. He didn't want to draw attention to himself. But now, when he squeezed his arms, he actually fancied he could feel the muscles going soft.

He threw himself full-length on the seat and closed his eyes. The click of the door latch brought him swiftly upright again.

'Relax. Here. . .tea.'

He gratefully accepted the cup of scalding amber fluid from McDonnell's hands. Binderhaven didn't usually drink tea, but at least this was something to relieve the endless tedium.

'I thought you were the dragon lady there for a minute.'

The 'dragon lady' was the Intourist guide assigned to

McDonnell in Moscow and inherited by Binderhaven when he joined the train at Novosibirsk. She was travelling hard class in a four-berth compartment down the other end of the corridor but she had a habit of looking in on them unexpectedly during the day, with her glassy stare and the porcelain white smile which only false teeth can give.

'Nary a sign. Relax. Hey, I checked with the *provodnik*. We're running behind schedule, like you thought. Now we don't get to Irkutsk until tomorrow morning. Early. Around six, she said.'

Binderhaven placed his glass on the window table and reached up to his suitcase for the map of Siberia.

'Another fourteen hours. If I don't get off this train soon I'm going out of my mind. Look. . .we have to go through one more big town. Angarsk. Did you ask what time we get there?'

'Nope. But looks like that's the last stop.'

'We should get there in the middle of the night. That can be our fallback if we have to quit in a hurry.' Binderhaven folded up the map and put it away. 'Any sign of the *schpick*?' he asked.

McDonnell shook his head. 'I wish you'd shut up about that guy. For Christ's sake, Kirk, give it a rest will you.'

Binderhaven fought down a desire to lash out at the younger man. McDonnell was twenty-eight, too old still to be in head-long exile from authority. In the short years of his manhood he had turned his hand to many things, including a captaincy in the elite Special Operations Group of the US Army. Nothing seemed to work out. Binderhaven was drawn to such men.

McDonnell had the kind of blond, blue-eyed college kid looks which a certain type of woman finds irresistible and Binderhaven thought cissy. Today McDonnell got on his nerves. So he made himself sit quietly and stare out of the window at the passing snowscape, the same white view which he had endured now for the best part of a day, until he felt calm again. In that short time the two men had already come closer to a fist-fight than either cared to admit. To make the adrenalin flow in a brawl would be a luxury, but one they couldn't afford.

'We've got one last hurdle to clear, Nat. We're going to move from one *oblast* to another during the night. That means a military check. My guess is they'll be KGB border guards.'

'KGB?' McDonnell was startled.

'You got to remember how close we are to Mongolia here. It's a hot spot. Don't worry about it. You've made it through three check points already on this fucking train and they haven't found a thing.'

'Yes, but KGB. . .shit.'

'Who in hell do you think that *schpick* belongs to? You think a couple of guys with American accents are going to walk aboard a Russian train without attracting a little attention?'

'Look, I told you, that *schpick* as you call him is probably some travelling salesman going home to his wife and kids. Leave it alone, will you?'

Binderhaven said nothing. His hands clenched and un-clenched without his being conscious of what he was doing. There was a man on the train and he was watching them. Binderhaven was convinced that his presence was no accident. He had joined the express at Moscow, along with McDonnell, and his compartment was next door. When Binderhaven went along the corridor to the john, the man was standing in the doorway of his compartment. When the two Americans went to the dining car, he followed a few steps behind. Once Binder-haven had raised a hand in greeting and been met with a frozen stare of unmistakable hostility. But as McDonnell pointed out, in Russia that meant nothing.

The *schpick* looked about forty, and physically fit. Binder-haven didn't know if he was armed, and McDonnell refused to treat it as a serious question.

'I need a drink. A real drink. You coming?'

McDonnell shook his head without looking up. 'I'll maybe join you later.'

Binderhaven opened the door and stood for a moment in the corridor, surveying the landscape. The view was just the same as from the other side of the train: an infinity of snow stretching to the thin black line of horizon where white joined grey. Somewhere out there, not so far at that, lay China. Binderhaven exhaled, and a small patch of moisture obscured his view. He had problems enough without China.

It was starting to grow dark. As he crossed over the noisy

coupling to the next car the lights came on, their feeble yellow glow doing little to illuminate the train's narrow corridors. At the far end of the second carriage he paused by the furnace, as if to warm his hands, and stole a look back the way he had come. The corridor was empty. The *schpick* must have stayed behind.

An alarm bell sounded in Binderhaven's brain. Maybe he should go back. . . He shook his head. He'd had it up to here with McDonnell. What he needed was a break. Let the mother-fucker look after himself.

Binderhaven took a seat in the dining car and ordered a half litre of vodka. At that time of day the dining car was unheated, which probably explained why he was the only person there. When the vodka came he poured himself a generous tot and knocked it right back, Russian fashion. The liquid descended to his stomach by the fastest route and there ignited the equivalent of an ICBM, which roared up into his head and exploded. Having survived the experience Binderhaven felt better, so he did it again. All over his body he could feel the tension loosen its hold. For the first time in two days he seemed in control of his own destiny. Maybe things would work out, after all. There would be someone to meet them at Irkutsk, and that someone would have concrete information for them, and something to hit the target with, and. . .

'Ah, Mr Concorde. . .'

The vodka made Binderhaven fractionally slow in reacting to his cover name. It was the dragon lady. Binderhaven resisted an impulse to groan. Part of the trouble between him and McDonnell lay in the latter's needling insistence that the woman had the hots for Binderhaven. Russian women weren't like that, not in Binderhaven's experience. They either didn't go for foreigners at all, or they went with a KGB gun in their backs. And they certainly didn't go along with the old joke about love at first sight.

He beamed at the woman and motioned her to the chair opposite. She treated him to her toothy white spread and sat down. Binderhaven vaguely remembered that Intourist staff are taught to smile more than the rest of the populace, because westerners expect it.

'I have to come to advise you, Mr Concorde.'

'Advise me? You want a drink, Miss. . .ah. . .?'

'Katskaya. No, thank you.' More teeth. 'Well, perhaps a small one.'

He filled his own glass to the brim and pushed it across to her, noting with satisfaction how she tossed it down. Miss Katskaya, he realised, was not unattractive, so long as you didn't mind your women Rubenesque. Miss Katskaya leaned across the table towards him. She was wearing a low-cut dress. Binderhaven allowed his gaze to fall on the widening gap between her breasts. They were what he called generous breasts. Forward, outgoing, *giving* breasts.

Binderhaven refilled her glass. Now her smile somehow seemed less glassy, more relaxed. The tension which had been dissipating itself through Binderhaven's body was starting to draw together into a highly concentrated and vulnerable spot. Miss Katskaya appraised him carefully, and this time when she smiled her lips did not part. He found that attractive. Their eyes met. Without quite knowing how it happened Binderhaven came to his feet, leaning heavily on Miss Katskaya's arm. To his surprise he saw that his left hand, instead of being round her shoulder where he had meant to put it, was squeezing one of her breasts.

He was aware of crossing the coupling into the next car but this time he did not notice the sudden traumatic blast of air. His body had settled down to a nice cosy temperature just below boiling point. As from a great distance he heard Miss Katskaya giggle, and looked down to see a disembodied hand run lightly over the bulge in the front of his pants. Then they were in a tiny cubby-hole of a compartment, its lights turned down low. Binderhaven supposed it was empty but he didn't greatly care. When he lurched forward Miss Katskaya fell across the lower bunk, her quiet giggle quickly dissolving into frantic licking of Binderhaven's ear. Her hands seemed to go everywhere at once. When he tried to kiss her the vodka bottle somehow materialised between them: he drew back, laughed, snatched it from her and drank. Her eyes seemed to advance and retreat like two bright stars which Binderhaven had strained too long to see. He swayed above her uncertainly,

132

trying to make the beguiling eyes be still.

He went from one extreme to another without a break. After a bout of scrabbling he was suddenly and instantaneously suffused with languor. A blank — then he was lying back, naked, while Miss Katskaya slowly divested herself of the few clothes she was wearing. Even when she stood beside him, completely nude, he was content to lie there and stare up at her, as if bloated with unsatisfied desire. Her skin was lightly tanned, he noticed; the breasts were as generous as he had hoped, the stomach flat, the blessed triangle above her crotch was rich and silky.

Miss Katskaya was clearly not on the point of losing her virginity. Through his alcoholic haze Binderhaven doubted whether she could even see that point over her shoulder on a clear day. Miss Katskaya knew a lot of tricks: that was the message coming from the creamy body next to his.

Suddenly, for no apparent reason, he seemed to lose interest. His mind floated away from Miss Katskaya and her cramped, stuffy compartment, drifting into the Russian night, flying over seas and whole continents, only lightly aware of its real surroundings, and the need to protect McDonnell. . .

Moonless night. Two men on the delta, their boat scarcely more than a piece of tree bark, the current running them fast downstream. The two men sit completely motionless, aware that the slightest tremor would be enough to tip them headlong into the flood, aware of hostiles without number on the invisible banks. . . A shot, a groan, 'Nat! Nat, are you OK?' One man is wounded, the other rises unsteadily to his feet, the boat trembles. 'Stand back!' But the man in the prow is upright, the frail boat rocks beneath his feet, falling. . .

A splash. From the river bank a sharp command in a foreign tongue, high and fell. Then white needles everywhere, two heads in the water, sinking, drowning. . .

Darkness.

Binderhaven opened his eyes. Miss Katskaya was sitting on the lower bunk opposite, fully clothed, combing out her hair.

133

Seeing his eyes open she smiled, a little uncertainly he thought, and said, '*Konchat?*'

Binderhaven smiled back at her. He had indeed finished: most likely for ever, the way his body felt.

To his surprise he realised that he was relatively sober. He sat up slowly, waiting for his head to start throbbing. Nothing happened. He reached out for his shirt.

'I have just advised your colleague, Mr Smithson. In half an hour there will be a halt. And a delay.'

'Delay?' Binderhaven frowned.

'Soviet trains are famous for their punctuality, Mr Concorde. The Trans-Siberian Railway especially so. . .'

He found it amazing, the way she prattled on as though nothing had happened between them. She could not seem quite to meet his eyes.

'The Rossiya Express, on which we are travelling, is more than ten minutes late in less than 0.3 per cent of all journeys in a year. But this is something beyond our control. In half an hour we cross from one military district into another. Our troops are conducting exercises. Defence exercises only, of course, you understand? But as part of those exercises there will be an inspection of the train.'

'Inspection?' Binderhaven stood up to finish dressing. Something was wrong, he couldn't place it. . .

Miss Katskaya lowered her eyes. 'A search.'

Binderhaven stared down at her in amazement. 'Well that's just great. That is. . .really. . .swell.'

His mind was racing. For the first time he felt genuine relief that he had insisted on travelling 'clean'. The only objects which might incriminate him and McDonnell were their knives, which could pass as penknives if the search wasn't too thorough, and the maps. . .

The maps!

'Please! A formality only. I am sure your position as honoured guests of my country will be respected.'

She leaned forward, as if to impart some great secret.

'And there is a special concession. The train will not be delayed. We shall pause only to pick up soldiers, then be on our way. The soldiers will leave the train further down the line. So

134

please. . .do not become upset. And afterwards, you will be the guests of Intourist for dinner this evening. Now I must go. Excuse me, please. . .'

Binderhaven was scarcely listening. The enormity of his folly reared up in front of him, for a moment almost threatening his reason. Russian women don't fall for foreigners. Or if they do, it's with a KGB gun in their backs. . .

She pushed past him into the corridor, eyes averted. Binderhaven was glad to let her go. He must get back to the compartment and destroy the maps, before it was too late. . .

It was only when he stepped into the corridor that his head went numb. The half litre of vodka had disappeared. Between them they must have drunk it all.

Get a grip on yourself. Somewhere miles away a voice was shouting at him: get a hold! Binderhaven took one step, then another. It was OK, he could walk. He made himself stand on the coupling between two coaches, a furious blast of cold air driving upwards and around him, until he could stand it no longer; then he stood by the samovar and held his hands against the furnace wall. He was all right now. He must have been crazy to drink, to fall for an old trick like that. But the boredom, the enforced inactivity, McDonnell . . .

A classic ploy. The oldest one in the book, run with a little help from the oldest profession in the world.

Binderhaven stumbled along the corridors until at last he reached his own compartment. He lifted his hand to the latch and paused. The memory of Miss Katskaya's guile made him rest his head against the panels, and listen above the pounding of the wheels beneath his feet. Inside the compartment, something was going on. Activity. Miss Katskaya said that she had already 'advised' his colleague of the impending search, maybe McDonnell was already cleaning up. Yes, that was it. . .

Binderhaven lifted the latch and walked in.

The first thing to catch his eye was the sight of McDonnell sitting stiffly in the corner seat furthest from the door, his hands clasped behind his head. For a split second Binderhaven thought he was doing exercises, callisthenics, then his glance strayed to the opposite corner and he understood.

The Russian from the next compartment, the *schpick*, stood

facing midway between him and McDonnell. On the seat behind him was an open suitcase; Binderhaven recognised his own. In the Russian's black-gloved hand was a pistol. It was pointing at McDonnell, but as Binderhaven met the Russian's eyes it travelled in a horizontal arc until it could comfortably cover the two of them. And in that second, any lingering doubts Binderhaven might have had about Miss Katskaya's role evaporated.

'Come in and shut the door. Quickly!'

Binderhaven reached behind him and pulled the door shut, keeping his left hand in the pocket of his coat.

'Now. What is this, eh?'

Without taking his eyes off the two Americans the *schpick* bent down to the open suitcase on the seat beside him and picked up a thick wodge of papers. Binderhaven recognised the maps and in the same instant his brain finally came to attention. He was stone cold sober and fighting for his life. . . which was how he liked it.

'I'll tell you what this is. . .' The Russian spoke with a thick accent but his meaning was clear enough. 'Military secret. How you get it, eh? And where?'

The folds of his puffy face half obscured tiny eyes which flickered backwards and forwards between the two men. Binderhaven sensed that he was nervous at the two-to-one odds and the narrow confinement of the train. He started to calculate distances. Between him and the Russian, say forty inches; between McDonnell and the *schpick* half that. . . Too far. The man's finger was curled round the trigger; a single wrong move and he could finish McDonnell before Binderhaven laid a finger on him. It was too early in the mission for heroic sacrifices. There had to be another way.

'You! Lift your hands like the other.'

Binderhaven cursed silently. He let go of the knife in his left-hand pocket and reluctantly raised his hands above his head. In the same instant another dimension occurred to him, and he frantically struggled to recall the precise lay-out of the compartment.

Suddenly they heard a short blast from the locomotive's whistle, followed by a long one, and with a squeal the brakes

136

went on. Binderhaven staggered against the seat and regained his balance only with difficulty. The train was decelerating hard now, and the whistle was blowing furiously. Binderhaven read relief in his captor's eyes and understood: they were approaching the military checkpoint.

'Soon we shall see. Sit down, you. Put your hands behind your head like the other one. We shall wait to see what the commandant of the Transbaikal Military District has to say about these secret maps.'

Binderhaven shot a look at McDonnell, praying for a response; got it; swung upwards on his toes scrambling for the light switch; found it; and plunged the compartment into total darkness.

In the cramped space the sound of the shot was deafening. As he launched himself forward Binderhaven had a fleeting impression that the flash was directed at the ceiling; then his hands closed round something hard and there was no more time for impressions.

'No blood!' he grunted savagely, and was relieved to hear an answering cry from McDonnell. He concentrated on finding the Russian's hands. Something solid landed on his right shoulderblade, causing him to wince with pain; then he heard the crash of the gun landing on the floor and knew the battle was almost won. He had one hand, then another. The Russian was powerful but after its recent experiences Binderhaven's body was screaming for action. His knee jerked upwards into empty air but the second jab made contact. The Russian's scream was lost in the squeal of brakes and the rattle of the wheels. As he fell forward, obeying the instinct to double up with agony, McDonnell encircled his forehead with his arm, and yanked backwards.

Binderhaven released the limp body very slowly, as if reluctant to abandon the game so soon after kick-off, and stood up. It took him a moment to find the switch and restore the light.

The Russian lay slumped on the floor between the seats. McDonnell was standing with his back to the window, rubbing his arm, lips drawn back in a grimace. But there was no time for first aid.

'The window! What's happening?'

McDonnell turned and released the window catch. Instantly the compartment was filled with freezing air and Binderhaven found himself shivering.

'We're coming in to some kind of halt. . . I can see soldiers. Christ, a platoon at least. . .all armed. Less than a hundred yards to go. *Fuck!*'

'Close the window. *Do it!*'

McDonnell fumbled with the clasp and managed to lodge the heavy glass panel back in place.

'Check where that bullet went.'

'In the ceiling. Look.'

Binderhaven followed McDonnell's pointing finger and registered the small hole next to the light bulb.

'Shit! We're going to have to plug that.'

'Screw the fucking hole, you stupid bastard, what about *him?*'

Binderhaven bent down to the body at his feet and retrieved the gun from where it had fallen during the struggle. He wiped it clean of fingerprints with his handkerchief and replaced it in the dead man's pocket, along with the maps from his suitcase. All his movements were fast but at the same time controlled, economical. As he stood up the long, heavy train finally ground to a halt with a squeal of couplings and overtaxed brakes.

After hours of relentless movement the silence was unnerving. Binderhaven and McDonnell looked at each other across the prostrate form of the *schpick*.

'What are we. . .?'

'Listen!' Binderhaven raised his head. He could hear shouting and the stomp of boots, the slamming of doors. 'They're boarding.'

Somewhere on the fringes of his consciousness the vodka stood ready for another assault, and for a mad moment he wrestled with the temptation to let everything go. Only for a moment.

'Maybe we could toss him out the window?'

'Are you crazy? They'd find the body almost as soon as we did it. That's a military checkpoint out there. And once they've found the body, we're a couple of dead ducks.'

'Under the seat, then?'

'They'll search there.'

'Then what the fucking hell are we going *to do?*'

Both men spoke in urgent whispers but there was no mistaking the insidious panic which threatened to overwhelm them.

'Kirk! We have got to get rid of that. . .that *thing!*'

Binderhaven cocked his head on one side. Somewhere not very far away — say the end of the corridor — he heard the tramp of boots, and the sound of knuckles knocking on wood.

'My God,' he said softly. 'My God, my God. . .'

14

Although it was still only mid-February the weather in Baku was hot enough to make Frolov open the windows of his taxi and loosen his tie. He had to admit that cruising down the Caspian coast road to Aljat was better than working. On his left was the sea, a deep navy blue, on the right the parched red hills of Azerbaijan. Every so often the car would descend to sea level in order to cross tiny tributaries of the River Kura, and Frolov caught a glimpse of children playing on the banks, or fishing in the slow-moving crystal water. For a man whose plane had been delayed three hours in Moscow because of a blizzard it was all very pleasant.

In Tbilisi Frolov ceased to be a uniformed member of the KGB and became a private citizen travelling for pleasure. Hence the taxi, rather than a chauffeur-driven official car. As the search for Povin's past tightened its grip on him he found that anonymity became increasingly attractive.

The drive took one and a half hours. At last the car turned

off the main road and began to bump down a stony track in the direction of the sea. Before they had gone more than a hundred metres they were brought up short by what looked to Frolov like an electrified fence and a sentry post.

He reached for his jacket and found his identity card, reflecting that although Stanov might have left under something of a cloud it did not seem to have diminished his Party status.

There were two uniformed guards on duty at the gate. While one of them inspected Frolov's credentials the other walked slowly round the car, examining it minutely, before opening the boot and peering inside. Frolov preserved both his temper and a genial smile.

The first sentry handed back Frolov's papers and saluted.

'You have an appointment with the Marshal, sir?'

'No. Do I need one?'

'Then excuse me, sir, but I must telephone the house.' As if conscious that this was not quite what a Colonel in the State Security Forces had a right to expect the man added apologetically, 'The Marshal is in mourning, sir. He has seen no one for three weeks.'

Frolov sat back and cursed inwardly. Of all the damnable luck! But irritation rapidly gave way to puzzlement. Stanov was a widower, childless. Why was he in mourning?

The sentry returned from the guard post, saluted again, and said, 'The Marshal will be delighted to see you, sir.'

The red and white rail swung upwards and the taxi moved on. Almost at once the track became a tarmacadammed road. As they rounded the next bend Frolov drew in his breath sharply. The view was magnificent. Below him was the house, a large white building in the modern style surrounded on three sides by a marble terrace overlooking the sea a hundred metres or so below. At one end of the terrace was a rectangle of cobalt blue, the swimming pool, around which were set sun chairs and a couple of beach umbrellas. The house was built out from the hillside, and as the car swept round the tight curve which led up to the terrace Frolov saw that underneath was a spacious garage in which were parked two cars: a Chaika and some other model which he didn't recognise but was in fact a Range Rover.

A white-coated steward was waiting at the foot of a short flight of marble steps leading up to the terrace.

Frolov indicated the boot of the taxi. 'There's a couple of cases of vodka in there. Bring them up, will you?'

'Vodka!'

Frolov looked up, shading his eyes against the monolithic reflected glare of the white house. Marshal Voldemar Pavlovich Stanov, seated in a wheelchair and wrapped in a rug, was waiting for him at the top of the steps. Frolov climbed them rapidly and stood to attention. Stanov extended his hand.

'I can't get out of this damned thing. The doctors say I'm not to walk in the mornings. Give me your hand, Frolov, I'm glad to see you.'

Over the hearty handshake Frolov took a good but discreet look at the former Chairman of the KGB. He had aged considerably since his last day in the office on the third floor at the Square. Most of his hair had gone, the cheeks were sunken and pale, and for all the balmy weather his touch was cold. His skin had that flaky-pastry feeling which Frolov always associated with extreme old age. Heavy bags under the eyes indicated only two or three hours' sleep a night.

'I think I came at a bad time, comrade Marshal. At the gate they said you were in mourning.'

'Ah, cretins. They had no business to say that, not to you. As far as my neighbours are concerned, I'm not available. For my friends, it's different. Come and sit by the pool. It's warmer there.'

Frolov's thick Moscow blood found the heat quite intense. He undid another button of his shirt and gratefully accepted one of the sun chairs, wiping sweat from his forehead.

'Let's have a drink.' Stanov rubbed his papery hands together, a look of overt greed in his eyes. 'What's in those crates?'

'Vodka. Stolichnaya, comrade Marshal.'

'Excellent! That's kind of you, Boris Andreyevich. Out here it's difficult to keep supplies up. Often we have to make do with "Starka". Aach! I must get out of the habit of saying "we". . .'

The steward brought up the boxes and opened one of them under Stanov's watchful, active gaze. They clinked glasses and drank; the steward poured again without being asked.

'You remember Yevchenko, Boris Andreyevich?'

Frolov coughed over his vodka, recovered, and assumed a pleasant, interested smile. Everyone remembered Yevchenko: Stanov's principal side-kick and crony for more years than you could count, an interfering old idiot who could safely be relied on to sneak to the boss over the slightest little thing. Not, of course, that he was going to tell Stanov that, not while Stanov could still remember his forenames after years of absence, and call him 'friend'.

'Of course. He retired about the same time as you did. How is the good Colonel?'

Stanov pointed along the terrace. Frolov followed his finger and noticed a newish-looking low structure of black marble on the other side of the pool, with flowers scattered around its base. About two-thirds of the way up the builder had carved a niche in which stood a small urn.

Frolov swallowed. 'Ah. I am truly sorry, comrade Marshal. A good colleague. How long. . .?'

'Three weeks. Cancer, of course. Who dies of anything else these days? Of the liver. Have another drink.'

Frolov winced and mopped his head. 'In a moment, perhaps.'

'I miss him. We'd been together a long time. I haven't taken it in that he's gone, yet. We'd always planned to retire together, you see. We were both widowers; it would have meant company. We chose this place, oh, ten years back. It was just a site then, of course. We used to come down once a year to see how they were getting on, the builders I mean. . .'

Stanov's voice tailed off in a croak, and Frolov looked away, embarrassed.

'You mustn't pay any attention. All past. We had four years down here together, I can't complain. Besides, I shan't be here much longer myself. Pour, Boris Andreyevich, pour the vodka and tell me what brings you here. How are things in the Square? Tell me all the gossip. How is Stepan Ilyich making out as Number One, eh?'

With relief Frolov put aside all thoughts of death, swallowed another drink, and started to ply his host with news. The old man was lonely and eager for contact with the outside world. By the time the steward came to summon them for lunch a bottle and a half of vodka had gone and Frolov was in danger of forgetting the real purpose of his visit.

The meal was served indoors, where it was cooler. Frolov was surprised to see that for all his diminished physique Stanov retained a voracious appetite.

'Ah, chicken pilau! You know the Azerbaijan cuisine, Colonel? It's the only food I really enjoy these days. Hot and spicy, I can't taste anything else.'

Frolov took an incautiously large mouthful and very nearly caught fire. His eyes watered, the veins stood out on his moist forehead and he groped for the glass of cold water which the steward, with forethought, placed by his side.

Stanov smiled maliciously. 'It takes some getting used to. Here, you must follow it up with a piece of bread. You know this stuff?'

Frolov shook his head, not yet trusting himself to speak.

'It's baked in a clay oven, like a cupola, with burning charcoal inside. They toss the flat loaves up so that they stick to the roof of the oven. But there's a trick to it. The temperature has to be a constant two hundred and seventy-five degrees Celsius, or the bread falls back on to the coals. Clever, eh?'

'Oh yes. And it's excellent, comrade Marshal, really excellent.'

'Try the local wine, why don't you? It's called Madrasa. Here, pour me a glass as well. . .'

By the end of the meal Frolov could hardly walk. He allowed himself to be guided back to his seat on the terrace, where he closed his eyes and sank into a contented coma. The steward left a flagon of Akstafa, the Azerbaijanian dessert wine, and retired into the house, leaving the two men alone.

'So now tell me. . .what brings you here?'

Frolov reluctantly opened one eye and saw that his host was if anything slightly more lively than before lunch. He propped himself up in his chair, striving to concentrate on the business in hand.

'Oh, I had some things to do in Baku and I thought while I was there I'd pop along the coast and pay my compliments.'

'No more than that?'

Frolov opened his other eye and saw that Stanov was still smiling at him.

'Well, nobody sent me, comrade Marshal.'

'I did not suggest they had.'

Stanov's eyes were gleaming. He lent forward in his wheelchair and gripped its arms tightly. 'You did not look to me like a man who has been sent, Colonel. You struck me rather as someone who urgently wishes to talk.'

Frolov devoted all his attention to pouring wine. Only when his glass was full to the brim did he risk a look at the old Marshal's face.

'If you are willing, comrade Marshal. Yes, there are a few things I would like to talk to you about.'

'Name them.'

Frolov took a sip of wine and replaced his glass on the table before replying. 'Something that has always intrigued me. The Kyril case. . .'

Frolov was disconcerted to see the old man throw back his head and laugh, without emitting any sound. . .a dry, hiccuping chuckle.

'Oh, *that!*'

Frolov hesitated, uncertain how to proceed.

'Go on.'

'Well, there are those — frankly, I'm among them — who look on that as the pinnacle of your career, if I may say so, comrade Marshal, and I was wondering whether I might, as it were, hear it from your own lips. If you have no objection.'

'Hear exactly *what* from my own lips, Colonel?'

'How you became so sure, at the end, of Michaelov's guilt. I mean, did he confess?'

Stanov shook his head. 'No. But he didn't have to. He was a *churka*, that one.'

'Strong language.'

'Ah, but you didn't have to work in such close contact with him as some of us. Ask Povin. He was on my list of suspects too, at one time, but Michaelov always led the pack.'

144

Frolov's eyes bulged. What with the wine and the vodka and the unaccustomed heat he wasn't sure that he had heard correctly. 'You suspected Stepan Ilyich? Really?'

'Oh, I suspected everyone above a certain level.' Stanov laughed, this time noisily. 'It seems incredible, doesn't it, suspecting old Povin? But that's how things were in those days, Boris Andreyevich. Why, there were even those who suspected me!'

He laughed again, and this time Frolov joined in heartily.

'Did Michaelov give you anything useful at the end? I mean, I assume you applied the usual, ah, pressures. . .?'

'Oh, yes. He never squawked, though. He was a tough nut, was Michaelov. I'm not sure how many people appreciated that. He said he was innocent right up to the end. Tried to incriminate a whole host of others, of course, people like Povin and so on, but that's common enough, as you well know, Boris Andreyevich.'

Frolov hesitated. He was approaching a highly sensitive area. And something about the last answer troubled him. What made Stanov look away as he spoke those words?

'There was that funny incident in the radio room. You remember? The cigarette ash. . .?'

'I remember, yes. He transmitted to England one night and left ash everywhere. Forensic identified it as his brand.'

'Did you put that to him under interrogation?'

'Of course.' Stanov frowned. There was a faraway look on his face, as if Frolov had stirred some sleeping memory. The Colonel waited in silence, but Stanov volunteered nothing more.

'And. . .?' Frolov prompted.

'And. . .he always refused to say where he was that night. It's a funny thing you should mention it, Frolov. We ran a check on his movements that night, so as to nail him. But nothing ever showed up. . .'

He tailed off. Frolov was starting to become excited, although he took good care not to show it. The old man was being very cagey. Deliberately so. But something was stirring in his memory. A word out of place might ruin everything.

'Could it matter?' he asked lightly.

145

Stanov viewed him from under a furrowed brow. He seemed to be weighing Frolov up. At last he reached a decision and leaned forward.

'I don't know why I'm telling you this, Boris Andreyevich, perhaps it's because I haven't got much life left and if I don't share it with you I'll never share it with anyone. But it's not for general consumption, you hear?'

Frolov smiled. 'I understand perfectly, comrade Marshal.'

'I wonder if you really do. I said it's not for *general* consumption. General, you understand? Clear?'

Frolov's smile sharpened. 'Clear.'

'All right, then. It's something I've never even discussed with. . .' Stanov jerked his thumb in the direction of Yevchenko's last resting-place. 'Another thing I always meant to get around to. After it was all over. . . I mean, after we shot him, but before the news got out. . . I had this letter. From Olga. Michaelov's daughter.'

Stanov broke off. Frolov took a long, leisurely time over taking out a cigarette and lighting it. He had smoked about a third before the old man resumed.

'It was very short. In her handwriting, I did check that. She simply said that she knew her father was innocent and if I was prepared to meet her she could prove it. She could prove it by telling me the events of a particular evening, when her father met someone — she didn't name him — at home.'

'And the evening was. . .?'

'Of course, it was the evening when Michaelov transmitted to London.'

There was a lengthy silence while the both men considered the possibilities which unfolded, and unfolded, and again unfolded in front of them.

'So. . .' Frolov tried to make his voice sound light. 'A child's attempt to save her father. Very commendable. But hardly a matter of any consequence. Hardly evidence.'

'You think not? Then tell me this, comrade Colonel. Why did I never get around to verifying her story? Why did I never even discuss it with Yevchenko, with whom I shared everything? Eh? Come now, what do you say to that?'

Frolov shrugged. 'You were always a busy man, comrade

146

Marshal. One cannot do everything.'

Stanov nodded, as though conceding what Frolov had said. 'It's true. Maybe you are right, Boris Andreyevich. Anyway, it's all in the past now.'

Frolov smiled. 'Surely you never had any doubt, though? About Michaelov being the traitor?'

Stanov's voice, when he spoke, was testy and sharp. 'Would it suit you if I had?'

'Suit me?'

'Yes. To think I had lurking doubts, that maybe I made a mistake. Is that why you came here, Colonel Frolov? To stir the stew once more?'

There was no mistaking the suspicion in the old man's eyes, but Frolov was prepared for this. He assumed a serious expression and leaned forward, as if to trade secret for secret.

'I don't have to remind you how things are in the Square, comrade Marshal. How people talk. The suspicion, the gossip. Every few years it's the same. "We're being betrayed," that's what they say. It happened in your day, it's happening in mine. But Stepan Ilyich's too much of an innocent. He listens, and smiles, and dismisses the talk as just that — talk. He needs looking after. That's why I'm here, comrade Marshal. The real reason. I want to kill the gossip before it spreads.'

Stanov continued to regard him with suspicious eyes. 'You can tell him,' he said at last, 'that I never had any doubts. I have none now. Michaelov was the traitor.'

Frolov stood up. 'Comrade Marshal, that's what I wanted to hear from your own lips. And now I've wasted enough of your time. I must go back to Moscow. But I shall remember today . . .this beautiful house, the wonderful meal. . .and all that you have said. Thank you, comrade Marshal. As a day it has been. . .remarkable.'

He held out his hand. Stanov took it after a scarcely perceptible pause.

'I, too, have enjoyed it. I hear nothing from Moscow now, you've brightened me up. If you get another chance, come back and see me.'

'I will.'

'And bring more vodka with you!'

They laughed, the mood of suspicion broken.

'I'll get Volodya to run you to the airport.'

After he had watched Frolov get into the Chaika Stanov wheeled himself to the back edge of the terrace, whence he could see the car climb the steep road up to the sentry post. For a long time after the sound of the engine finally died away he remained there, sunk in thought, one hand resting lightly on the urn which contained Yevchenko's ashes, so as to draw up the comforting warmth left in the metal by the day's sun.

'Nothing ever changes,' Stanov muttered to himself. He patted the urn gently. 'What should I have done? Told him the truth? Yes, you would say that, that's what you always said. . .'

His face darkened.

'They're all the same. They *never* change. And we're well out of it, old man. You and I.'

While in an upstairs room of the house the steward, having finally made his connection with GRU headquarters in Moscow, identified himself by number and asked to speak to General Mironov.

15

Captain Kalinin's orders were short and precise: he was to search the train and all persons found thereon, without exception, including the locomotive and its crew. This took time. He dealt with the Russian-speaking passengers first, and it was thus some twenty minutes after he and his men first boarded the Rossiya Express that he knocked on the door of Berth 16, Car 5.

'Come in.'

Captain Kalinin did not understand English but Miss Katskaya did. With a timid glance at the officer's face, as if to seek his approval, she reached across him and pushed open the narrow door.

Kalinin consulted his bundle of passports. Canadians. His instructions obliged him to come down heavy on citizens of the United States but they said nothing about Canadians.

Two men sat opposite each other at the far end of the compartment, reading. Both looked up with the inane, pseudo-friendly smiles against which Kalinin had been warned so many times at officers' training school.

Binderhaven allowed his glance to linger for a second on the Captain's dark green shoulder boards before looking away with apparent unconcern. But inside he was nervous. Chief Border Guards Directorate. The worst.

Kalinin motioned a soldier forward, and the man started to search the compartment. He was very thorough. He made the two occupants stand up while he searched under the seats, then undid the beds and rifled through the sheets. Next he combed the luggage racks while Binderhaven and McDonnell said a silent prayer that no one would look at the ceiling and notice the bullet hole.

During the search Kalinin stood in the corridor and surveyed the Canadians. They conveyed the same kind of mild irritation mixed with anxiety which he had noted in aliens many times before. Their papers were in order, their luggage 'clean'. The compartment, with its blind drawn down against the cold night, exuded peace and warmth. And yet. . . Something was not quite right. Kalinin had a nose for these things. Perhaps it was nothing major — a little petty smuggling, maybe, or a currency violation — but there was something.

He waved the soldier aside and stepped into the compartment, Miss Katskaya hovering nervously behind him. He spoke a few quiet words over his shoulder and she hastened to translate.

'I am afraid. . .the Captain wishes to search your persons. A formality, you understand. . .'

For all her bright bonhomie, Miss Katskaya sounded less than convinced. To her relief she saw her charges raise their arms with good-natured smiles on their faces.

Kalinin took his time over it. He liked to smell a man when

149

he was doing a body search, and analyse the odours he was giving off — fear, or anger, or sometimes even revulsion at being touched so intimately by a stranger. But these men wore the perfume which so many westerners seemed to like, on the face where they shaved, and so Kalinin learned nothing new from mere proximity.

He found the knives and held them up.

'What are these?'

Binderhaven heard Miss Katskaya's breathless translation with a patient smile and turned back to Kalinin, who listened expressionless while the Canadian spoke.

'He says they are promotional gifts, comrade Captain. From his company. He tells you to keep it, as a sign of the mutual benefits which will stem from their pleasant visit to the Soviet Union.'

Without taking his eyes off Binderhaven's face Kalinin opened one of the knives. The blade was extraordinarily sharp for a penknife. He paused for a long moment, waiting to see what changes appeared in the faces of the two men opposite him, but they remained calm and unruffled. Reluctantly Kalinin closed the knife and gave it back. Binderhaven attempted to refuse, but Kalinin shook his head and spoke a few words of Russian.

'The officer asks me to tell you that he is not allowed to accept gifts from any person. . .but he thanks you for the gesture, Mr Concorde.'

The first part of the translation was authorised; the second was not. Binderhaven smiled innocently at Miss Katskaya and shrugged his shoulders.

Kalinin pushed the two men gently aside and walked over to stand with his back to the window. His hand knocked against the blind, causing it to sway and flap against the glass. He was suddenly aware of tension in the two men, a tension that was new.

'Why are you travelling by train?'

Kalinin waited until Miss Katskaya had finished translating, then immediately spoke again without waiting for an answer.

'Tourists fly to Irkutsk. It has an excellent airport. The train is slow.'

'Please tell the officer that we are not tourists, we are here on business. And we are travelling by train because we're both train freaks. All our lives we've wanted to ride the Trans-Siberian. We may never get another chance.'

Kalinin listened to the translation with his head on one side, staring at the floor. He was missing something. It might be something trivial, but it was also something obvious. It would come to him. Sooner or later.

He took a last, cold look at the two Canadians who wanted to travel by the famous train and stalked from the compartment. Miss Katskaya remained a second longer to shoot her 'guests' a glance of mixed relief and gratitude before following him out and closing the door behind her.

For a few minutes the two men held their positions, then McDonnell tiptoed across to the door and placed his ear against it.

'They're talking. At the end of the passage. Now it's quiet.'

He eased the door open and took a swift look. The corridor was empty both ways. McDonnell slammed the door shut and gave Binderhaven the all-clear signal.

At the same moment the locomotive's whistle sounded three long blasts and the train began to slow.

'They're through. They're getting off.'

With one accord the two men launched themselves against the blind. It rattled upwards to reveal the *schpick*'s body on the other side of the glass, where they had suspended it with strips torn from a spare sheet. Binderhaven lowered the window and they hauled the heavy corpse aboard, grunting under the strain. It had been easier to drop him out, suspended by the wrists from the window catch, than it was to recover him.

'Where. . .?'

'Under the seat.'

A few minutes' frantic work and the deed was complete. Binderhaven raised the window and pulled down the blind as the train once more shuddered to a stop. They listened in silence while outside the troops were lined up in the snow, ready to move out. Above the sound of escaping steam the harsher noises of warrant officers' voices and heavy transport were clearly audible in the compartment. For what seemed an

151

eternity the train remained stationary, while Binderhaven looked at McDonnell across the narrow space between the seats. Then they heard three more blasts on the whistle; the couplings clanked; a shudder ran the length of the train. . .and they were moving.

McDonnell slumped back in his seat. 'Oh shit, oh shit, shit, shit.'

Binderhaven said nothing. His heart was racing. He stretched out along the seat and closed his eyes, waiting for the spasm to die away.

'I really thought we'd had it back there. I mean, suppose they'd ridden the outside of the train?'

'They wouldn't. Not in this weather.'

'All it would have needed was for one guard to look out of a window. Just one, that's all.'

Binderhaven opened his eyes. 'That Captain kept them too busy. His orders were to search the train. No one said anything about the outside of the train. But, oh brother. . .no more like that. Hey God, y'hear me? No more, not this trip.'

'Yeah, but what do we do now? We can't just leave him under the seat.'

'We don't.'

Binderhaven's heart had returned almost to normal. He swung his legs off the seat and sat up.

'We're going to wait for a tunnel. There's several on this line between here and Irkutsk, they're shown on the map. Hell, the maps!'

He got down on his hands and knees and reached under McDonnell's seat. A moment later he emerged triumphantly, holding aloft the maps which they had hidden in one of the *schpick's* pockets.

'Then we toss him out. In the tunnel. Chances are they won't find him until we're way clear of town.'

McDonnell frowned. 'I don't like it, Kirk. That guy's supposed to report in somewhere. Maybe at Angarsk. If he doesn't they'll send someone to meet the train when it gets into Irkutsk.'

'You're guessing. I've been watching him, remember. He got off precisely once, and that's the only time he could've used a phone or reported in somewhere. Now that we're so close to Irkutsk I'm betting he wouldn't have reported again before we got there. Besides, we have to take that chance. What's the alternative?'

'We could take off during the night, make it to Irkutsk some other way.'

'Too risky. It'd cause too many problems at the other end. Our "Emily" is expecting us on this train. We don't know what she looks like or how to make contact with her any other way, and we'd lose too much time trying to find out. Our best bet is to stay put. Remember, we satisfied the KGB back there. That's as good as a guarantee any day.'

McDonnell nodded reluctantly. He didn't like it but the alternative to staying on the train was worse.

Binderhaven unfolded the largest-scale map. 'It's impossible to know where we are right now. We were late before and the hold-up didn't help any. But there should be at least three tunnels between here and Angarsk. Still quite a way off, though. So why don't we rustle up the dragon lady and take that free dinner she's offering, then say we want an early night 'cause we got business to do tomorrow.'

While he spoke these words he studiously avoided meeting McDonnell's eyes. The other man was still too het-up to notice.

'You're going to leave the body here? Unguarded? I think I should maybe pretend to be sick and stay here.'

Binderhaven shook his head. 'We've got to act normally. It's our only hope. I know we're taking a chance, but hell, this whole thing's leaking like a sieve anyway. One more hole isn't going to make that much difference.'

He clapped McDonnell on the shoulder, making him wince. 'Hey, sorry. Your shoulder. . .you got hurt in the fight?'

'Yeah. A sprain, is all. I'll live.'

'Good boy.'

Binderhaven smiled, but as they walked along the corridor his mind was troubled. You have to be fit, that's what he'd told his recruits. Or you may as well forget it.

Neither he nor McDonnell got much sleep that night. Somewhere around two in the morning the train entered a long, winding tunnel and the *schpick* made his final exit. Between two and four they dozed. By the time the Rossiya Express eased its way to a halt in Irkutsk station the two men were long since packed and ready to go.

Binderhaven surveyed the busy platform from the window of their compartment.

'Over there by the bookstall.'

McDonnell followed the direction of his companion's gaze and saw a red Intourist flag held aloft on a white pole by a tiny, fur-swathed figure.

'Got it.'

'Ah, you are ready. That is good.'

Miss Katskaya's responsibilities evidently did not end until she had delivered the two men to the next link in the Intourist chain. They followed her down the corridor and, with a shiver of regret, left the comfortable warmth of the express for the last time in exchange for the freezing cold platform.

'This is Miss Anna Petrina. She will be your guide for the next few days.'

'Hi. . .hello.'

The tiny fur-clad figure put down her pole and brushed the hood of her coat aside. With a start Binderhaven saw, as he took her hand, that she was young, no more than twenty-five, and that her face was beautiful. He had been expecting a guide in the classic Russian winter mould: frumpy, bespectacled, old and pasty-faced from the long, dark months. But Anna Petrina was none of these things.

'Hello.'

She had a small voice to match her body, but there was nothing timid about either. She carried her head upright and Binderhaven found the steady gaze of her wide green eyes oddly disconcerting. They seemed to say to him, 'I see what happened with Katskaya last night, but I give no judgement'; his imagination, of course. She spoke softly, but with confidence, as if used to warning people that they were not to be misled by her size. As she led them to the waiting car Binderhaven couldn't decide whether he ought to be despondent or reassured by the sight of their Siberian contact.

The three of them sat in the back seat. It was an easy matter

154

for Binderhaven to show her the note he had written while still on the train and then at once pocket it again. 'Emergency,' it read. 'Urgent. Must talk.' Anna kept up an uninterrupted flow of small-talk about their journey, the weather, Russian trains, the delights of Irkutsk; her eyes flickered downwards for long enough to read the note without a second's break in the professional patter. Binderhaven felt the reassurance grow. She had obviously been well trained. They were dealing with a serious organisation.

The car drew up outside the Hotel Angara in Ulicia Sukhe Bator. Checking in was accomplished with a smooth efficiency for which his previous experiences of Russia had not prepared Binderhaven. Before he knew it he and McDonnell were being shown to a double room on the first floor. It seemed comfortable enough. He tried one of the beds and found it firm.

'Bathroom?'

The floor-lady pointed along the corridor. Anna Petrina smiled and said, 'Come, I will show you.' She turned to the floor-lady and jabbered in Russian; the woman nodded and went off. Anna beckoned, and Binderhaven followed her into the corridor. As they rounded the corner furthest from the stairs, where the floor-lady kept watch in her lair, Anna took out a pass key and opened a door which had no room number on it.

'Quick, we cannot afford to be away long. This is the room where the KGB come to collect my reports on guests. It is not bugged. Speak freely and fast.'

Binderhaven complied. As he spoke Anna raised her hands to her cheeks, a look of horror dawning in her lovely green eyes. When he had finished recounting the events on the train she shook her head slowly from side to side, and her first words merely confirmed what Binderhaven already knew.

'This is terrible, terrible, I cannot think what to do. . .'

'We have to get out of here. Fast. Have the others arrived yet?'

She nodded.

'Then your organisation can move us out. You have instructions for us? Arms, maybe?'

'Organisation!' Anna laughed. Normally, Binderhaven

fancied, that would be a sound worth hearing. Now it sent a shiver up his spine.

'What organisation? The organisation is *me*, do you understand?' She beat her clenched fists against her breasts and looked up at him through frightened eyes. 'This is Siberia we are in, not Paris or Berlin, or even Moscow. This is Irkutsk! Apart from me. . .no one.'

The look in her eyes was now reflected in Binderhaven's own.

'But that's incredible. Impossible. How can. . .'

She cut him short. 'Listen. Be quiet. We have only a few more seconds here. I have a message for you.'

'The weapons!'

'Yes. They are coming into the country tonight. Your cover story. . .it is the same here as it was in Moscow: you come to demonstrate high-insulation outer clothing to the director of the industrial co-operative. This you will do by surviving two nights in the tundra. I have all the documents. In fact, of course, the director is not expecting you, has never heard of you. That does not matter. My instructions from Intourist are to deliver you by truck to a disused fur-trappers' outpost tomorrow morning, early. Later tomorrow I must report to the KGB. What happens after that is not my concern, except that somehow I must get your weapons to you. I had thought of a way. Now, everything is ruined.'

'How long before they discover the body of the man we killed?'

'I don't know. Nor does it matter. When he fails to report the hunt will start. I shall be questioned and watched as soon as you disappear. You are the obvious culprits. They will start to track you. . . I must have time to think. Now we have to go back to your room. Already the floor-matron will be suspicious.'

She hurried him out of the room, no bigger than a closet, and locked the door behind her. As they returned the way they had come she resumed her bright, bustling delivery.

'What I suggest, Mr Concorde, is that this morning you and your friend should rest, and at lunch I shall introduce you to some Americans we have staying here. That will be nice for

156

you? Until lunchtime then. . .'

'Americans?' McDonnell had picked up Anna's final words as she hurried down the corridor towards the stairs.

'Apparently,' said Binderhaven casually. 'Of all the things, you travel round the world to the back end of beyond and find yourself shacked up with a bunch of Yankees.' He yawned and stretched. 'I didn't sleep much last night, Nat. Guess I'll take a rest.'

'Think I'll do the same.'

Binderhaven lay down on the nearest bed, but he did not close his eyes. Instead he reached into his overnight bag and pulled out a pad of paper. Each sheet had the logo of a fictitious company — 'Tog-Lo-Tights Inc.' — at its head; it was the kind of promotional memo pad carried by salesmen everywhere. Obviously the room was bugged, so Binderhaven used the top sheet to scribble a message to McDonnell. As Nat read it a look of infinite depression crept over his face. With a grimace he tore off the sheet and ate it, repelled as always by the sickly-sweet taste of the rice paper.

For the rest of the morning they dozed. At 12.30 Anna returned to take them down to the dining room.

They sat at a table laid for five. Faber and Mannheim were already there. As he saw them Binderhaven knew a moment of elation at the knowledge that the group was now complete. He quickly suppressed it. There must be no indication that he and McDonnell knew the other two.

Anna made introductions, and while they waited to order the four men improvised small-talk. With every appearance of genuine interest Binderhaven learned that the two Americans were fur buyers visiting Irkutsk to set up a deal involving sables. McDonnell did a passable impression of a clothes sales-man, and Joe Faber took out a note book to write down the name of his company. They were helped by the fact that neither group was aware of the other's chosen cover story. Not even Binderhaven knew beforehand what Faber and Mann-heim were officially supposed to be doing in the middle of Siberia.

'Why Tog-Lo-Tights?'

'Tog is a unit of clothing insulation. Tights because we've

developed a close-hugging material which keeps sweat and skin irritation down to a minimum. It's a breakthrough. We reckon there's one almighty big market for warm work-clothes here in the Soviet Union. . .'

A waiter placed a large menu in front of Binderhaven. He opened it to discover eight pages of dishes, printed in English as well as Russian, and his mouth watered.

'I shouldn't bother to finish reading it if I were you.'

He looked up to find Mannheim smiling at him.

'This place is like everywhere else in Russia. Nine-tenths of the things aren't on. It's best just to ask them what they've got, and have that.'

'Well, what have they got?'

'Fish and cabbage. It comes in different combinations, but that's about it.'

Mannheim turned out to be right about the food. Binderhaven spoke little during the meal. He was concentrating on trying to discover the level of his men's morale. As far as he could tell, they were in pretty good shape. They'd need to be, he reflected grimly.

After lunch they were scheduled to have a guided tour of the city. At Anna's suggestion they decided to walk. Binderhaven kept Faber a pace or two behind the others as they set off from the hotel. After they'd been walking for about five minutes he said, '*This*. . .is Irkutsk?'

'Uh-huh. Grim, isn't it? Concrete junk and electric cables. There are some good things, though.'

'What do they do here?'

'Furs. Some industry, a little gold mining, but mainly furs.'

Binderhaven lowered his voice. 'How's it going?'

'Pretty well. We've actually done some business.' He grinned. 'You wanna buy some sables? But seriously, Kirk, it's getting awful late. We're supposed to be leaving tomorrow morning. That's when we jump off. So far we've got a target but nothing to hit it with.'

Anna's voice interrupted them.

'On your left, the White House of Irkutsk. This used to be the Governor-General's residence. Its porticoes and six Corinthian columns go back to the nineteenth century.

Nowadays it houses the University's scientific library. . .'

She walked quickly. Binderhaven had not expected her petite body to hold such reserves of stamina. Now they were climbing a hill, but her steps never faltered.

'What's the latest on weapons?'

'Express delivery from Moscow tomorrow, if all goes well. Anna's going to get them out to us on the tundra, don't ask me how.'

'There's something you've got to know, Joe. . .' Binderhaven spelled out the bad news while Faber's face lengthened.

'That's bad. You told Anna yet?'

'Soon as we got in.'

'What'd she say?'

'That she needed time to think.'

Faber made an unobtrusive gesture with his hand towards the others. 'Better catch up.'

Anna was several yards ahead of McDonnell and Mannheim. As Binderhaven and Faber rejoined them they heard McDonnell mention Anna's name and Mannheim laughed quietly.

'You notice how none of the Russian men look at her?' he whispered.

'No kidding?'

'She's too small for them to bother with. You know the Russian saying: "Tits and half a *pood* of ass"? That's how they like 'em. Stacked.'

'You wouldn't think they'd be that fussy out here in a dump like this,' said Joe Faber, and Binderhaven looked at him with a sudden incomprehensible stab of dislike.

'Hey,' said Mannheim, 'did I ever tell you about Norilsk Roulette?'

They slowed, letting the distance between them and Anna lengthen still further.

'Shit, no. Where's Norilsk, anyway?'

'Way up above the Arctic Circle. North of the Putoran Mountains, if you know where that is. They get the women together and make 'em kneel in a circle, facing inwards. Then the guys work round screwing. The winner's the one who *trakhnuts* the most.'

'Trak — what?'

'Aw, you know. Fucks.'

'You're kidding.'

'No way. Pity there ain't no Irkutsk Roulette. I'll bet you couldn't even get a whore round here. The floor-ladies shoo visitors out of your room at eleven o'clock, did you guys know that? Not like Moscow. . .'

'Why, what's so great about Moscow?'

'Sex is easy, that's all. You just go to the National restaurant or you pick up a cab in the evening after dark, there's always a whore around. The cab driver'll take you both out to Sokolniki Park, somewhere like that. He gets his cut. Or you take the steamer down the Moscow River to Klyazma. It's got cabins. You can always get a woman there. . .'

Binderhaven let them talk. He didn't want to alarm them, not yet. His time was better spent trying to fashion a cast-iron plan of what they did next. Trouble was, he couldn't think of one. They were utterly dependent on Anna Petrina, a young girl working on her own without a back-up organisation or the kind of muscle that could sometimes jerk strings behind the scenes, even in places like Irkutsk. She couldn't even get them what they most needed: hard intelligence. Had they found the body in the tunnel yet? When would the weapons arrive? How would they ever get through customs? Binderhaven shook his head. Let the men talk sex all they wanted, for now.

He plucked Faber's arm. 'You'd better tell Mannheim about the *schpick*.' Faber nodded.

'This. . .is Znamenskaya Hill. The monument you see is to the historian Schapov.'

They hurried to catch up, shamefacedly putting schoolboy thoughts from their minds. It's not so unlike a school outing, thought Binderhaven: sites of interest and thoughts of sex. . .

The view from the hill was excellent. Binderhaven took Anna's arm and gently led her aside from the rest. He looked over his shoulder. They were the only people at the monument, braving the cold; from the top of the hill they would see long before anyone could approach.

'This mission,' she said, before he could speak, 'it is important?'

Binderhaven hesitated only a second before deciding to tell her the truth. It was essential to win her trust, her absolute dedication to the cause. He kept it simple, and stark.

'Some of your Generals have stolen an American plane. The most technologically advanced, the most sophisticated military aircraft ever to fly. As long as the Americans can keep its secrets from your people, they will always be on top. A decision has been taken. The plane must be destroyed before your scientists can inspect it. If we do not do it by stealth' — he held her shoulders so that she had no choice but to face him — 'there could be another world war.'

For a long time she stared into his eyes, trying to assess what she read there. Binderhaven found the moment timeless. She was beautiful, beautiful with a precision of line that was almost hard, as though the material had been refined over and over again, until at last the craftsman was satisfied.

'I'm glad,' she said eventually. 'Glad that it is important, I mean. I would not like it to be less than vital.'

She broke away from him and went to stand by the low wall overlooking the city. After a moment he joined her, suddenly unable to restrain his curiosity.

'Why are you doing this, Anna?'

She did not look at him. 'Because of the debt I owe.'

'Debt?'

And now she did look up, to reveal two tiny tears swelling in the corners of her eyes.

'For America. . .there is nothing I would not do. Nothing. And to hit back at those. . .those monsters. Nothing!'

Her outburst astonished Binderhaven. It was impossible to doubt the sincerity in her voice.

'I don't understand. Why. . .?'

She smiled, and wiped away the tears as if they were precious, not lightly to be disturbed.

'It's a long story. There was this woman. American. She used the train a lot, a sort of unofficial guide for other Americans. We became friends. Then one day, she helped me.'

'Helped you? How?'

Anna turned away so that he could no longer see her face and had to strain to catch the next words.

161

'I had a cousin. We. . .were in love. But his parents had permission to emigrate. He was young, he had to go too; besides,
it would not have been safe for him to remain here when his
mother and father were gone. We wrote to each other, for a long
time. He hated it, America I mean. All he could talk about in
his letters was coming home, to me. And then one day. . .'

She faltered. He left her alone for a moment, then said, 'One
day. . .yes?'

She recovered and went gamely on, as if determined to finish
once and for all. 'He was arrested. There was talk of deporting
him. It was terrible, terrible.'

Binderhaven was silent. He could see what was coming, and
it revolted him.

'He wasn't wicked, please understand that, only young, and
foolish. I. . .went to my friend. The woman on the train. She
promised to try and help. She did. Later I saw the newspapers,
she sent them to me. He was cleared. And. . .they did a deal.
They sent him back to Irkutsk. Voluntarily. Only. . .'

'Yes?' But he did not really need to ask.

'Only the Soviets broke their word. He was arrested. Sent to
camp. Now I do not know whether he is alive or dead.'

She raised her tear-stained face to Binderhaven's, seeking for
reassurance, for comfort.

'It was not the fault of the Americans. They kept their word.'
Her face darkened. 'It was my own people who lied. . .
betrayed.'

A tidy operation, he was thinking. The newspaper reports
must have cost something to fix, but there were ways. He had a
sudden sharp vision of the cousin, living in Idaho with a wife
and four kids, mowing the lawn and reading *Time* on Sundays.
A hard nugget of imperishable anger was growing inside him
so as to threaten his peace of mind. Now he had no choice but
to build on the foundation of deceit which had been so lovingly
and carefully laid. They were lucky, that was what his brain
kept telling him. But his heart was bitter.

He wanted to say something to her, offer at least a word of
consolation, of healing. Nothing came. He turned abruptly
and walked off down the hill, not looking back to see who
followed him.

Dinner was more or less a repeat of lunch, served in a slightly different order. After the meal Anna assembled them in the lobby and for the benefit of the hotel staff made a great show of handing out travel documents and itineraries for the following day. It was not until he had climbed the stairs to their bedroom that Binderhaven found the message tucked into his travel folder.

'Sixty hours to reach target. Wait until 1800 tomorrow. If I do not reach you, go on.'

He burned the scrap of paper and washed the ashes down the plug hole of the wash basin.

Bearing in mind the kind of terrain they would have to cross, that was not a lot of time. In the hour before dinner Binderhaven had studied the maps. The air base was about ten miles from Achiny, itself some eighty miles from Irkutsk. Much would depend on how far Anna was able to take them next day. Where was this abandoned fur trappers' post? He frowned. They would have to split up right from the start, that was obvious. One party could follow the foothills of the Primorski Mountains, which bordered Lake Baikal on the north-west, while the others made their way up a tributary of the River Angara, separating when they were. . . Binderhaven used his forefinger as a rough measure. . .less than fifteen miles from target. But the route would take them over vast tracts of exposed tundra. He shook his head. Say they had to stay under cover during daylight, which seemed likely — after all, the military would have helicopters. The nights were long, but even assuming Anna took them twenty miles next day, they were going to have to cover thirty miles a night to get to the target by dawn in two days' time. Maybe there would be some taiga; if so, they would be able to move by daylight underneath the trees. But he couldn't guarantee that. . .

There was a knock on the door. McDonnell and Binderhaven exchanged uneasy glances.

'Who is it?'

'Joe Faber and Frank Mannheim.'

At a sign from Binderhaven McDonnell rose from his bed and went to open the door.

'You guys fancy a little cards? There's this Russky game I picked up in Leningrad last season. *Duraki*, they call it. . .'

Binderhaven noticed that each man had brought his pad of rice paper and smiled approval. While the others settled down he busied himself covering a couple of sheets of paper with figures, to be found in the waste paper basket next day and so pass for scores.

Faber outlined the rules of the game. Mannheim shuffled the cards and dealt. Under cover of the usual card-players' banter the men began to exchange notes.

By the time Binderhaven had finished his written briefing there were glum faces all round the room. Faber picked up his pad and wrote: 'If we can trust the girl — and I say we can — she'll get us out of this. We're slated to be picked up here by car tomorrow at 0700 and taken to the airport. The driver's OK: he's going to have a breakdown (cash transaction). You go by and offer us a lift. That way, the search goes in the direction of the airport. We turn round and head north. Anna swears she dropped us off outside the terminal building. Simple!'

Binderhaven looked, then wrote on his own pad: 'Weapons?'

Faber shrugged and shook his head.

McDonnell wrote: 'Who's driving us to Base One?'

'AP — I think.'

McDonnell wrote again: 'Dangerous,' allowing raised eyebrows to stand for the missing question-mark.

'What choice?'

Binderhaven sketched out preliminary plans for the morning and circulated them. There were no questions. Soon after ten Faber and Mannheim left the other two to prepare for bed.

Several times during the night McDonnell awoke, each time to find his chief sitting by the window, looking out, a cigarette in his hand. The room was hermetically sealed and with the central heating set to full in order to combat the bitter Siberian cold the atmosphere was stifling. McDonnell tossed and turned on the surface of sleep, unable to keep his mind from dwelling on the next day. It was nearly four o'clock before both men, overwhelmed by fatigue, lost consciousness.

They had been sleeping for less than an hour when there was a knock on the door. Binderhaven was the first to hear it. He sprang from sleep to wakefulness in a single bound, his heart beating wildly. The knock was repeated, more urgently this time. He looked at the face of his luminous watch. Four-fifty. They weren't due to be woken for another hour yet. What the hell . . .

McDonnell was awake now, sitting up in bed. As he heard Binderhaven throw back the covers he switched on the light and felt for the knife beneath his pillow. Binderhaven waved him down and reached for his dressing gown.

'Who is it?'

'Miss Petrina. Open, please.'

Binderhaven hesitated an instant longer, then reached out for the door handle.

Outside in the corridor stood a crowd of people. At the head of them, in the doorway, McDonnell quickly identified Anna and the floor-matron. Behind them . . .

Behind them stood a tall, brown-uniformed officer with the blue shoulder boards and four small gilt stars of an officer in the Komitet Gosudarstvennoy Bezopasnosti.

'This,' said Anna Petrina tersely, 'is Captain Yuri Dmitrevich Boychenko of the KGB. Get dressed, pleased. There has been a change of plan.'

16

Frolov was thoroughly fed up at the prospect of having to go out again that night. So was Ilinichna, his wife. She had gone to no end of trouble to welcome her Boris home after his trip to Baku: there was steak from the 'closed' store on Furmanova, and a bottle of good burgundy from her husband's last trip to Europe. She had been looking forward to dinner followed by cognac round the fire and bed with — who knows? — a little romance. Boris could be very romantic when he was in the mood, which usually happened when he was well fed and the children had been amusing.

There was nothing wrong with the meal, and the children behaved exquisitely, but romance was out. Boris made that perfectly clear when he came home in a foul temper and immediately laid into her for opening the wine without his permission. Ilinichna pouted.

'I thought you'd be pleased. I've worked all day getting this meal ready for you.'

'Well, *molodsti*.' Bully for you.

'And the children have worked so hard, too. Volodya has been appointed *zvenovoi* of his link in school.'

Ilinichna fully expected this to be a trump card, but for once she was disappointed. Mention of their eldest child merely deepened the furrows of anger across her husband's brow.

'So he's going to learn how to be a little sneak, is he? *Molodsti* for him, too. Why don't we put him straight into a special vocation school and train him up for the KGB, eh? Instead of wasting all this precious time in teaching him to count. . .'

'You're so hard on them,' said Ilinichna, turning away so that her husband would not see the tears which sprang unbidden to her eyes. 'They are our future. . .'

Frolov softened. 'You're right.' He put his arm round his wife's shoulder and hugged her gently. 'I'm sorry. It's just that I've been working hard lately. . .'

Ilinichna clung to him, cradling her head on his chest. 'You work too hard. Nobody else works the hours you put in.'

'Maybe. We should think about taking a holiday, you and I. Just the two of us. We'll leave the children with *babushka*. Only. . .'

'Only what?'

'It'll have to be a week or two before we go. I'm tied up at the moment.' He sighed. 'That's why I have to go out again to-night.' His face hardened at the thought. 'I'm going to see someone else's child, darling. A child who had everything in life, and then had it taken all away. Sad, eh?'

166

He was rocking his wife to and fro, her eyes half closed. 'Mmm. . .very sad.'

Ilinichna smiled into Frolov's uniform, so that he did not see. She could usually play the children card and win, even if it did take a little time.

So they had the steaks and there was no more fuss about opening the wine. Frolov even managed a small glass of cognac before he put on his overcoat and hat, kissed Illinichna hard on the lips, and went down to collect his car.

He drove the same grey Moskvich he had used on the night of his visit to the Klimovs. Frolov found it possible to run two cars, apart from the official Chaika which the State provided. The Moskvich was usually garaged at home so that Ilinichna could drive it, and indeed Frolov had thoughtfully registered the vehicle in her name when he first bought it at the used-car market. Frolov himself, however, found the anonymous vehicle very convenient on unofficial occasions such as the one on which he was about to embark.

His second car was a Mercedes-Benz imported from West Germany and paid for in the magical 'certificate roubles'. Frolov had managed to lay his hands on quite a few of these in the course of his career. Most of the time the Merc was out on the roads paying for its keep in hiring fees. It was particularly popular with married couples as a means of conveying them from one of Moscow's numerous Wedding Palaces up into the Lenin Hills for the family photographs and reception. For the right price, and the right couple, Frolov sometimes threw in the services of a KGB driver, who received his cut of the takings. (It was more of a paring than a cut.)

Gasoline was not a problem, because Frolov had a special arrangement with a moonlighting tanker driver. This *sha-bashnik*, who worked for the Ministry of Defence, used to call once a week on his way out to the ring road and siphon off whatever Ilinichna ordered in exchange for meat, or fresh vegetables, or vodka, or even occasionally certificate roubles. Over the course of a year the Ministry lost a good deal of petrol in this way, not only to the Frolovs. The accountants had a word for it. They called it 'evaporation'. Recently the KGB tanker drivers had also started to report 'evaporation'. Frolov disapproved of that. There ought to be a clamp-down. . .

He drove the Moskvich along Gogol Boulevard as far as Kropotkinskaya Square where he turned south-west on to the street of the same name. In Zubovskaya Square he joined the traffic on the south-bound carriageway of the inner ring road until he came to the intersection with Konsomol Prospekt, where he again turned south-west. He pulled up just short of the railway line and looked at his watch. He was late. As he lowered his arm someone tapped on the offside window. Frolov unlocked the doors, front and back. He waited until the two men were seated before pulling out into the traffic stream and continuing down the Prospekt towards the Lenin Stadium.

'This is the man you told me of, Major?'

The man in the seat beside Frolov answered. 'Yes, sir. He took a bit of finding but we managed in the end.'

'He knows where the girl is?'

'Yes. He's supposed to be meeting her in half an hour's time.'

Frolov grunted. 'Good.'

A few minutes later he pulled off the highway, past the large swimming pool, and drew up in the shadow of the Museum of Physical Education and Sports. Away to the left of them the huge edifice of the sports arena loomed up like a modern version of the Roman Colosseum. On the other side of it, Frolov knew, a thicky-wooded park led down to the Moscow River.

'Smoke?'

Frolov offered a pack of Chesterfields to the man in the back without looking over his shoulder. He had only the vaguest impression of his passenger, gleaned from the driving mirror while they were still travelling along the brightly lit Prospekt. He seemed young, about twenty-five, and he had a beard. Major Voznoy vouched for him as a reliable *stukachi*, or informer. For the moment Frolov didn't need to know any more.

For a few minutes the three men smoked in silence, while Frolov framed a series of questions.

'How did you first meet this girl?'

'At the Motherland Cinema, just over a year ago.'

Frolov knew all about the Motherland Cinema, near

Izmailovo Park in the north-eastern sector of the city, where drugs changed hands nightly.

'Were you buying or selling?'

The *stukachi* took a quick drag on his cigarette and spat out the smoke. 'I was present.'

Frolov smiled. 'Did she tell you her name then?'

'Not then.'

'But you saw her again.'

'Yes. After a while someone told me her name. She was well known up there.'

'She is an addict?'

'No. She smokes hash now and then, and I've been there when she's taken a couple of LSD trips, but that's all.'

'We have no record of her taking employment. As you know, that is a crime. Where does her money come from?'

The young man in the back seat laughed.

'Her body, mostly. She's on the rent.'

'Foreign tourists?'

'Strictly not. Too much attention.'

'She told you that?'

'Yes. She doesn't like the KGB or the militia.'

'You sound like pretty good friends.'

'We were close at one time. She used to drift around. As soon as she thought she'd stayed too long with the same person she'd move on. She stayed with me for six months.'

'Without official permission.'

'Ask Major Voznoy.'

The Major spoke up for the first time. 'I leave him alone as part of the deal. He always tells me who he's got staying with him.'

Frolov nodded. 'So she makes her money whoring. Good money?'

'Not bad. Fifteen roubles for straight sex, twenty-five for the night, extras by negotiation.'

'She has a protector?'

'Not at the moment. She has a knife instead.'

'Has she ever had to use it?'

'I don't know. I shouldn't think so. She's a tough kid, and picky. I've seen her sweet-talk several men before choosing.'

169

Frolov extinguished his cigarette. 'She gives value for money?'

The young man grunted. 'You bet. Anything you want, if she likes you. Nothing's too far out.'

'All right. Let's go. Major, you come too but stay out of sight.'

As they got out of the car Frolov had to adjust his underpants slightly to accommodate the swelling in his crotch. He noticed that his heart was beating a little faster than usual. Like many Russians of his generation, sexual repression vied with the lurid fascination of loose, promiscuous, perhaps even deviant desire, in his complex make-up. The prospect of meeting Olga Michaelov suddenly both attracted and repelled him.

The young *stukachi* guided Frolov round the corner of the giant stadium and the two began to walk in the direction of the river. Ahead of them on the Lenin Hills Frolov could see the red star atop the University building and used it to get his bearings.

The Lenin Central Stadium is something of a monument to Soviet constructional engineering. The whole thing was built in fifteen months on an empty tract of marshland known as Luzhniki, and as a result the ground level had to be raised one and a half metres before building could start. Under the grandstands of the largest arena there are changing rooms, doctors' surgeries, training and work-out rooms, a hotel, a restaurant, and much else. These facilities are in constant use.

But the stadium also offers other facilities, which do not appear in the official guide book distributed by Progress Publishers. After nightfall the trees which separate the buildings from the river shelter a number of sporting events for which as yet no Olympic medal has been struck. Officially, prostitution in Russia does not exist. Anyone who wishes to compare the official version with reality can visit the stadium after dark and see for himself.

Frolov knew all this, of course, just as every militiaman and KGB officer knew it. The fact of the matter was that prostitution was here to stay and unofficially the Moscow city authorities acknowledged it. The next question, therefore, was how to contain it, and the stadium provided a useful answer.

Over the years it had acquired a sort of quasi-respectability. The militia cleared out the undesirable types as soon as they showed their faces on the riverside walks, and the KGB monitored whoever was left. With proper control came an influx of money; it was by no means unusual to see a Chaika parked by the sports arena along with the lesser Zhigulis and Moskvichs and Volgas. Frolov would not have been surprised to see a familiar face under the trees, nor did the prospect of being recognised by a colleague bother him. For what he was about to undertake such recognition provided the best cover going.

'Over there.' The young man spoke softly. Frolov looked down an avenue of trees and saw a dark figure seated on a bench about fifty metres away.

'You'd better wait here. She's only expecting me.'

As the *stukachi* moved off Frolov reached out to grasp his sleeve. 'Remember. . .you we can trace without difficulty.'

'I know.'

Frolov released him, and watched as the young man walked down the avenue, hands in the pockets of his jeans. Jeans and a short leather jacket. . . Frolov shivered and stamped his feet on the impacted snow which covered the footpath.

The dark shadow on the bench did not get up as the informer approached. He stood talking to her for several moments, during which time she did not move, then returned the way he had come. As he approached Frolov found that his heart was beating faster than ever.

'Go ahead. She's expecting a wealthy client with *blat*.'

Frolov could hardly help smiling. KGB Colonels had money, and influence enough.

'See the Major. He's got something for you.'

The *stukachi* disappeared into the shadows. Frolov waited until he had disappeared before starting on the short walk which separated him from the next link in the chain.

Ever since leaving Baku he had wondered how to begin this conversation. In his person he represented the *vlasti*, those in power, the men who had shot her father for a crime he did not commit. Disillusionment with the State had followed. Olga Michaelov, daughter of a proclaimed traitor, dropped out of school before she could be pushed, left home hours before the Ministry arrived to take possession of it, and then disappeared into the murky depths of drugs and whoring. How did someone like Frolov bridge a gap like that? What could he say or do to make her trust him?

He sat down on the opposite end of the seat, away from the girl, and studied her. She was slumped down low, hands in pockets, looking straight ahead. In the dim light of a far-off street lamp Frolov discerned long fair hair, a pointed nose, a padded jacket, jeans. . . Then very slowly she turned towards him.

He was looking at a skull. That was his first thought. Two round black holes for eyes, a dead white face, a grinning mouth half open in what was presumably meant to be a come-on smile but which scarcely concealed the contempt she felt.

'Cigarette?'

She did not react. Frolov was just starting to feel foolish sitting there with a packet of American cigarettes held out when the girl removed one hand from its pocket and stretched towards him. Frolov edged closer.

'Take the pack.'

'Thanks.'

Her voice was rough with fatigue and nicotine. Frolov knew from the way she refused a light, the speed with which she removed the cellophane, the casual expertise over the wax Vesta, that his informant had been wrong about one thing. Olga was an addict — of sorts.

The girl drew hard on the cigarette and let out a little smoke, inhaled again, puffed out some more, drew in for the last time and held the smoke down in her lungs. Frolov looked on in wonderment. He could not have done that without making himself sick. Then he noticed that the girl had rested her left leg on her right knee, so that the sole of her left shoe was presented to him. That was where the prostitutes marked their price tags.

He shook his head. 'Never mind that. How much does it cost to talk?'

She took another deep drag on her cigarette, threw back her head, and exhaled to the sky. Then, without a word, she stood up and started to walk away from him.

172

'Olga. . .'

She neither stopped nor turned.

'Olga Michaelov, daughter of the General who was betrayed and murdered.'

She stopped, but did not turn. For a long minute Frolov held his breath, willing her to turn.

'Go away.'

But still she did not move. Frolov stood up and took a step towards her. Then another.

'Go away!'

He stopped and looked down. The steel blade seemed to grow out of her hand, barely visible in the semi-darkness under the street lamp.

'This is not official, Olga. Just an attempt to set the record straight. Right a wrong. That's all.'

The blade hung there between their bodies, unwavering.

'Who are you?'

'My name is Boris Frolov. I am a Colonel in the KGB. . .'

The knife seemed to shiver in the dim light.

'I work for the Chief of the First Main Directorate. . .'

'Povin.'

Her voice cut across his as roughly as her knife would have hacked open his belly.

'Yes. . . Povin.' Frolov made himself take one deep breath, hold it, then expel it with a sigh. 'Why not come and sit down?'

He became aware that, without appearing to move, the girl had somehow pocketed the knife.

'All right.'

They sat closer together this time, as if for mutual protection.

'You knew Povin. In those days, I mean.'

'I knew him.' With exercise her voice was losing its hoarse, tarry croak. 'He used to come once a month for dinner. The first Friday. Always the first Friday. Stepan Ilyich. Always smiling. You know that rather ironical smile he has? As if he was prepared to listen tolerantly to your drivel on the clear understanding, of course, that none of it mattered.'

She had finished the first cigarette and was lighting a second from the butt.

173

'You disliked him.'

'No.' She rested her elbow on her knee and sat forward, as if to concentrate on some surprising new idea. 'What made it tolerable was that the irony extended to himself. Do you understand? He knew that everything he said, that anyone said, was rubbish too. I quite liked him for that.'

Frolov hesitated, then decided on another tack. It was too early to go for target.

'I've just come up from Baku. Marshal Stanov lives there now. He told me about your letter.'

He heard her breath escape in a sudden rush of air. 'So. . . You meant it, then. Things are serious.'

'Very serious.'

'Then why aren't we meeting face to face across a table in the Lubianka, comrade interrogator?'

Frolov swallowed bile. 'Because, as I say, this isn't official. Yet. We're trying to find out whether we ought to make it official.'

' "We"?' There was no mistaking the bitterness in her voice. 'Who. . .*exactly*, Colonel. . .are "we"?'

'Me, then.' Better not to lie.

The girl laughed, meaning it for an insult. 'That's what I thought. Looking for a little promotion, Colonel? Or. . .'

A new thought seemed to strike her. She sat up and looked him directly in the face, somehow by-passing the darkness which concealed his expression.

'Or did he send you?'

'Send me? Who?'

Olga sat back and continued to smoke her cigarette in silence. 'Did old man Stanov tell you what was in my letter?'

'Yes.'

'What was it, then? Tell me.'

'You offered to prove your father's innocence by revealing something about a meeting he'd had. With an unnamed person.'

'He told you that did he?'

Something in her voice drove a sudden, sickening wedge through Frolov's self-confidence, splitting it neatly in two. Stanov lied. Stanov told the truth. Stanov. . .

'That letter was stuffed with information. About a certain man. I named him, all right. But it's hardly surprising Stanov denied that. It's not the sort of name you say out loud. Not now. Not then, really.'

She regarded him mockingly while he strove to regain his courage. It took some minutes.

'What name is that, Olga?'

'Give me one good reason why I should tell you, Colonel.'

'You want to rehabilitate your father's name, perhaps?'

'He's dead. You can't rehabilitate a corpse, can you? Why not try money, Frolov? A lot of money. Enough to buy me out of all this. . .' She waved an airy hand in the direction of the avenue. 'Enough to find my mother. If she's alive. Say a hundred thousand roubles.'

Frolov's voice became businesslike. 'Your mother is dead, Olga. She died of starvation. In a camp. What did you expect?'

For a long moment there was silence underneath the trees. The red star on top of the University tower continued to wink on the periphery of Frolov's vision. When he first heard the sound he thought someone was approaching; then he thought it was tears; then he identified it. Olga was laughing.

'Why, that's very good, Colonel. Very shrewd. But you've forgotten something. My father was a General in the KGB. That's higher than a Colonel, I think? I know you'll tell me if I'm wrong. . . More *successful* than a Colonel. And he taught me a lot about the Organs. . . Fuck, what a name! Organs. . . He taught me how to wind someone with words. Tell them a lie, a lie so big they think it must be the truth. For instance, tell your suspect her mother's dead.' Again the sinister, near-silent laugh. 'No, Colonel. You fuck off. I'm going.'

She made as if to rise, but before she could complete the movement Frolov had her pinned to the bench.

'Before you do. . .' He fumbled in his coat pocket and brought out something which he stuffed into the girl's hand. 'A memento. Of our meeting.'

In spite of herself she looked down. He had given her a folded sheet of paper with something inside, something solid.

'Take it over to the lamp. Read it. Then you can go.'

The girl wrenched herself free, and for one nauseous

175

moment Frolov thought she was going to hurl the paper back at him. But she didn't. Instead she walked over to the pool of light and stood with her head bent, reading. When she had held the same awkward position for five full minutes Frolov realised that she was his.

'A death certificate.' He came slowly up behind her, so as not to frighten, and his voice had quite lost its earlier rough edge. He might almost have been talking to Ilinichna, or Volodya, or little Katrina. . .and after all, what was this girl but a grown-up daughter of someone? 'They can be forged, of course. That one happens to be authentic, though I don't expect you to believe it. But I could hardly forge the ring, could I? The ring that your mother tried so often to take off during her lifetime, so that your father could have it properly cleaned. . .but which would never come off. Would it, Olga? Because your mother's fingers had swollen too much for it ever to be removed. . .'

'You could have cut it off her finger. . .' The words came out borne on the crest of a flood of tears.

Frolov folded the weeping girl in his arms and held her tightly, rocking her a little, as earlier he had rocked his wife. 'Come, dry your tears. Come. . .' He led her back to the seat and when she was calm again gave her a cigarette.

'Your father, your mother. . .these things didn't just happen. They were made. Tell me, Olga. Tell me the truth. It's never too late. Let's begin again.'

The girl leaned forward to rest her elbows on her knees, took several puffs on the cigarette, and dropped it in the snow.

'My parents were supposed to have gone away for a few days. To the Black Sea. I had the house to myself. That evening I. . . I had a boyfriend. To stay the night.'

Frolov leaned forward so that they were sitting in the same position. 'Yes?'

'We. . .we were making love when. . .we heard a car outside. It was my father. He hadn't gone after all. We were terrified, both of us. I expected him to come storming up the stairs, but he didn't. Fortunately we hadn't left any lights on. I made the boy be quiet and went to the head of the stairs. My father was talking downstairs, to a man I didn't know. He kept calling him Oleg. . .'

176

Frolov stiffened. 'Oleg. . .'

'It was Kazin. I didn't know it then, but it was Kazin.'

Very, very slowly, so as not to attract any more attention than he had to, Frolov turned round. He moved his body 180 degrees to the left, then the same to the right. He was aware of an irritating click in his throat. However hard he tried he couldn't make it stop. He was cold, colder than he had ever been.

Kazin had been one of Stalin's principal executioners. Somehow he had escaped the aftermath. There was a saying about him: he had survived 'from Ilyich to Ilyich', from Lenin to Brezhnev. It was no mean achievement. No one ever talked about Kazin, because he spent as much time out of favour as in it, and you could never be sure where he stood at any given moment. One day he'd be seen in a black Zil as it hurtled through the Borovitsky gate into the Kremlin; the next you'd hear of him in exile, or under house arrest. But wherever he was, his views didn't change. The Revolution must go on. The West must be obliterated. Anti-Soviets must die.

One thing was quite clear now: why Stanov had lied to him the day before. If Frolov had received a letter making accusations about Kazin he would never have disclosed the fact to a living soul. And something else was explained, too: why Stanov had not followed up Olga's letter. So much safer just to leave things alone. . .

'You're quite sure?' Frolov spoke very quietly, as if keen not to be overheard.

'I'm sure.'

Suddenly Frolov wanted only to get out of this place, go back to his warm apartment, and Ilinichna and the babies.

'You listened. Tell me.'

'They spoke for a long time. After a while I went and got a blanket and wrapped it round me and crawled halfway down the stairs to listen.'

'The boy. . .did he hear any of this?'

'No. He was hiding under the bedclothes.' There was a touch of the former contempt in her voice. 'Shivering.'

For a moment Frolov said nothing. His sympathies were entirely with the boy.

'Go on.'

'I remember. . . Father was being stupid that night. Everything had to be explained to him five or six times — there were moments when Kazin got really angry.' She shook her head from side to side at the memory. 'You should have heard it. . .'

The last thing in the world Frolov wanted was to be anywhere near Kazin in one of his celebrated paroxysms of rage.

'Because it was all done so thoroughly I managed to pick most of it up. They talked about Povin, mostly. Kazin had evidence that he was a Christian, can you imagine that? A page from his confidential dossier. . .'

Frolov's breath escaped in a hiss.

'Stanov and Kazin were sworn enemies. Even we knew that, at school. Kazin wanted the old man out, so he could take his place. Then he knew it wouldn't matter who was nominally in power, Kazin would reign. So he'd vowed to discover the traitor before Stanov did. He had men working on it night and day — those were his very words. They had a sign for recognising each other's handiwork. . .'

For all his self-control Frolov could not resist breaking in. 'Was it a hand? A human hand?'

'That's right.' She did not seem at all surprised that he knew. 'A little picture of a hand. Kazin was inviting my father to join him. He told him straight: Povin was out to throw the guilt on to Michaelov, and Stanov had already begun to fall for it. At first my father wouldn't believe him. But as the night went on. . . Well, I don't know about Father, but Kazin convinced me. He said he had a lot of evidence. Hard stuff, the kind of thing you can't lie away.'

'And your father agreed?'

'Oh, yes. You don't disagree with Kazin, not openly. Kazin made him promise not to talk about their meeting, not to anyone, no matter what happened. He was very keen on that, I remember. There was going to be hard times ahead, difficult times, but Father wasn't to crack because that would ruin everything. And Father agreed. And I thought Kazin agreed, too. But at the end, when Father needed him. . . Have you got another light?'

Frolov looked and saw that she had dropped her matches in

the snow. He flicked open his lighter. In the glow of the flame her face looked ghastly.

'Why didn't Father tell, at the end? I've asked myself that over and over again. When he saw they were going to shoot him anyway, why not then, at the end. . .?'

'Do you know who shot your father? Who pulled the trigger, I mean?'

Olga shook her head.

'It was Stanov himself, or possibly Yevchenko. They were the only two there at the end. No one else. Suppose your father told them everything. Do you think Stanov would be interested?'

Frolov's mind was working. It was all becoming clear. Like the girl, he had been puzzled to know why Michaelov didn't break, and tell the truth. Now, he was convinced he knew.

'Kazin would never have trusted your father with concrete *evidence*,' he said slowly. 'By doing that he'd merely enable him to put the finger on Povin himself, and then claim all the credit. . .' Just the sort of thing Michaelov was always doing, he added to himself. 'Nothing your father said to Stanov and Yevchenko ranked as *evidence*. There were no documents. Everything was circumstantial. Do you understand me?'

'I think so.'

'And look at it from Stanov's point of view. He'd found the traitor, *a* traitor. Against that he was being asked to weigh the frantic babblings of a condemned man. Dangerous babblings. Isn't the real question: why did *Kazin* desert *your father*? Why didn't he produce whatever it was he had, and convict Povin then?'

'Kazin's a shit. You're all shits, all bastards. All of you.'

Frolov said nothing. He was not a fool, nor did he lack imagination. In the course of a few minutes he had destroyed this girl's last remaining hope of seeing her mother again and made her go back over the memory of her dead father. The price he exacted was enormous.

But the merchandise was. . .perfect.

'Is there anything else you can remember?'

Olga shook her head. 'Oh. . . One thing. I remember how I felt, later, knowing what I did and being unable to do anything about it. Not the slightest little thing. All that knowledge. Useless. Useless to save my father's life. Can you conceive of that, Colonel? How for days I dragged myself around, thinking up how I could contact people up top, who I should write to, while all the time I never knew if it was too late. . .?'

Her head sunk on to her chest. Frolov stood up.

'Thank you,' he said. 'I'll do what I can for you, Olga Michaelov. Not a hundred thousand roubles, I'm afraid. But look. . .here's a hundred.'

When she did not raise her head he laid the money on the seat beside her.

'There's other ways I can help you. Not money. More important things than money. It may take a little time.'

Olga sat upright very slowly. 'Good night, Colonel,' she said wearily.

'I'll remember. I promise you. . . I'll remember.'

She did not answer. But as Frolov began to walk away down the avenue, towards the stadium, he heard her say something indistinct, lost in the cold wind from the Moscow River.

He stopped. 'What?'

'I said. . .if ever you're lonely, Colonel. You know where to find me. After nine. . .'

For several moments he just stared at her, slumped in precisely the same position in which he had first caught sight of her emaciated body: hands in pockets, legs stretched out in front of her, face shrouded in darkness. Then he turned his back on her abruptly and began to walk down the long avenue, double-time.

Ilinichna was asleep when he crept into their apartment. Frolov undressed in the dark, but before going to bed he stood for a long while in the doorway of their children's bedroom, looking down on their peacefully sleeping faces. Volodya and Katrina. . .such babies. At eight and six respectively, such tiny, tiny babies. . .

When Ilinichna awoke to urinate, half an hour later, she found him still in the same position and led him, unprotesting, off to bed.

180

17

Ground Traffic Control kept the Ilyushin Il-86 waiting at the far end of the runway while the black Zil slowly approached behind a set of self-propelled steps. The pilots watched through the windscreen, curious to know why they had been denied permission to taxi in. It was very early in the morning, the passengers and crew had had a long flight, everyone was tired. Now this hold-up a mile from the nearest airport building, it was too much. . .

The occupant of the Zil's back seat was screened from prying eyes by black curtains. The nearside front door opened, and the pilots saw a thick-set man wearing a grey fedora pulled well down over his eyes get out and run quickly up the steps. A few moments later he reappeared in their field of vision, carrying three briefcases. He walked smartly back to the Zil, threw the cases into the front seat, and got in. At once the huge car drove away, gaining speed across the tarmac in the direction of the squat, ugly building which housed the KGB's immigration department at Moscow's Vnukovo II airport. The steps were removed. Only then did the tower permit the Il-86 to taxi into its parking bay. The captain looked at his co-pilot in silence, and both men simultaneously shrugged. With Zils you did not argue; questions were best left unasked. Each pilot knew that the other would somehow omit to log the incident in his flight report.

The Zil pulled up in the grey half-light of the February dawn outside the KGB building. This time it was the back door that opened, and General Povin who emerged carrying the cases. He knew his way without having to ask directions. With

Victor, the man in the wide-brimmed hat, a pace behind him, he walked at a leisurely pace down a long corridor, turned left, ascended a gentle ramp and so entered the office of Major Yevgenni Romanovich Avdeyev, station commander attached to the 11th Department of the Second Main Directorate of the KGB.

The Major rose to his feet with a genial smile and saluted. Povin acknowledged his welcome and shook Avdeyev's hand warmly. After the initial pleasantries there was an awkward pause. Both men were perfectly well aware of what business had to be transacted. Neither was keen to appear enthusiastic about it.

Povin humped the briefcases on to the table. Avdeyev looked at them and smiled appreciatively.

'Very nice,' he murmured. 'Very nice indeed, General. Real leather.' He ran his fingers lightly over the surface of the nearest case, enjoying the feel of the hide. Povin did not reply. His eyes remained fixed on Avdeyev's face. He opened the lid of one of the other cases a fraction, keeping it between himself and the Major, and slid his hand inside. Suddenly his eyes widened in mock astonishment and Avdeyev's face dissolved into a smile. He vastly enjoyed these little pantomimes, which were the source of an infinite supply of stories for telling at intimate dinner parties with his friends. The rich, the clever, the well connected. . .somehow none of them could ever bring themselves to be quite straightforward about what was, to Major Avdeyev, merely a business arrangement. It amused the Major greatly, but he was careful not to let it show. A deal was a deal; and in his line of business you'd only have to upset the wrong client just once to find yourself posted as officer commanding internal customs on the Mongolian border. Avdeyev had no intention of upsetting anyone at all.

Povin slowly withdrew his hand. Avdeyev looked at the magazine and his eyes popped in a beautiful imitation of shocked surprise.

'*Screw*,' he murmured. 'Such interesting names they have, General.'

Povin smiled. 'Shall we put it down as. . .literature?'

Avdeyev pursed his lips. This was the part he enjoyed most,

but it required skilful handling. With an apologetic smile that bordered on the obsequious he very slowly shook his head.

'The truth is, General, that here in the Soviet Union we have so much literature. So many books and articles on such a wide variety of subjects that, well. . .frankly. . .' Avdeyev shook his head again and sucked his teeth. 'I don't know. Really I don't.'

Victor had been lounging against the door. Now he stood upright and slowly placed his right hand in the pocket of his overcoat. Fortunately Avdeyev was at the end of a long night shift and he did not notice the peculiar hue which had suddenly suffused Victor's face.

Povin's smile did not falter. He closed the lid of the case and said quietly, 'On page eight there is something which I think even you, Yevgenni Romanovich, would regard as being fresh, and new. A variation on an old, old theme. Please look.'

Avdeyev raised sceptical eyebrows, but did as he was told. Pinned to the top of page eight were twenty ten-dollar bills. His smile widened, and this time there was no pretence. Povin had a reputation for being open-handed in his dealings.

'Literature,' murmured the Major as he pulled a pad of blue forms towards him. 'Culture,' he breathed reverently, unscrewing the top of a gold fountain pen. (Avdeyev had many nice possessions.) 'How can one ever have enough of it?'

Victor removed his hand from his pocket and sank back to lounge against the door once more. Avdeyev finished writing out his clearance, signed it and tendered it along with the magazine — but minus the money. Povin accepted the clearance and gently rejected *Screw*, indicating that Avdeyev could keep it. The Major smiled and inclined his head. As Povin lifted the cases from the table he rose from his chair and came round the desk to open the door with a polite bow.

'A moment, General.'

Povin stopped. The expression on his face had scarcely altered since he entered the office. Now he was aware of a minuscule tic at the corner of his mouth, and across the space which separated them he could feel Victor tense. Avdeyev reached out a hand as if to touch the nearest case, his expression thoughtful. Povin made an almightly effort and did not jerk away.

183

'There is a good market for this stuff? The "literature", I mean?'

'Excellent, yes.'

Avdeyev's hand still stroked the leather, up and down, up and down. . . 'I was wondering. . .'

Povin swallowed but managed to keep his smile intact. 'Yes?'

'The cases. When you have finished with them, I think I might know of someone who would be *very* interested in purchasing them.'

'I'll have to think about that, Yevgenni Romanovich. It's tempting. But now, if you'll excuse me. . .'

Avdeyev withdrew his hand. 'Of course. Good day, General.'

'Good day.'

Povin led the way down the ramp at a brisk pace. As he turned the corner, however, his confident stride faltered and he almost fell back against the wall, his eyes closed. Without a pause Victor snatched the cases from him, linked one arm through his and half dragged Povin on towards the exit, looking fearfully over his shoulder. The passage was empty. No one saw.

By the time they emerged into the fresh air Povin had almost completely recovered. Only his grey face remained as a testimonial to the terrible ordeal of the past five minutes.

'Go,' he breathed, shoving the blue form into Victor's hand.

'You will be all right?'

'Yes! *Go*.'

Povin leaned heavily against the side of the Zil and watched Victor as he walked quickly off in the direction of the internal departures building. Only when he became aware of a nearby guard looking him over with an expression that was half respectful and half suspicious did he make the effort to climb back into the car and slowly arrange the rug across his knees.

The black Zil accelerated smoothly away, bearing Povin off to his office in Dzerzhinsky Square and the numberless, fretful days which lay ahead.

18

The two men dressed in silence. Anna, the KGB Captain and the rest of the group stood outside, occasionally exchanging a few words in low voices. By tacit consent Binderhaven and McDonnell decided to ask no questions but await events.

When they had finished dressing they went out to the corridor.

'Your baggage, please. We shall be leaving almost at once.'

They packed, again in silence. Binderhaven was puzzled by what he had seen outside their room: there were no troops with the officer, the remaining members of the little party being hotel staff sent up to carry the bags. If this was an arrest it had some unusual features.

Downstairs in the lobby Faber and Mannheim were already waiting. They looked tense and worried. Binderhaven wished they'd talk among themselves, like normal people. Four men with American accents in an Irkutsk hotel, wearing apprehensive expressions. . . Not good.

'We shall obtain breakfast at the airport.'

Anna was by the main entrance, the officer at her side. He was smiling. Something about the way he stood told Binderhaven that his connection with Anna was not merely professional; there was a distinctly proprietorial air about the way he listened to her announcements, rather as a proud parent hears a favourite child recite in a language he doesn't understand.

'During the night there has been much snow. Roads are closing. The airport has activated de-icing procedures now, but more snow is anticipated and no flights are guaranteed out of Irkutsk after one p.m. The officer here has very kindly offered to help by getting my party through. But we must go now, not at the stated time. Mr Concorde. . .you and Mr Smithson will accompany us, please, and after the airport the officer will take you on to your rendezvous.'

She flashed a typical courier's in-house smile at him and turned away. Binderhaven was paralysed. He couldn't think what to do. If they accepted, all chance of striking out on their own was gone. If they refused. . .but they could not refuse. And what's more, Anna must have known that before she set up this crazy scheme. So what in hell's name. . .

Mechanically he picked up his bags and followed her from the hotel. There had to be a way out of this. To come so far and then be casually picked up by the KGB under pretence of giving them a lift. . .

His thoughts were interrupted by a long, low whistle.

'Jeez. . .will you look at that thing!'

It was Faber who spoke. Binderhaven looked up; for a second he couldn't comprehend what he saw, and then it dawned. There was a solution to every problem. His was parked outside the Hotel Angara.

At first sight it looked like a tank, with its long, low-slung body and six-wheeled tracks, but Binderhaven identified it at once: a GT-T Over-Snow Load Carrier, the kind of thing Soviet planners usually assigned to logistical support and medical back-up services. As its name implied, it was custom made for travel in Siberia: four men could ride inside without difficulty but in considerable discomfort, because only a canvas collapsible roof separated the occupants from the elements. Binderhaven sized up the vehicle through narrowed eyes. Four men, the officer, the driver, maybe; the luggage and Anna as well, no. . .

His head swivelled. Parked behind the snowcat was a black Volga. Binderhaven saw that it had been fitted with chains and his lips pursed. If the roads weren't too bad it might be possible for the Volga to tail them most of the way to the trappers' post. But how bad were the roads? What exactly was the weather forecast? He shook his head, mentally cursing his lack of hard information. The Volga might not even belong to Anna.

186

On that point at least his mind was soon put at rest. Anna clapped her hands and started to allocate placings.

'Two people in the Volga with me, please. We shall fill the boot with luggage, as much as it will hold. The other two will please ride with the officer and the rest of your cases.'

Binderhaven nodded his approval. The car did not come equipped with a chauffeur, he had already checked that, so Anna must have managed to change part of the overnight plan. She was good. In Binderhaven's mind she was becoming very good. If only the KGB officer didn't stand over her like that. . . No, he was being dumb. He ought to be pleased she had friends in the KGB. Without them they'd never have gotten access to a GT-T. Two men in with the driver and the officer should be enough. The Volga would trail along behind. Somewhere on the road to the airport the GT-T would temporarily leave the service of the Soviet Union and enter the inventory of the United States' armed forces. After that. . . Binderhaven couldn't think what might happen after that.

He turned to Joe Faber, who was lifting a suitcase inside the snowcat, and touched his arm.

'You know the first thing I'm going to do when I get out of here? I'm going to drink myself a whole bottle of Red Eye, two of Bacardi and I'm going to smoke my way through a couple of packs of Luckies.'

Faber smiled frantically as his brain struggled to recall a code from way back, when he and Binderhaven last worked together. 'Yeah,' he laughed. 'Sure thing. No kidding.' His flickering eyes stilled, and came into focus. 'Count me in on that.'

Binderhaven nodded pleasantly, and walked over to where Anna was holding the Volga's door open from her place in the driver's seat.

'OK,' he said as the car pulled out behind the huge GT-T, 'what the hell is going on?'

It took her a while before she could trust herself to speak. Binderhaven studied her profile and didn't like what he saw. Her face was white except where a blotchy spot of red pulsed in time with her heartbeat, her forehead was moist and every other second she would lick her lips, which were cracked and dry.

'He and I. . .are friends.'

Inside Binderhaven something gave a wrench. He made himself ignore it.

'He has done this before. When the weather is bad, and they have not much work on. He helps me out by taking people places where they want to go.'

'Who else knows about this?'

'At KGB headquarters they will have a record of where the snowcat is today. And who is driving it.'

'How long before they miss it?'

'Not before this afternoon. Why? You can't seriously. . .'

'Just watch the road, Anna. Now tell me something. Couldn't you have stopped this?'

Her hands clenched the steering wheel. Several times she opened her mouth before the words came out. 'He . . .insists. He is. . . I don't have the words for it. . .'

Deep inside Binderhaven the same thing wrenched again, only this time in another direction. 'You mean he's trying to make a pass at you. Make love to you.'

She nodded, and the car skidded on a patch of hardened snow.

'Like I say, Anna, just watch the road. Is it all highway between here and the airport?'

'Not all of it. They are extending the road but it fell behind plan in the summer. Everything is being diverted north, to the construction of the Amur Railway.'

'Is the road built up? Are there houses, I mean?'

'There is a stretch before the turning to the airport which goes through fields.'

'Good. Watch out for that stretch. When we get there, that —' Binderhaven gestured at the tracked vehicle ahead — 'is going to slow down and stop. Pull in behind it, as far out of the traffic lane as you can safely go. The two of us will get out for about ten minutes. I want you to use the time by checking and re-checking the map until you're sure you can take us to the trappers' hut. You'll have to use your own judgement about the state of the roads but I want you to go by the backways as far as possible. Any questions?'

She shook her head. Binderhaven saw a tear roll down her

cheek and gritted his teeth.

'I'm sorry, Anna. We'll think up a story, you can say we overpowered you, something like that, but this is the way it has to be.'

She banged her hands on the steering wheel.

'You're mad, mad, mad. You can't take on the whole of the KGB like this. What happens when they send out the search parties, the helicopters? They're bound to find you. That thing leaves traces, tracks. . . It will be like following a straight road, from the air. . .'

'We need the vehicle, Anna. If we're to have any hope at all of making our target in time, we have to use it. It would take an army to patrol the area from here up to Bratsk and if what you said about the weather is right, no one'll be flying anywhere. By the time they do, our tracks will be covered. Now watch the road ahead, and be ready to pull in like I said.'

Binderhaven wished he could believe any of it. He knew the girl was right. Even if the weather was on his side, the loss of the snowcat would result in them doubling, trebling the guard round the air base. And as yet he hadn't even told her the worst of it: that she must return to Irkutsk and sit it out until the weapons arrived. If they ever did. Then she must deliver them to the task force, wherever it might be.

Anna Petrina had suddenly become expendable. Binderhaven would have done anything in his power to prevent that happening.

They were skirting the city limits on a ring road. The snow had stopped but the grey sky made for poor visibility and their speed was slow. Ahead of them three white lights flashed on the side of the GT-T, and Anna indicated a turn.

'This is the airport spur. From now on we travel in open country.'

'How far is it?'

'Not far. Three kilometres, less.'

The snowploughs had been at work on the airport road but it was still treacherous in places. High walls of crushed snow prevented Binderhaven from seeing more than a glimpse of the white wilderness on either side.

'Careful now. He's slowing.'

Binderhaven swivelled in his seat to look out of the rear windscreen. Traffic was light. After a couple of cars and a truck the road stretched away to the junction, black and deserted. Ahead of the car the snowcat wobbled, swerved almost into the path of an oncoming lorry, righted itself and halted in a narrow lay-by carved out of the snow wall.

Anna stopped the car.

'These are the maps. Study them carefully. If anyone stops to see what the trouble is, tell them the truth about us and explain that the driver up ahead is having a little trouble. Get rid of them as quickly as you can.'

Binderhaven and McDonnell got out of the car. Anna watched them as they approached the GT-T and disappeared into the cab. When nothing else happened for about a minute she unfolded the map and with trembling fingers tried to find the road she wanted.

Ten minutes went by, the longest that Anna had ever endured.

At last a movement by the snowcat caught her eye and she looked up swiftly, a frightened little animal who hears the hunter's tread in every sound. What she saw made her heart contract. An officer wearing the uniform of the KGB was coming towards her over the snow.

Her relief when she recognised one of the Americans was so profound that it was several moments before she could respond to his gestured instruction to wind down the window.

'Sorry if I frightened you. Have you found the route yet?'

'Yes. It's not so far away.'

The man went back to the GT-T. A few minutes later Anna saw Binderhaven and Faber climb down from the cab and walk to the Volga. She waited until they were all seated before asking, 'Well?'

'No problem.'

'But what happened to. . .'

'Like I say, Anna, it's not a problem. Now this time you're going to lead the way. The snowcat'll follow. It can't do more than forty kilometres an hour top, and in this weather it'll be less than that, so watch your speed. Keep looking in the mirror and make sure you can always see the others. OK. Drive.'

The convoy started off again. Anna drove until they could see the airport buildings, then made a left turn down a side road. Here the snow ploughs had not penetrated but the carriageway had been cleared some days before and the snow did not lie thick. The wheels slithered a little; then the chains gripped, Anna regained control, and they were off.

The journey took two hours. The roads were never better than treacherous but they had to stop only twice. The first time the Volga was rescued from a drift by all four men pushing while Anna hung on to the wheel and wrestled the car back on to the road. On the second occasion they had to break out the shovels from the snowcat and dig.

'How much longer can we keep this up?'

Binderhaven looked up wearily from his last shovel load of snow and found Joe Faber at his side.

'As long as it takes.'

'This thing is due back in a little over an hour, if what the girl says is right. When do you think they'll start looking for it?'

Binderhaven dumped his shovel in the back of the snowcat and did not answer.

'Sky's heavy as lead, but there's nothing to stop a chopper picking up those tracks right now. And once they find that stiff you and Nat left in the tunnel. . .'

'Get back in the car, Joe.'

'Look, Kirk. . .'

'*Get back in!*'

Binderhaven was surprised to hear the anger in his own voice. He had picked a good bunch of boys, the best. But he didn't need any pessimistic assessments of their chances just then.

The last thing he did before climbing back into the car was survey the sky. Cloud hung low and black as far as the horizon. He strained his ears to listen. Apart from the low moan of the north-east wind there was nothing: no sound of rotor blades, no engines. But, Christ, what a country. Nothing but snow wherever he looked, with a smudge of black on the far horizon which might have been taiga. To think that people eked a living out of this wilderness, this white desert. Binderhaven shook his head and shivered a little. The next forty hours were going to

191

be rough. What happened then was. . .irrelevant.

'How much further?' he asked, slamming the door.

'A kilometre, maybe. Then we must walk.'

'Walk? How far?'

'One kilometre again.'

Binderhaven frowned. 'You can't get any closer with the car?'

'No. I am sorry, but no.'

'OK. We'll leave you there, so long as you can direct us.'

'I can do that.'

'Then you head back into town.' Binderhaven studied his clenched fist and very slowly made himself unclench it. 'And we'll see you back here before nightfall.'

Before she could respond Joe Faber put his arm on the back of Binderhaven's seat and leaned forward.

'Say, you can't ask her to come back. She's been great, fantastic. I've been thinking it all out as we came along, she goes back and tells them that the crazy Canadians and Americans got into a fight, see, and Captain Whatsisname tried to pull a gun on them, and he got killed. . .'

'Killed!'

Anna's breathing had become very fast. The red blotch on her cheek pulsated in time with her heartbeat, and the sweat had broken out again on her forehead.

'Ah. . .' Joe Faber lowered himself back into his seat and fell silent.

Anna swallowed a couple of times and licked her lips. 'Yes, I see, he was killed, all right, all right. But the weapons, that's what you want, isn't it, you must have the weapons, the weapons. . .'

Binderhaven spoke gently. 'We can't do it without you, Anna. I agree with Joe. You're fantastic. You've done more than we had any right to think you ever could, or would. But without you, we're helpless. We need those weapons. Unless we have them our mission fails. Anna, remember what the failure of this mission means.'

She nodded her head very fast: a shiver of assent.

'It could mean a war between the peoples of our country and the peoples of yours. Many would die, Anna. We can't imagine the horrors that would come out of such a war. We have one chance of preventing that. Just one. The chance is that those weapons have come through, and we can get our hands on them. That's all.'

For a few moments she continued to stare out of the windscreen while her fingers toyed with the wheel, and Binderhaven wondered what she was seeing in those pale middle distances. Then she suddenly raised her hands to her eyes and her small body seemed to heave in a single, wracking sob. It had an indescribable effect on the two toughened men sitting in the car with her: it was as though something small but immensely powerful, a weary child's body taxed beyond all endurance, finally gave out. Binderhaven saw tears oozing between her fingers and looked away.

'The weapons. Of course, you must have the weapons.'

Binderhaven turned his head and saw her hastily wipe her eyes with a handkerchief. Her voice, when she spoke, was rapid, and she looked more embarrassed than he felt.

'I will bring food also. Is there anything else you require?'

'Nothing. Food would be nice, but don't worry about it. We have tablets, and we're trained to survive on them.'

She managed a wan smile. 'Like the astronauts?'

Binderhaven nodded without smiling. 'Like that.'

'I will find you here?'

'In the place where you drop us off, which you say is a kilometre away. One of us will find you, but you may not see us when you first arrive.'

'You do not trust me?'

'You I trust. The people who may try to use you if things go wrong. . .no.'

At a sign from Binderhaven Anna started the engine and engaged gear. The road was growing progressively worse. It took them a long time to cover that final kilometre.

At last they stopped. At a sign from Binderhaven Faber got out of the car. McDonnell leaned out of the snowcat's cab and hollered, 'Thermometer says ten degrees below. Better move it!'

Binderhaven nodded without taking his eyes off the car as it manoeuvred gingerly round to face the way they had come.

193

'Break out the snow gear. Shoes and goggles only for the moment, we'll change outer clothing when we get to the hut.'

The Volga chugged off down the track, its black exhaust staining the snowbank, and Binderhaven lifted a hand in farewell. Only when it turned a corner and disappeared down a hill did he return to his men.

'Joc, I want you to take constant bearings. Each man needs to be able to find his way from the hut to the road and back in total darkness by compass alone.'

'Check.'

'OK. Let's ride. Stow and board.'

It was after two o'clock when Anna drove past the University and turned into Ulicia Garcena, at the far end of which Intourist had its regional offices. She felt exhausted after hours of struggling with icy roads, Siberian traffic and the pathetic shreds of her emotions. Nausea gripped her stomach at the thought of the blind alley down which those men on the tundra had led her. She could not go forward, she could not go back. They were relying on her. He was relying on her. . .

Anna jabbed angrily at the horn and the driver of the Zhiguli which had tried to cut in trod on his brakes instead, cursing all crazy women. He, he, he. . . Why out of all those warmongering spies did one face insist on coming between her and the road? The thought of Binderhaven was enough to madden her, with his calm assurance that she would do his bidding, go back to the city, run errands, return. . . There was no god but there was a devil right enough, and he was an American with the most endearingly crisp, brown eyes. . .'

Anna felt herself growing uncomfortably warm and switched off the heater which had been running at full blast ever since they had left the Hotel Angara. With the noisy fan no longer functioning she became more aware of her surroundings. Cars hooted, engines whined, somewhere close by a militiaman blew his whistle. Anna craned ahead, planning where to park. Damn! A lorry had stopped outside the front entrance of her office.

As her eyes lighted on the lorry its tail board crashed down and men began to pour on to the pavement. Uniformed men. . .

KGB troops. Anna braked hard. Maybe they were nothing to do with her. Perhaps they would march off round the corner, out of her life. . .

But already she knew she was fooling herself. Without lining up on the sidewalk the troops began to move inside the Intourist building, leaving two sentries on the door. Anna instinctively put the wheel hard down, made an illegal left turn under the outraged glare of the militiamen directing traffic and accelerated hard.

Home. She must get home.

The Volga made a right, then immediately forked left, heading as far away from the Intourist building as her instincts could ensure. She looked in the mirror. No one was following her. The militiaman might put out an alert for her, but somehow she didn't think so. Siberia was like everywhere else in that respect: if the traffic police caught you for a violation they dealt with you, if they didn't catch you they forgot the incident. But the KGB were looking for her, that was plain. They had found the body on the railway line. The snowcat had been missed. Anything could have happened.

To go home was dangerous but after her initial decision Anna never hesitated. She had told Binderhaven the truth when she said she would pay the debt she owed America. Especially if it meant revenge on the brutal, heartless autocrats who had betrayed her.

Especially — she faced it at last — if it meant seeing him again.

Whatever happened now, she knew she was finished. By helping the Americans she had compromised herself beyond all hope of saving. She knew she could never withstand the kind of interrogation to which they would subject her. The only hope was to keep moving as long as possible, and then throw in her lot with Binderhaven and his men.

Anna thought she knew something about spies, and how they worked. They would have an escape route all worked out: maybe a plane was coming for them, or they had a safe house. When they escaped, she would go with them. But she must plan. There would be no second chance once she left her apartment.

195

Food. That was the first thing. Warm clothes. Anna shivered at the thought of the steppe at night and pushed it out of her mind. Her skiing clothes would do. She had nearly thrown them away, thinking never to wear them again, but something stopped her. What luck! And the weapons. . .

Her hands whitened on the steering wheel. Suppose these mysterious weapons had been delivered to her office. They would find them at once, you couldn't hope to hide such things. No point in worrying about that. Just keep your eyes on the road and drive, *drive!*'

She made herself do two full circuits of her apartment block before being satisfied that no one was waiting for her, and even then she parked the Volga round the corner, out of sight. She tapped the glass of the fuel gauge, which was faulty. The car was very low on petrol. She could buy more on Intourist coupons, but they were back at the office. Anna held her hands up to her eyes and said, very loudly, 'I. . .will. . .not. . .cry!' It would be all right. She would get as far as she could on what fuel was left, then she would hitchhike. Or walk.

As she ran inside the first snowflakes whirled around the forecourt, heralds of the oncoming blizzard. She used the back door of the building, which was deserted at that hour. No one tried to stop her. The *dezhurnaya*, a lazy old woman whose job it was to guard the entrance, was taking her usual afternoon nap. Anna vaulted up the stairs three at a time, not thinking that the click of her shoes on the lino ran far ahead of her. As she emerged on the landing of the fourth floor, latch key in hand, a man stepped out of the shadows to stand between her and the door of her flat.

'Anna Petrina.'

She stared up at him. In his black overcoat and fedora he seemed to tower above her; a tall, threatening nemesis. For a split second it crossed her mind what a fool she had been to think they were not watching her home, and then her round eyes dissolved in floods of tears. She half turned back towards the stairwell, in what her brain already told her was a futile move, but before she could take the first step a strong hand closed round her arm and she fell to the ground, weeping and cursing her own stupidity. Far, far above her, on the outer

196

fringes of the black void which rose up to engulf Anna Petrina, she heard a voice hiss, 'KGB. Don't try to run.'

19

Ilinichna was astonished when her Boris rang from the office to say they were going out to dinner that evening. It wasn't her birthday or any other special occasion that she could recall. Perhaps it was Boris's name day. . . No, that was in June, a long way off yet. And the Aragvi Restaurant, on Gorky Street: nothing but the best, although. . .

'I didn't know you liked Georgian cooking,' she said doubtfully. 'Whenever my mother makes *shashlyk*. . .'

'The chefs at the Aragvi,' he interrupted her brusquely, 'know what they're doing. Unlike your mother. I'll meet you in the foyer at eight-thirty sharp. Don't expect me to hang about if you're late.'

But Ilinichna was early. She stood outside the ladies' cloakroom, watching the under-managers' desperate attempts to control the queue of people vainly fighting for a table, and wondering if Boris would mind that she had gone out to buy herself a new dress. A noisy rumble from her stomach made her look at the clock on the wall. Eight-thirty, he'd said, and already it was twenty to nine.

A Chaika drew up outside the restaurant and disgorged Boris Frolov with his warrant officer of the day, who proceeded to shoulder a path through the mass of worthless humanity milling between Frolov and his dinner.

'Hello, darling. Did the traffic hold you up?'

Frolov grunted. He was in a bad humour, she noted: say little and smile a lot, then. The manager himself escorted them to their table. Boris stalked ahead looking to neither right nor left, while Ilinichna would pause every so often to exchange gushing greetings and kisses with acquaintances. In consequence Boris was already ordering vodka by the time she reached the table and sat down.

Ilinichna didn't much care for the table, which was tucked away out of sight halfway behind a pillar, but Boris didn't seem to mind, so she kept her mouth shut. She was not to know that her husband had earlier paid good money to reserve these very seats. Ilinichna began to look about her.

'Why, look over there. Isn't that Stepan Ilyich?'

'Tzhut! Keep your voice down, can't you.'

Boris made large inroads on the vodka, but this time Ilinichna was not to be silenced.

'But it is! What a coincidence, darling, that your boss should be here. Who are all those people with him?'

Warily Frolov stole a discreet glance at the large round table in the very centre of the restaurant. Povin was sitting a little way apart, the usual placid smile on his face, deriving quiet satisfaction from the noisy revels going on around him. Several empty bottles of champagne — the best champagne, Ilinichna noticed — stood on the table, and Povin's party was evidently determined to have a very good time indeed. Four women, three other men, that face was familiar, no it couldn't be, yes, yes *it was!*

'Boris! It's Stolyinovich! With Stepan Ilyich, would you believe it? Oh, darling, we must go and talk to them. . .'

Her husband grabbed her arm. 'Stay where you are,' he snarled. Ilinichna was about to protest when the waiter arrived and, faced with the necessity of ordering immediately or losing the chance for at least another hour, she gulped and buried her head in the menu.

Ilinichna found Boris very tiresome that evening, though not one half as tiresome as he found her. He scarcely touched the excellent food, but sullenly smoked and drank his way through his wife's energetic attack on everything they put before her. Throughout the meal he scarcely took his eyes off Povin.

That morning, quite by chance, Povin's diary secretary had let slip that Stolyinovich was giving a party to celebrate the start of his next foreign tour, and the General was going.

198

Frolov at once resolved to go too. Now he was regretting it bitterly. The meal was costing him a fortune, and Lenin only knew what he'd expected to get out of it: Povin was hardly likely to transmit morse code messages to the West with a knife and fork. Added to which his wife had gone out and bought herself a new dress with money they didn't have, doubtless hoping he wouldn't notice, and she was now pestering him to walk right up to Povin and say, 'Stepan Ilyich, please do introduce me to all your illustrious friends. . .'

Frolov stubbed out a half-smoked cigarette, sending large flecks of ash fluttering over the white tablecloth.

'Get your coat,' he said. 'We're leaving.'

Ilinichna was on the point of opening her mouth to argue when Boris turned to face her squarely and she backed off, aware of something unpleasant, more than unpleasant, in his expression. Without a word she rose and made her way to the far side of the room, and the *Tyalet*.

'Interesting sight, isn't it?'

Frolov turned his head. Seated alone at the next table was a fat, jolly-looking man with his eyes, two little buttonholes, fixed firmly on Povin. Frolov was about to give him the brush-off when he saw the fat man rearrange his greatcoat, which was lying on a chair beside him, in such a way as to reveal the shoulder boards of a Lieutenant-General, and his demeanour abruptly changed.

'Very interesting, comrade General.'

The fat man stood up and slouched across to Frolov's table. 'Mind if I join you?'

He sat down without waiting for Frolov's answer. The Colonel looked longingly at the bottle of French cognac in the fat man's hand; as if reading his mind the fat man smiled and snapped his fingers. Within seconds a glass appeared on the cloth in front of Frolov, who swallowed uneasily. After a pause he gingerly held out his hand, and said, 'Er, Boris. . .'

'Frolov, yes. Have a glass of this.'

The Colonel struggled to clear his head. He had a problem. He didn't know what it was, or how big, or why, but indisputably he had a problem. When you can feel the shit rising over your ankles, details cease to matter.

The fat man poured generously from the bottle and replaced the cork with a snap before raising his glass.

'Progress,' he said. 'Here's to it.'

Frolov said nothing, but drank deeply. For the first time in a long while he was starting to miss Ilinichna very badly.

'D'you like stories, Frolov? Fairy tales and suchlike?'

'Well, I. . .'

'Of course you do.' The fat man laughed, a merry sound, and Frolov relaxed a fraction. 'Two children, both at school, doing very well I believe. Volodya made *zvenovoi* just the other day, or so they tell me. What father doesn't like a good story?'

Frolov's head was beginning to pound. If only he hadn't smoked and drunk so much. . . Too late now. A crisis was dawning and he was in no fit state to deal with it. He had absolutely no idea of who he was talking to, or how that person came to know so much about him, or what the hell was going on at all. For once, the roles were reversed; and Frolov didn't like it one bit. Damn Ilinichna, he thought, where is she?

The fat man gestured in Povin's direction, and Frolov strove to concentrate.

'Now he'd be interested in this story. It's just the kind of thing he's supposed to take an interest in. He and his deputies, of course. . .'

The fat man stole a sly glance at Frolov before raising the glass to his lips and draining it with a backward toss of his head. If he was worried about losing Frolov's attention he needn't have been. The Colonel's eyes were riveted to his own.

'Now you will bear in mind, won't you, that this is only a *story* that I'm going to tell you. . .'

The fat man smiled genially, as if seeking reassurance. Frolov swallowed and nodded.

'Well then, imagine this. Nineteen-fifty, or thereabouts. Good Party family: father away in Siberia on State business, although he needn't be; mother left at home with the only child. A boy, newly commissioned into the KGB. Follow me?'

The fat man glanced at Frolov to ensure that he was still paying complete attention, uncorked the brandy bottle, and poured again.

200

'Mother seeks consolation in, of all things, religion. Gets it badly, too. Fanatical.'

The fat man paused and drank. Frolov, as if mesmerised, did likewise.

'What to do? Mothér has kept her secret from just about everyone — except the son, who promptly goes to pieces. He knows he ought to turn his mother in. But before he can do anything, someone tells the father what's been going on. . . Are you awake, Frolov?'

'Yes, comrade General.'

'Good. Drink up, then. . . That's right. Now, what was I saying? Oh, yes, the boy. He knows the KGB are shortly going to pick up his own mother. In real desperation he seeks out his mother's confessor, a zealous priest called Father Michael. Who persuades him to do nothing, let things take their course. The good comrades bring the woman in for questioning, rough her up a bit. She recants. The son undertakes to be responsible for her good behaviour. Everything is hushed up. You know how it is, Frolov, where a good Party family is concerned. But, shall I tell you a curious thing? The boy, the young Lieutenant. . .he rose to a position of great power, a good and useful servant of the Party, and you would think such a one would be quickest of all to forget the past, would you not?'

Frolov nodded assent.

'Yet he does not forget. Instead, he visits this Father Michael, and they talk, sometimes for hours on end.'

Frolov stared at him. 'But. . .the risk?'

'Certainly.'

'If ever it came to light he could be for the *gulag*, surely?'

'Without a doubt.'

For a moment Frolov sat in silence while his imagination struggled to come to grips with such incomprehensible folly.

'Then why on earth. . .?' he said lamely.

'Is not the answer obvious?'

Frolov looked up to see that the fat General was smiling at him, his head cocked to one side.

'I'm sorry.' Frolov shook his head. 'I just don't. . .'

'Because he loved his mother! And his guilt goes beyond anything he's ever known.'

'Love. . .guilt?'

'Of course. He let her be arrested, didn't lift a finger to prevent it. Well, how would you feel? And of course, the only other explanation, that the son is now himself a Christian, well, it only has to be stated to be dismissed as treasonable rubbish.'

There was a long silence.

'How do you know all this?' Frolov asked irresolutely.

The fat man shrugged. 'That would be an excellent question — if this were anything but a fairy story. Which it isn't.'

Frolov bit his lip. Over the fat man's shoulder he could see his wife approaching. Damn and blast! When he needed her she stayed away, and now that he would have given anything for a few more minutes, seconds even, of this man's time, she was coming back.

'Why are you telling me this?' he said urgently. But for answer the fat man merely raised his glass and said, 'Progress. You're doing well, Frolov.'

'Please, darling Boris. . .who is your so-charming friend?'

The two men lumbered to their feet and Frolov introduced his wife.

'And this is General. . . General. . .'

'Such a pleasure to have met you, comrades. . .'

The fat man struggled awkwardly into his greatcoat, shook hands with Frolov, bowed to Ilinichna, and turned to go.

'Mironov,' he said over his shoulder.

20

Anna Petrina's first coherent thought after falling at the top of the stairs was that she was sitting on a chair in her own kitchen with a cup of evil-smelling liquor in her hands. The man in the black overcoat and fedora sat opposite on the very edge of another chair, hands in pockets, a frown creasing his ugly face.

'You are all right now?'

She stared at him, speechless.

'Go on. Drink it. Right down.'

Mechanically she obeyed. A scalding fire ignited in her larynx and flooded into her stomach: she choked some of the liquid out and swallowed the rest, gagging. The man laughed.

'Polish *śliwowica*. To keep the cold out. Siberia. . .ai-ee!'

Something was wrong with his voice. It came out between a deep hiss and a croak. When he moved his head slightly his collar rode up to reveal scars on his throat which looked very old. A fight, cancer. . . She found him terrifying, and it had nothing to do with his job.

'I thought you were going to scream out there. That would have been very bad.' Again the movement of the head and she saw that he was nervous. It was ridiculous. What did he have to be afraid of?

'It's bad enough having to come all this way from Moscow without a hysterical woman waiting at the end of it.'

'You. . .you're from Moscow?'

'Yes. Mine was the last flight in today. Except for some military brass, that is.'

'But I. . . I don't understand. You're not from Irkutsk?'

'Look, woman, would I fly in from Moscow if I was from Irkutsk?'

She watched while he poured a shot of *śliwowica* for himself and knocked it back with a shiver.

'You're Anna Petrina, right?'

She nodded, too weak to reply.

'Yes.' His eyes flickered from her to a square of cardboard in his hand and she realised that he must be looking at a photograph of her. 'It looks like you. You're expecting something, no?'

Inside Anna a tiny spark of hope was feebly struggling to life with the help of the oily Polish spirit.

'You have something for me?'

The man did not answer. Instead he jerked his thumb at three attaché cases standing by the kitchen door. Anna stood up unsteadily and walked across to them.

'Careful now. . .'

'Why? Can't I look?'

The man laughed, a tired humourless croak. 'Not unless you want to kill us both. You've heard of an auto-destruct mechanism? No? Those cases each have a device built in to them, see. When it's set — and it's set right now — if anyone comes along and interferes with them — wham! Napalm-based. Everything within fifty metres turns to powdered ash.'

'But how can I. . .?'

'I'll tell you, woman, if you'd stop interrupting. These things here, see, are combination locks. Each one has three digits. Look now. . .they're set at nine all the way across. Use your thumb and turn them together, like this, watch. . . That's the way. Now they're pointing to eight and it's safe. The big thing is to make sure they all turn together, that none gets out of phase. Do you understand?'

She seemed not to hear. The man waited for an answer, got none, shrugged and rose to his feet.

'I'm going now.'

She did not react in any way. Her brain was racing.

'Look, what's the matter with you? You mind getting out of my way?'

'How did you get here?'

The question, so sharp after so long a silence, caught the man on the hop. 'By taxi. . .'

'It's still waiting?'

'It'd sure better be.'

'Right.' Anna stretched out her arm and grasped the door lintel, barring his way to the hall. 'Sit down, comrade. Your cab driver can just wait a little longer, that's all.'

'Look, what is this? I've done my job. All I want to do is get out of here.'

He moved to push her aside, but Anna was quicker. She transferred her hand from the door jamb to the man's sleeve, and to his surprise he found that this attractive little kitten had a grip like a steel vice.

'I mean it, comrade.'

Her voice had changed, too. Before it had been timid with fear, the fear which the initials KGB usually provoke in all Soviet citizens. Now it was hard and low, the voice of a woman who knows what she wants and sees her way to getting it.

'Sit down. Pour us another drink. Two minutes, that's all I ask.' She pointed at the three innocent-looking cases. 'I have to deliver those. Handling them is probably the single most important thing either of us will ever do. To carry out my duties, I need transport. I'm out of petrol and have no means of getting any. So you're taking me for a ride. . .comrade.'

She held his eyes with her own, and saw doubt written there. Someone had told this man to be very careful. Someone had chosen him for his quick-wittedness, his resource, his trust-worthiness. With sudden instinctive certainty she knew that he had been instructed to offer whatever help she needed, and she hesitated no longer.

Anna pushed past her visitor and made for the bedroom. Moments later she emerged muffled in a thick padded jacket and wearing snow boots, thick mittens on her hands. She pushed past the man, now busily taking anxious gulps from his tea cup, and opened the tiny fridge. There was not much on the shelves but she took what there was, adding to the pile some dried goods from her store cupboard. A hollow space over the cupboard yielded a knapsack containing a scarf and thick over-gloves. Anna stuffed the provisions into the knapsack and looked around her. Time was running out. She could wait no longer. Seconds could make that vital difference. . .

No. There was one thing. Under her bed she had been keeping a bottle of good Stolichnaya vodka for years. A special occasion, that's what she was saving it up for. A special occasion. Well, here she was leaving her home for the last time, with a prison cell or worse as her next likely resting place. If that was not a special occasion. . .

When she emerged from the bedroom for the second time the anonymous stranger was standing by the front door looking at his watch. 'You're ready? I thought you'd never finish.'

Anna nodded brusquely and slammed the door behind them without looking back.

As they came to the front entrance Anna took a quick look out in to the street before joining the man at the door of the taxi. The driver was arguing. When Anna dumped her three precious cases on the back seat he swore at her, ordering them both away from the cab. Anna gathered that the argument concerned money. She scrabbled in her purse, found a twenty-five rouble note and was about to hand it to the driver and cut the thing short when suddenly her companion drew his hand out of his pocket and, with his lips drawn back in a malicious snarl, showed the driver a red-covered pass. For a second three pairs of eyes focused on the State seal and the unique signature beside it, then suddenly the air was full of sweetness and light, there was help with the cases, the money was more than enough, and where to. . .?

The man looked at Anna, who thought quickly. It was important not to leave a trace. She named a village further along the road on which she had dropped Binderhaven and his men earlier that day. She could always stop the cab before then, or she could go to the village and walk back. . . But she could not think straight, because although she had occasionally seen red-covered passes before, in the course of her work, she had never seen one bearing the seal of the Soviet Union authenticated by that mythical name, and she knew that the men who carried them could be numbered in hundreds rather than thousands. . .

As the cab pulled out from the kerb, an army lorry rolled by and made a U-turn, slipping into the space occupied until a moment ago by the taxi. Anna looked out of the rear window to see men drop down from the back and pause to straighten their uniforms before walking purposefully towards the apartment block she had just left. Her eyes closed in relief; but when she opened them again it was to find the stranger's stare full on her. Very deliberately he turned to look out of the window, as she herself had done, and treated the diminishing lorry to a long, expressionless look. Even at that distance it was possible to make out the grey uniforms of the state security troops.

The man turned back to her. Anna was hypnotised. She knew, she just knew that any minute now he was going to order the driver to stop, go back, say to her, 'I think you have some explaining to do. . .'

He opened his mouth. For a sudden chilling instant Anna knew with perfect clarity that if she had a gun, she would kill him.

'Fucking bandits,' said the man conversationally.

21

For Binderhaven and McDonnell the cold had become everything. It penetrated, broke in everywhere, through the tiny eye slits in their white masks, the all but invisible gaps between arm and elasticated sleeve, between the hood of the parka and the hairline. So scalpel-thin and sharp was the blade of cold that it could slit their flesh through white padded outer-garments, through woollen underwear and silk cling-suit, right down through the last layer of dry cotton which protected the skin from chafing. Neither man had ever experienced anything remotely like it for intensity, and the deadening of the soul.

It had been a long, endless day. Once they heard the rotors of a small helicopter, high above them, and wondered anxiously if the pilot had seen their tracks, but there was nothing they could do. The rotors clattered away into silence, which thereafter remained unbroken. On the tundra, nothing moved. It was a dead land.

Now it was evening, and already the light was fading, all too fast.

'My God, look!'

McDonnell swung round in the direction of Binderhaven's pointing arm and saw where on the far horizon a thick grey bar seemed to rise out of the snow, its upper edge rippling with swirls and eddies and gusts. 'Snow,' he breathed. 'The one thing we needed.'

Binderhaven nodded. 'No wonder that chopper didn't hang around. Weather must have warned him of snow coming and told him to high-tail it back to base. You'd better get up to where the tracks leave the road and take a bearing. Make sure you've got one bearing, all the way to the hut. I'll wait here. Someone's got to wait for Anna.'

As McDonnell began to trudge up the road Binderhaven raised his glasses to his eyes and tried to gauge the blizzard's rate of progress. It was like watching a tidal wave roll its relentless way forward. The grey bar had already become a grey wall. Isolated snowflakes flurried around him in the half-light, and as he watched them Binderhaven marvelled that the tons of snow which would shortly bury all their traces could deliver themselves to earth so lightly. He held out a gloved hand and caught a few flakes, watching them gather silently in his palm. Yet add them all together and that ethereal lightness became a massive killer, a grave, a hundred thousand tons of ice multiplied over and over again. . . 'We will bury you,' the few drops of snow on his glove seemed to say. 'Give us time. Wait. You may clear us away as much as you wish, as you can, but we are patient. In the end, when finally you grow tired, we shall bury you. . .'

Far away, in the opposite direction to the one taken by McDonnell, he heard a cry. He looked up quickly to see a black figure, no bigger than an ant, struggling against the backdrop of the oncoming grey wall, which was by now so close that it threatened to overwhelm the tiny black ant before she could reach him. Binderhaven knew without having to be told that the figure was female. Something about the sight churned his stomach. The blizzard wall towered over her minute form, a huge confused mass of currents and visible streams blown relentlessly onwards by the rising gale, while she staggered on through the snow to greet him. As he ran towards her he saw that she was weighed down with luggage and as he made out the three briefcases for an instant his heart soared.

They met just as the blizzard struck. She dropped everything and hurled herself into the protection of Binderhaven's outstretched arms. For a second he held her, surprised, not knowing what to: then he looked down into her eyes and everything suddenly became marvellously simple, after all. While the snow whipped past them in a horizontal howl he tore away his silk mask and kissed her, enjoying first the feel of her cold lips on his, then the moment of resistance followed by sudden surrender and the warmth of her mouth on his tongue. . .

He was the first to pull away. The snow was already starting to pile up over their boots, the cases reduced to white-coated lumps on the ground. They swept up the baggage between them and linked arms before lowering their heads and setting off on the long trek to join McDonnell.

Darkness and snow came together. Within minutes Binderhaven knew that they were lost.

He couldn't understand it. The road was bounded from the tundra by two ridges of snow. All they had to do, or so he reasoned, was find one ridge and follow it in the direction McDonnell had gone earlier.

But there was no ridge.

Binderhaven did not let Anna see how disturbed he was. He counted while they struggled onwards against the blinding snowstorm which by now had totally engulfed them. Fifty paces. They halted.

'McDonnell!'

The wind drove Binderhaven's shout back against him. Anna tugged his sleeve and said something. He bent down. 'What?' he shouted. 'I said. . .I can't hear you. It's this wind. . .'

'I said. . .where are we going?'

'To find McDonnell. Then on to base camp. Don't try. . .to talk. . . Too. . .tiring.'

They struggled on in the direction Binderhaven guessed they wanted to go. Fifty paces.

'McDonnell!'

For the next half hour they repeated the operation over and over again, never deviating from the line on which they had started. All around them the white wall, a maelstrom of circling snowflakes, hemmed them in, destroying perspective and sense of direction. Binderhaven knew they were navigating on blind faith. Beside him Anna seemed to shrink smaller and smaller under the weight of their combined burden. With mounting desperation Binderhaven knew that she was not as well protected against the cold as he was, that slowly he was losing her.

Fifty paces more. Then they must stop, scoop a shelter, huddle together, and wait to see who would be first to die: the blizzard, or them.

'Forty-eight, forty-nine, fifty. Halt. *McDonnell!*'

The first answering cry seemed only a pale echo of his own shout. Binderhaven shook his head to clear it, and tried again.

'McDonnell!'

'Over. . .here.'

Anna was falling. He caught her up roughly, together with the cases, and began to drag her in the direction of the other man's cry.

'Here. . .here. . .here. . .here. . .'

McDonnell kept up a regular, rhythmical shout, like a directional beacon. Sometimes the gale defeated him, so that he seemed now nearer, now further away, and several times Binderhaven had to pause until he was sure of the line to follow. Then suddenly the white wall broke, and three people stood at the centre of the maelstrom where seconds before there had been only two.

McDonnell held out both hands to touch them, just for a second, and Binderhaven knew how he felt.

'The bearing,' he shouted. 'You've got the bearing?'

McDonnell nodded the whole upper half of his body three times, in a kind of jerky bow, to indicate easily visible assent.

'Then let's move it!'

For a full minute McDonnell stood stock-still with the compass cupped in his hands, his gaze shifting slowly between the luminous dial and the snow wall. Then he raised his arm to give the line. Binderhaven placed himself at the extremities of McDonnell's fingertips, facing outwards, and waited while the other man guided him gently on to the precise bearing. At last all was ready. McDonnell tapped him on the shoulder, and Binderhaven began to walk.

For a while the going was easier. There were now three of them to share the load which Anna had brought with her, and the psychological fillip of finding McDonnell lent them all new strength. But every fifty paces they had to stop, and recheck the bearing, and with every halt Anna wilted a little more. Not once did a single word of complaint escape her lips, but all the same Binderhaven knew she was failing. He concentrated on preserving her; for the moment, that was enough. When they reached camp he knew there would be other problems: there was no room on their mission for an untrained woman. Somehow she would have to be returned to civilisation. That could wait. For the moment, all that mattered was survival.

The first flurries of snow had brought a warmer flow of air but now the temperature was steadily falling again and the cold was greater for the contrast. Only iron will power prevented Binderhaven from shivering. He knew that once he began he would be unable to stop. Every so often Anna's body, linked to his at the elbow, would suffer an almighty shudder which transmitted itself through Binderhaven's own frame. Somehow she managed to struggle on, her eyes tightly closed against the blinding, driving snow. She could not feel her feet, or her hands.

Fifty paces. Compass. The outstretched arm. Fifty feet. Compass. . .

Binderhaven had lost count of the number of times they had taken the bearing. He had no idea of how far they had gone since leaving the road. Surely they must be almost at the edge of the forest? Because how much longer could they go on?

Fifty paces. Compass. The outstretched arm. . .only now McDonnell was gesturing with his hand alone, unable to muster the strength to raise the whole limb.

Anna could no longer feel anything very much. Sometimes when Binderhaven's body lurched against her own she crossed fully into the world of consciousness, only to return the next second into the darkness which numbed her brain. Her feet seemed like two heavy weights which she was condemned to drag after her through the stiff resistance of the snow. Every time they stopped the snow deepened. She was not wearing snowshoes, so that Binderhaven had to work harder all the time to help her through the drifts. Soon she would not be able to lift her legs at all.

Fifty paces. Compass. McDonnell's hand feebly pointing.

The cold seemed to reach Anna's heart. All of her body was frozen, she was blind and deaf, she could no longer move. All she wanted to do was rest, and as the word crossed her mind it seemed to expand to fill it to the total exclusion of everything else: to rest, to go to sleep, to lie, to lie, to lie. . .

Her knees buckled. Anna Petrina knelt down in the snow; for a second she was conscious of a man's voice screaming inside her head; something hard flung itself against her. . .and then there was nothing.

The lift doors glided open and Povin stepped out into the oppressive heat of the richly carpeted corridor.

His surroundings were comfortable, more than comfortable. During the week he occupied a stylish new apartment on the first floor of a high-rise block in Kutuzovsky Prospekt. It was a plush address. Andropov himself lived just down the road at Number 26, although his quarters were not quite as up to date as Povin's. There were more practical advantages, too. It was handy for work, and his status entitled him to a generous cut from the *kremlevsky payok*, the Kremlin ration of food and other goods denied to the masses, so that he could actually send out for a meal from the Kremlin kitchens and have it delivered while still hot. The 'closed' store at Number 2 Granovsky Street was but a short car-ride away, and there at least he could be sure of a regular supply of whisky. On the material side he had absolutely nothing to complain about.

But still it wasn't home.

For Povin 'home' was a comfortable country *dacha* in Zhukovka which he had 'owned' for many years. He used to have an apartment in a block on the very site of his present town flat, but four years ago they had torn it down to make room for something more modern. That was the official version. In fact this demolition coincided with the closing of the Kyril case and Povin always thought privately that they wanted a look inside his former pied-à-terre: the kind of look which involves stripping the plaster from the walls and ripping up floorboards. Marshal Stanov, the last Chairman of the KGB, had a big flat in the same building, and no doubt it was advantageous to take a good look round that as well. Those had been troubled times. Povin thought they had gone for ever. Now they were back.

As his eyes strayed round the comfortable room he wondered, not for the first time, what Stanov would have made of the new regime in Dzerzhinsky Square. The old man might have ended his career on a note of glory by nailing the traitor, General Michaelov, but he was edged out all the same. Not that Stanov ever admitted it. He had many excuses for leaving. He was getting old, he was sick, they were tearing down his apartment and making him live in Sivtsev Vrazhek, his staff were becoming so incompetent that it was impossible to carry on. . . Then his dog died and Stanov, a widower, now finally without an ally in the world, gave in. Part of Povin still missed him.

He missed his old flat, too. The new seven-room apartment on the first floor was adequate, even luxurious, viewed simply as living space. There was a grand piano on which Stolyinovich could play to him in the evenings. The pianist had a Moscow residence permit now, and lived in an imposing mansion in Aleksei Tolstoy Street, not far from Podgorny's old house. It was a poor week when Povin did not see his friend at least twice. . .

Povin closed the outer door of his apartment and double-locked it on the inside. For a moment he stood in the hallway, undecided what to do; then he very gently lowered the brief-case to the floor and released his grip.

The apartment was empty and silent. The General listened with his head on one side. Nothing moved. No one spoke. Solitude retained its melancholy sway, and Povin at least was grateful.

He took off his coat and hung it up carefully in the cupboard before carrying the briefcase through to the living room. He placed it upright on the desk, and backed slowly away, keeping his eyes upon it.

No sound marred the unruffled surface of the surrounding silence. He really was alone, as alone as it is possible for any citizen of the Soviet Union ever to be.

Povin turned to the drinks trolley and poured whisky. He held the cut-glass tumbler up to the light and watched the amber fluid shimmer gently against the crystal. The relentless, tiny movement depressed him. There must have been a time when his hand was steady, but that was long ago.

A leaden weight seemed to hang suspended from his heart: during the day, a constant dead presence; at night, as he lay on his back, a dreary never-ending awareness of the terror that was just around the corner but could not be named. Normally he could cope. Today was different.

Povin put down his glass and went over to the hi-fi. He chose Chopin, a nocturne played by Stolyinovich. An involuntary spasm ran down the side of Povin's face to waste itself in the knotted muscles of his neck, and he grimaced. Lack of control. It was beginning to manifest itself too often, in too many diverse ways. Especially today.

He swallowed some more whisky. The spirit left an un-pleasant taste in his mouth as a reminder that drink, his last consolation after God, was deserting him. And Povin was no longer sure about God. Tonight he proposed to put his trust in a man.

Frolov knew.

In the world of the spy, certainty, knowledge can never be more than relative concepts. A wise man does not trust his own reflection in the shaving mirror. Povin acknowledged this, but it didn't detract from the certainty that Frolov knew his chief's mother had once been an Orthodox Christian, perhaps even knew that Povin himself was a believer.

Their daily meeting had begun as usual. His deputy seemed distracted but that was nothing new. Then Povin became aware that Frolov was staring at him without making any attempt to conceal the look of hostility on his face.

Tanya.

The name, which happened also to be his mother's, had dropped easily into the conversation, where it belonged. Povin was about to move on when Frolov slowly repeated the name, lingering over each separate syllable and keeping his eyes fixed on Povin's face. He repeated it again. And without pause or transition Povin went from ignorance to knowing, from anxiety to terror.

Frolov knew.

Several times more he had gone out of his way to introduce the name into the discussion, only now the name didn't belong anywhere. It had become a probe, a long, perilous needle of shining steel which Frolov slipped under Povin's guard at will, prodding and poking his chief further and further back against the walls of his own deceit. . .

Povin poured more whisky, seized with an avid desire to sluice away the memory. From now on all that mattered was the timing. Given another two days, one more day, he would be safe. But. . .did he have another day? Another hour?

He looked at his watch. Pyotr was late. How like him. A smile wrinkled the General's dry lips, unbidden. Once, only once, had he been on time. . .their second meeting, when all things still were new. Povin arrived early and from some professional instinct hid himself in such a way that he could watch the rendezvous unobserved. Pyotr Stolyinovich came quickly, one minute before the appointed time, sniffing the air, looking about him like a dog who seeks his master, and Povin's heart leapt for an inexplicable second of what he later recognised with hindsight to have been joy. But still he did not move. Some inner reserve, some devil, kept him from walking forward to greet his new friend. Instead he continued to watch, fascinated. Before many moments passed the pianist's vivacious enthusiasm had visibly waned. His body, hitherto alert, became slack and still. His eyes wandered between the faces of the passing throng with a look of assessment, as though he had already half written off his new-found friend and was searching for a new distraction. Eventually his gaze fell upon a brightly-lit shop window. The centre of the display, its focal point, was a pair of calf-length soft leather boots. As Povin watched the pianist's whole frame seemed to quiver into stillness, all the palpable nervous energy of a few minutes ago now channelled in upon itself. When at last he could bear it no longer Povin emerged from his hiding place behind a column of the arcade, and walked silently to stand a few paces from Stolyinovich, who remained oblivious to his presence, all his attention centred on those beautiful products of western craftsmanship. Then, as if suddenly overwhelmed by knowledge of the closeness of another human being, he swung round to face the General, and for a long, long moment Povin saw reflected in his eyes not himself. . .but the boots.

In that long moment, something happened to Povin. He knew that he had not, after all, been designed as a lover of men. And with that knowledge came a tiny seed of ineradicable regret.

'Come,' he said, linking arms with Stolyinovich. 'Let's go and buy them.'

The smile faded from Povin's face. Only that once did Stolyinovich come on time. Never again. Since that day Povin had kept his heart carefully sealed up, offering merely affection to one who craved not love but lovers, and lacked even the penny-price of loyalty. The General poured himself more whisky and stared vacantly into space, wondering how much longer he would have to wait this evening.

Frolov knew. No good thinking about that. He looked at his

watch, took it off his wrist, held it up and shook it violently. Frolov. . .no. He was about to give his watch another shake when the door bell rang.

He leapt to his feet, heart pounding like a fish in its death throes, and went quickly to stand by the door, head on one side, listening.

'Who is it?'

'Pyotr.'

Povin flung open the door and hustled the pianist inside, darting quick glances up and down the corridor to make sure he had not been followed. For a moment the two men looked at each other; then they embraced.

' ". . .For truly to see your face is like seeing the face of God. . ." ' Povin could hardly force the words out. Stolyinovich stood back and held him at arm's length for long enough to take the measure of the anguish on the General's face; his eyes and hands fell together and he moved on into the living room, without speaking.

Povin gave him whisky and sat down heavily. Stolyinovich shaded his eyes with his hand and did not look up at his host. While a doom-laden silence seemed to harden its grip on the two of them Povin rolled the tumbler between his hands and sought vainly for the words which would encapsulate all that he had endured over the past few days.

'I'll put another record on.'

He chose a recording of his friend playing the Tchaikovsky No. 1 Piano Concerto and turned up the volume. Stolyinovich at once recognised the simple anti-bugging device and his face grew longer. Povin pulled his chair close up beside him and quietly began to talk.

'It's all right, Pyotr. Things are still all right. Just. We have to make plans. It's time for us to go.'

Stolyinovich opened his mouth to speak, but Povin held up his hand.

'Let me talk. I've got a lot to say, and it simply wasn't possible in the restaurant last night, not in front of all the others. The first thing you'd better know is that while I was away my deputy, Frolov, has been looking into you. Certain of your. . .activities. In private life. I can't prove it, but I'm sure it's happened.'

217

Stolyinovich could no longer contain himself. 'But you promised. . .'

'I didn't have to promise. You know very well that your status puts you above the KGB and the regular police as far as. . .as far as those things are concerned. No, it's something else. They're starting to get on to me. Frolov. . .' Povin bit his lip. 'It doesn't matter. But we've got to leave, Pyotr. Soon. Now listen. . .'

For the best part of an hour Povin spoke. He knew his man, knew that if he was to command his undivided obedience over the next few days he had no choice but to entrust him with the truth. He told of Geneva, the theft of the plane and its terrible significance, the deal he had struck with Binderhaven, the terse confirmation received from London that very day — 'Sale agreed'. When at last he finished the pianist's face was haggard with strain.

'All these things. . .' he whispered. 'They're terrible, terrible. My God, my God. . .'

'Yes. This is the biggest thing we've ever had to face, you and I.' Povin struggled to inject into his voice every ounce of calm he could summon up. 'The strategic importance of that wretched aircraft transcends all belief. At this moment we stand between peace and war, Pyotr. But I can't. . .' His voice broke. 'I *can't* face it without you. You'll need all your courage. Are you with me, Pyotr. . .?'

He could not keep the beseeching tone from his voice, and while he waited for the reply the anguish of a whole unhappy lifetime seemed to hover between them like a black angel, sword upraised.

The record had changed; Tchaikovsky had given way to *Tosca*. Stolyinovich raised his eyes to Povin's face and stared at him for a long time. Both men simultaneously became aware of the climax of *E lucevan le stelle*; in the moment of silence before that glorious burst of hope, *Ah! Franchigia. . .*, Stolyinovich bowed his head, as if pronouncing his own safe-conduct from the beloved country of his birth.

'Yes.'

Povin closed his eyes. For several minutes he could not speak. At last he recovered enough to sit up; when he spoke his voice had recovered some of its old timbre.

'Good. Then I can plan with a clear conscience. You're leaving for Athens. . .when? Two days' time?'

'Yes.'

'Perfect. By then everything will be finished here one way or the other. Since I've just come back from Switzerland and have no plans to go abroad again, there shouldn't be any problem over your exit visa. Leave that to me.'

'I'm supposed to collect it tomorrow.'

'Once I know you've got it I can open up a route for myself. Not difficult, that. No one'll be surprised if I decide to pay a weekend visit to Stanov, for old times' sake. Only I'll stop off in Tbilisi and two hours later I'm in Turkey. All we need do is fix the co-ordination. Once you know I'm safe you can run for the nearest American Embassy, and the thing's done.'

'You make it sound so simple. Like a day trip to the country.'

'Don't talk like that, don't even think it. Nothing is simple.'

Behind them the opera reached its climax and the hi-fi set automatically switched itself off. While Povin changed the records Stolyinovich made as if to rise.

'I must go.'

At the door Povin embraced his friend. 'Careful as you go out,' he said. 'Better not wake up the *dezhurnaya*. She spends so much time spying on me that she has to catch up on her sleep in the evenings.'

The two men stared at each other, half-smiles upon their lips. Povin's face cracked; he could feel the fortress of his face begin to crumble. The two men embraced once more before sharing a whispered blessing, and a farewell.

23

Povin was right about Frolov: the Colonel had no intention of ignoring his chief's devoted Christian background. But Frolov was a methodical if somewhat pedantic worker. 'One thing at a time' was his motto. For the moment his whole attention was taken up with something else.

It took him most of the morning to establish that he wasn't going to get hold of Kazin's address.

At first he couldn't understand the difficulty. He wanted to interview Oleg Kazin. As a senior officer in the KGB, Deputy Head of a Main Directorate, that was, or should have been, his right. Therefore he required Kazin's address, and Senior Lieutenant Valyalin was dispatched to Central Registry to find it. He returned half an hour later, empty-handed. Frolov shrugged. To him this omission was no more significant than the discovery that a telephone subscriber was ex-directory would have been to his opposite number in America or Britain. The information would be in the Confidential Registry but Frolov didn't intend to tempt fate by going back there again in a hurry. No, there were other ways.

He telephoned a couple of cronies in the Kremlin, without result, and as a last resort a contact in the Kommandant. The latter was brusque: Oleg Kazin was, and would remain, strictly off limits to ordinary members of the KGB. Frolov, on the point of retorting that he was hardly an 'ordinary' member, recalled who he was talking to and rang off just in time.

The First Main Directorate's encyclopedia of offbeat information did not help, and counter-intelligence over in Second did not know, or claimed not to know, which came to the same thing.

Frolov was puzzled. He had never come across anything quite like this before. After ten minutes of sitting and staring vacantly into space his eye lighted on the drinks cupboard. Reluctantly he shook his head. Vodka didn't give you ideas, it stole them. There had to be another route to Kazin.

The vodka. . .

When the idea first struck him Frolov was inclined to write it off as a waste of time, something out of one of the cheap detective novels published by the gross every year under the imprint of the Writers' Union. But it was worth a few phone calls, surely. . .?

He spoke first to his deputy in Tbilisi, republican capital of Georgia, who produced the names of the two principal suppliers of Georgian wines to Moscow. Then a couple more calls to the respective heads of the *pervy otdel*, the 'First Department' of each shipper, and he had a list of all those 'closed' shops in Moscow which had received a supply of a certain commodity in the past twelve months.

At this point Frolov took his feet off the desk and got down to some serious work. There were only six outlets to choose from. Three he wrote off at once, on the ground that their class of clientele was way beneath the one he was interested in. Of the other three, only one had received a regular monthly supply from Tbilisi in the past year. Frolov jotted down the name and address on a piece of paper. Thirty-eight Ulitsa Pushkinskaya, not far from the Bolshoi. He hesitated. The shop was known to him as being patronised by families of Politburo members. For a mere Colonel like himself getting past the door would be more than a formality.

Frolov picked up the internal phone and dialled the underground car park.

'Is Milovidov there. . .well get him. Now, not the middle of next week.'

While he waited he drummed his fingers on the desk, trying to calculate the risks involved in what he was doing. His eye chanced to light on the doll above the fireplace and his expression hardened. He had come too far, too close, to worry about odds.

'Hello. . . Milovidov. Frolov here. Listen, I want the

221

hearse. . . Now. . . I don't know, not more than an hour I should think. . . Well just *do* it for once. . . You think I don't know that? You think I value my own job so little. . .'

The man at the other end of the line was reluctant. It took Frolov five minutes of hard talking to make him see reason.

Frolov replaced the receiver and wiped his palms on his handkerchief. He was sweating profusely, although the office was not particularly warm that day. His eyes strayed longingly to the drinks cupboard but with an effort he checked himself. There would be time for that later. First he had to swallow his pride and do something which, in all the circumstances, he resented very much.

He walked along the passage until he found himself outside Povin's room and knocked.

'Come in.'

Povin did not look up as Frolov entered. He was writing at his desk, all his attention focused on the papers before him.

'I wonder if I might slip out for half an hour, Stepan,' said Frolov apologetically.

Povin said nothing, but continued to write.

'It's Ilinichna. . .she asked me to collect some money from the bank. Normally she'd do it, but with one of the children ill, and her mother coming to stay, and you know how it is in the lunch hour, Stepan, with all the stores crowded to bursting-point. . .'

Nervousness, or rather a combination of nerves and white-hot anger that he should be compelled to stand here like some clerk, begging for time off, made his throat dry. But that was Povin all over. That represented everything Frolov most loathed about his boss. In any other Directorate he would simply have taken off, without a word, leaving the Chief to whistle for his deputy. But in First you could not do that. You had to stand stiffly in front of General Stepan Ilyich Povin, like a delinquent hooligan before the militiaman, begging. . .

'I sometimes think. . .'

Povin broke off for long enough to correct a word in the document before him, and resumed.

'I sometimes think that there ought to be a rule in this organisation. . .'

He looked up, face expressionless.

'No married men.'

For a few seconds he treated Frolov to a stony glare, then his face broke into a boyish grin.

'What the hell are you waiting for, Boris? Get the fuck out of here.' And he laughed, a hearty, good-natured sound, to anyone but Frolov.

'. . .and give Ilinichna a big kiss from me, next time you see her.'

But Frolov had already closed the door and was making for the lift, his face red with suppressed rage and resentment, first, that Povin should tease him like a school child, and secondly that he should make light of his wife, that he should dare. . .

By the time he arrived in the basement he had mastered himself again. It was necessary, above all, to remain calm for what was to happen next. Frolov was about to put his head in a noose.

In Russia, almost every car numberplate means something. The prefix MOC indicates that the vehicle belongs to or is used by a member of the Party Central Committee. To usurp a numberplate to which one is not entitled can be a very serious offence, depending on the rank of the person thus usurped. Frolov was about to drive away in a car with the numberplate MOC 255 A. He was not entitled to it, and if he was caught it would mean the end of his career. Or maybe worse, Frolov could never be sure about these things.

It was not the first time he had done this, although on each occasion he promised himself never under any circumstances to do it again. Officers of the KGB sometimes found it not merely useful but indispensable to pretend to a higher ranking than they in fact possessed. One of the props available for this charade was a black Volga with a Central Committee number-plate, which could be changed within seconds in case prying eyes came along. Because of the risks attached to its use it had collected the ill-starred nickname of 'the hearse'. Normally it was kept blocked into a far corner of the underground car park, out of sight, but when Frolov arrived it was standing in the middle of one of the lanes, its engine already running and the driver's door open. Frolov looked around. The area was deserted. No one wanted to be a potential witness when the hearse was taken out.

Frolov took a final look round, got into the Volga, slammed the door and roared up the ramp into the street.

Fortunately he had not got very far to go. He went north up Dzerzhinsky Street, turned left into Varsonofjevskiya and headed for Petrovka Street. At the junction between Petrovka and Petrovskiya Ulitsa a militiaman raised his arm to stop him, saw the numberplate and, with abrupt change of heart, waved him through. Frolov grinned. Driving the hearse had something of the exhilaration which he associated with piloting a bobsleigh. So long as you kept moving, and in the right direction, you were OK; let yourself think for one second about what you were actually doing and you ended up on a slab.

Moments later Frolov pulled into the kerb just short of 38 Ulitsa Pushkinskaya and switched off the engine. He was in a no-parking zone but that was the least of his worries: no militiaman was going to risk his neck by peering too closely through the tinted glass of a Central Committee car. Frolov hitched his greatcoat a little more securely over his shoulders and drew a deep breath. He had come to the point of no return.

He extracted the keys from the ignition and got out of the car.

The front door presented fewer problems than he had anticipated. The guard was an MVD man, with no particular love for KGB rivals, but Frolov's rank coupled with his red-covered pass proved enough to secure entry once the guard had established that the Colonel was going inside in order not to shop, but to see the manager.

Stepping inside was like entering another world. Frolov was familiar with high-grade shopping facilities by virtue of his own position, but not on such a grand scale as this. For a moment he looked around him with ill-concealed astonishment. From floor to ceiling the walls were taken up with wine racks: row upon row of green and yellow and red bottles, winking in the dim light. Behind the long counter at the far end were the spirits. Frolov approached across the thick pile carpet, his eyes bulging. There must have been at least fifty different brands of vodka standing upright on the shelves. To the right was a cabinet full of cigars and western cigarettes. It was like entering Aladdin's cave.

'Yes?'

The young girl behind the counter gazed at Frolov with indifference. She could tell he did not belong. A woman wearing a long sable coat turned away from the cigar cabinet and subjected him to a long, casual stare.

'I'll take these,' she said before Frolov could open his mouth. With a stab of irritation he realised that to the women his blue shoulder boards and collar tabs meant nothing. He waited until the fur-clad customer had paid for her purchases before approaching the counter.

'I want to see the manager.'

'Wait here. I'll see if he's available.'

Frolov smothered the sudden blaze of anger and looked down so as to conceal his feelings. The top of the counter was a sheet of thick glass, beneath which miniature bottles were laid out in rows: French cognac, liqueurs, Scotch whisky. . .

'What do you want, please?'

Frolov looked up to see a middle-aged man standing at the top of a little flight of stairs which led off the shop floor to an office at the back of the premises. Without taking his eyes from the man's face Frolov walked slowly to the foot of the stairs and climbed them. He noted with satisfaction that the manager lacked the women's assurance; his glance flickered repeatedly to the officer's insignia, and as Frolov approached he licked his lips, quite unnecessarily, for they were already moist. Frolov recognised a man with something to lose, and experienced a moment of sympathy with him.

'Lev Rudolfovich Sheskin?'

The man nodded.

'I wish to ask you some questions. Shall we go into the office?'

Before the man could protest Frolov pushed past him into the narrow room and appropriated the chair behind the desk where Sheskin usually sat. He was aware of the shop girl's eyes upon him, and he looked up coldly. This time the girl was first to look away.

Frolov waited until the door was shut, then he said, 'Certain interesting questions have arisen on your accounts, comrade Sheskin. Smoke?'

After a moment's hesitation Sheskin came forward and accepted a cigarette. He felt awkward. There was nowhere for him to sit in his own office.

'Not your fault, we think.' Frolov kept the tone light, conversational almost. 'No one's anxious to make a stink. A small rearrangement of staff, that's all. But someone has a racket.'

Throughout the foregoing Frolov kept his eyes firmly on Sheskin's face. His reaction was precisely what Frolov anticipated. Of course there was a racket going on, how could there not be in a shop of this kind. The man was working out his best approach. A bribe, maybe. Full co-operation. . .yes, that was it — Frolov saw it dawn in the man's eyes — give the Colonel all the help he wanted. . .

'I'm. . .astounded, comrade Colonel. Colonel. . .?'

'The problem is that we need to see a list of your Georgian suppliers. It's wine, I can tell you that. Not spirits. If it was spirits I wouldn't be here. Not my line at all. No, as usual, it's the good stuff they're after. Kinzmarauli. . .'

The man's face went dead. Frolov could hardly credit the change which came over him.

'We sell very little. A bottle here and there. It's very scarce. Good Georgian red wine, it's. . .well, it's not easy to get. And there's very little call. . .'

'Ah, yes, the call. . .that I grant you. Not since the passing of Iosif Vissarionovich, eh?'

At the mention of Stalin's forenames the manager's face twitched, but he said nothing.

'Very few customers, I dare say,' Frolov went on. 'But some. You would agree, some?'

The man shook his head.

'But you have deliveries once a month, comrade Sheskin. Where does it all go, eh?'

Sheskin said nothing. By now the colour had drained from his face, leaving it a peculiar shade of grey. Frolov studied him with interest.

226

'Tell me,' he said softly, 'tell me, Lev Rudolfovich. . .which of the Beloved Father's many friends continue to drink his favourite wine?'

Sheskin was trembling. He had a habit of blinking very slowly, like a tired animal.

'You make regular deliveries. Don't bother to deny it, comrade. We know. What I want is very simple. I want your delivery sheets.'

'No!'

Frolov allowed himself to appear surprised at the sudden outburst. 'Why, comrade. . .you're shaking. Sit down, why don't you.' Frolov rested his legs on the desk while Sheskin's eyes fluttered round the room in search of a non-existent chair.

'I cannot give you my lists. They are. . .confidential.'

'And that is your last word?'

'Yes.'

Frolov sighed and swept his legs off the desk. 'You struck me as a sensible man when I came in, Lev Rudolfovich. Get your coat. You'd better tell them in the shop you won't be coming back for quite a while.'

Frolov paused to see what effect his words had on the shop manager. His tongue flickered over his lips a couple of times, his eyes went everywhere except to Frolov's face, but he stood firm. The Colonel waited while he took his coat and hat from a tree in the corner of the room, then followed him out into the main shopping area. As Sheskin stopped to give a few nervous orders Frolov casually inspected the cigars in their cabinet with the air of a calm Party servant who merely does his duty.

Inside his shirt, however, the sweat was trickling down his back. Everything depended on the next few seconds. Frolov had bluffed many people in the course of his career, but never with so much at stake. Inwardly he trembled as much as Sheskin.

Now the two men were at the door, passing into the street. Frolov laid his hand unobstrusively on Sheskin's arm and wheeled him in the direction of the black Volga.

Something about 'the hearse' sounded a warning to passers-by. It stood parked half on and half off the pavement, the only stationary car in the busy street, but no militiaman came to take notes, no one stopped to stare. Indeed, as people walked past they tended to turn their heads and study the shop windows, anxious not to be caught out over something that was none of their business. The Volga stood alone, as if surrounded by an invisible *cordon sanitaire*. Frolov felt Sheskin stiffen beside him, but he was taking no chances. They were about twenty paces from the car. Frolov jogged his companion's arm and pointed discreetly at the numberplate with another loud sigh.

'You see, comrade, what you are getting yourself into here?'

They reached the car, and Frolov opened the rear door with a gesture to show Sheskin where he was to sit. But Sheskin stood rooted to the spot, his hands in his pockets and his head shaking from side to side.

'No. I. . . I. . .'

Another loud sigh from Frolov. 'Get in,' he snapped. 'You can tell them in the Lubianka.'

At the sound of the dreaded name Sheskin's resolve finally broke. He reached out to grasp Frolov by the arm and was suddenly babbling. 'No, no listen to me. Hear me, comrade! I have a wife, two children. . .'

Frolov automatically filtered out the spiel as they walked together back to the shop. He had heard it all before: the wife, the children, the sick grandmother in the Ukraine, the mounting debts. . . All he knew was that the hearse had worked again. But for the last time, positively for the very last time. . .

The delivery sheets were kept in the safe. Sheskin brought them out with trembling hands and thrust them across the desk at Frolov as though they were poisonous snakes. Frolov shuffled rapidly through them and there, sure enough, was the name. Kazin. Next to it, an address. It was the work of an instant to memorise the number, street and district. Frolov flicked the sheet of paper back across the desk, and rose to his feet.

'You'll be hearing from us,' he said as he went out. 'Don't talk to anyone about my visit. In particular, comrade. . .' Frolov paused in the doorway and looked back. Sheskin was sitting at the desk with his head in his hands, still wearing his overcoat and hat. 'In particular, don't talk to any of the people mentioned in those sheets. Understand?'

Sheskin nodded. Frolov went down the little flight of stairs, across the shop floor and out into the street. In the doorway he paused to adjust his hat and pull on his gloves. As he did so something caught his attention down the street. Two militiamen and a Major from the Procurator's office were standing by the hearse, arguing. While Frolov hesitated in the doorway a car drove up and disgorged another Major with a plainclothes detective. Frolov hesitated no longer, but turned and began to march briskly in the opposite direction, his brain in a turmoil. What he needed more than anything in the world was a drink, plenty of drink. . .and he must think as never before. . .

Back inside the tiny office at the top of the flight of stairs a badly frightened man replaced the telephone receiver on its rest and cradled his head in his arms on the desk in front of him. Time passed. Down in the shop customers came and went. Nobody noticed when one of them climbed the little flight of stairs for a moment, for he was well known in the shop; nobody noticed when he left. No one, in fact, noticed anything in the least unusual until half an hour later the shop girl went to the office to ask permission to go to lunch, and found Sheskin still sitting in the same position, with brains and fragments of his bloody head scattered on the desk in front of him.

24

The last people into Irkutsk before the blizzard closed everything down were the two Lieutenant-Generals, Kronkin and Mironov.

'Have you met this Grigorenko?'

Mironov leaned forward to close the sliding partition of the car that had met them at the airport while he considered his chief's question.

'Hardly in my class, *mon cher*. A real career soldier, that one. He's spent more time in staff college than in barracks, I can tell you that.'

Mironov liked to call his friends *mon cher*, because the great national hero, General Kutazov, used to do it.

'How old is he?'

'Sixty-eight. He's been commander of the Transbaikal Military District for ten years now.'

'So he got the top job young.'

'If you can call it the top job. He's not going any further.' Mironov laughed, the usual catarrhal gobble which, in his present frame of mind, was more than usually irritating to Little Adolf.

'Where does he stand on. . .us?'

Mironov stuck out his lower lip. 'Hard to say. No one's ever approached him, as far as I know. Why? You think we may be in for trouble?'

Kronkin squeezed his hands together in a gesture of exasperation. 'I don't know,' he said. 'How should I know?'

The car drew up outside military headquarters in Barrikad Street and two soldiers materialised by the rear doors, their forms swaddled in greatcoats and fur hats. The snow had already begun to settle in the road as Kronkin got out, his eyes moving instinctively to the uncooperative sky above. Flying weather. He had to have good flying weather. . .

Mironov touched his arm and nodded. 'Grigorenko.' Kronkin's gaze focused on the steps leading up to the high-porticoed building in front of him where a short, grizzled old man was waiting under a huge umbrella.

'General. . .'

The old man shook hands with Little Adolf and Fat Hermann, treating each of them in turn to a long, questioning stare. 'Your message puzzled me, comrades.'

The Lieutenant-Generals remained silent.

'But I've done what you asked. This way. . .'

He led them to a briefing room on the second floor overlooking an inner courtyard. Five men were waiting. As the

Generals entered they stood up, and Grigorenko performed introductions. Kronkin was relieved to see that he had complied with the request to restrict attendance to only the most senior officers.

He took his place on the podium, resting his hands on the lectern in front of him, and looked down at their tense, expectant faces. Kronkin was sensitive to atmosphere. He felt hostility at the massive GRU presence which had so suddenly and unexpectedly descended into these ordered lives; hostility mixed with reluctant, restless curiosity. Not since the day he succeeded Peter Ivanovich Ivashutin as Head of the GRU had Kronkin faced a task as sensitive as that which now lay ahead of him.

'A difficulty has arisen,' he began quietly. The faces remained unchanged. Inside Kronkin the deep, obsessional secrecy which had protected him for so many years fought a desperate rearguard action against the need to seek help from these plodding fools; his hands gripped the lectern convulsively; then he began to speak.

'In the last few days, comrades, four foreigners have entered the Transbaikal Military District. Two of them are, and acknowledge themselves to be, Americans. The other two purport to be Canadians but we think they are from the United States as well. They entered legally, with business credentials which on their face entitled them to come to Irkutsk.'

At the back of the room Mironov finished with the large, old-fashioned projector and raised his hand. Kronkin nodded briefly and said, 'Put them up.'

On the wall behind him the four faces appeared, their features indistinct in the artificial light of the room. A Colonel stood up and went over to extinguish the lights. Kronkin couldn't tell if he was motivated by military courtesy for a senior officer or nascent interest in the subject matter. Unlikely to be the former: the GRU was well used to being universally hated.

The four faces on the wall assumed new clarity. From the darkness Kronkin spoke again.

'In connection with these men a crisis has arisen.' Kronkin dropped his voice so as to lend emphasis to his next words. 'I

231

would not like you to think I speak lightly, comrades. Crisis is the word I want.'

For the first time he felt a rustle of interest in the room below him. Now the attention was more than just polite. He went on quickly, before he lost them again.

'They have all disappeared. On the same day. Without explanation. The usual searches were at once put in hand by our. . .*colleagues*. Fruitless, of course. . .'

Now there was a murmur, half humourous, half contemptuous, at this reference to the KGB. If the Red Army did not much care for its own chief intelligence directorate, it cared even less for the civil equivalent.

'With these men, on the same day, disappeared an Intourist guide, a Captain in the KGB, a driver in the KGB's motorised transport corps, and a GT-T snow vehicle. None of them can now be found. What *has* been found is the body of a KGB officer who was supposed to be monitoring two of the Americans on the Trans-Siberian Express.'

Kronkin strained his eyes to see into the darkness of the room. With a little shudder of relief he saw that none of the officers was looking straight at him; their attention was held by the four faces projected on the wall. He felt a cold, creeping dislike radiate out towards the rostrum, but it was no longer directed exclusively at the GRU. It enveloped these foreigners, these aliens who had penetrated Soviet territory and there made away with good citizens, valuable equipment. Kronkin smiled. He had not been obliged to draw the connection. His audience had done that for themselves.

'You may ask, how does this concern us? The KGB, the MVD, it is their job to find such people, and deal with them. Spies — for they are spies, comrades, no doubt about that, we have checked those photographs thoroughly — are not our problem.' Kronkin shook his head. 'There is more to it than that, comrades.'

He paused, sensing their reactions. With every passing moment their commitment increased. He must move quickly now.

'In Moscow, where I have come from today, they have a theory. They think these men are going south, to the border with Mongolia, there to stir up some incident which will put

232

the Soviet Union in a bad light.'

Somewhere in the darkened room a chair scraped on the floor. Mongolia was a sensitive subject in Transbaikal.

'I know better. We have sources denied to others, comrades. We have to know things which for the most part are not known by most of the people. Now I am going to share some of our knowledge with you.'

Kronkin leaned forward to rest his elbows on the lectern.

'Approximately thirty-six hours from now an aircraft is coming into this military district from north-east Siberia. It is a very special aircraft, and secret, so secret that the pilot will not be told where to land until after he has taken off. When the plane arrives, some of our most senior scientists will be on hand to examine it. After they have finished, then we shall return the aircraft to its true owners.'

Kronkin stood upright and swept a strand of hair from his forehead. The silence in the room was electric.

'I think I do not have to tell you who its true owners are.'

He could almost hear their brains at work: not wanting to admit their ignorance, not caring to know too much either, for who knew who might be asking questions later on? But these Americans. . .the KGB. . .aircraft. . .true owners. . .

'The resources of the State are limited, comrades. We all know that there are people whose duty it is to look after such things. But there comes a time when it is necessary to take out insurance. To turn to the experts. And then the answer is really very simple. One turns to the Red Army. Where there is trust.'

He allowed a long pause, giving them time to absorb the message.

'Those Americans have not gone south, to China. They have gone north. They are making for the air base which we know as TDM-13. It is reasonably big and well equipped while at the same time out of the way and hard of access, even in the summer. Now it is completely isolated, which is precisely why the aircraft will land there thirty-six hours from now. Those Americans would prevent that happening if they could. So I need your help. I need to catch those men, alive if possible, but in any case, I need to catch them. Can we have the lights back on, please?'

In the few seconds which followed the shock of the neon flicker Kronkin watched their faces narrowly, before they could settle into their usual fixed masks. What he saw pleased him.

'The first requirement, the obvious one, is to double, treble the guard on TDM-13. This can be done?'

It was Grigorenko himself who supplied the answer.

'That depends.'

Kronkin's tone was icy. 'On what?'

'On that.' The old General pointed at the window. Through the darkness it was still possible to make out the perpetual thick screen of snowflakes which fell between the men in the hot, stuffy briefing room and the Siberian steppe.

'If we can fly them up there, well and good. I can put two men every ten metres along the perimeter fence for you and still have enough over to comb the tundra. But I have a question or two.'

Kronkin's heart sank. Mironov had been right about Grigorenko: a soldier of the old school, attentive to detail, a typical *polkovnik* — born to be a Colonel.

'First. What have we got to fear from these Americans? Are they armed?'

'We don't know.' Kronkin tried not to let his unwillingness show. 'They passed through the usual border checks.'

Grigorenko snorted. 'And we all know who conducts *them!*'

'They are known to be travelling light. Hand guns, perhaps.'

'So. That suggests to me that if we guard the outer perimeter of this wretched base properly, there's no need for me to waste my men's energies in the tundra.'

Kronkin studied his hands. Under the cruel neon lights they looked wrinkled and old. 'Some attempt should be made to round up these people. . .'

'This is the middle of winter, General.' Grigorenko spoke kindly, his voice that of a parent who explains to an impatient child why he can't go to the zoo today. 'Everything I have is either down south of the border, being overhauled, resting up, or on stand-by. I'll tell you what I'll do, though. When this weather lifts, I'll fly up a batallion to the base. Once they've secured the perimeter, they can scout about at will.'

'And that's all?' Kronkin was aghast, and this time it showed.

'After that we'll have to see. You know how it is. Ten helicopters to a division, that's the rule. A third of my choppers are undergoing repairs, half my planes are grounded for the same reason, and we'll want the rest to ferry men up to this base of yours. Then you can have the Ka-25s until someone else needs them.'

Kronkin shook his head. 'I need a division. On the steppe. I need one whole division, General, spread out in a fan between that base and Irkutsk. Nothing less is of the slightest interest to me.'

'For four Americans armed with pistols?' Grigorenko threw back his head and laughed. 'Allow me to tell you, General Kronkin, that your *demands* are not acceptable to me.' The laughter drained out of his eyes. 'They are also absurd. You have my offer. In all the circumstances it is generous. Of course, if you don't want to take it up. . .'

Kronkin looked at each face in turn. In some of them, particularly those of the younger staff officers, he read concern and an eagerness to help. A bit of excitement, they seemed to imply; something real to do at last. . . But no one spoke up against Grigorenko. Kronkin, furiously angry, kept his rage well hidden. It took a little time to organise the ways of dealing with people like Grigorenko.

'Thank you, General. I am sorry you think my request absurd. But I am grateful to you for your offer. I accept it with thanks.'

'Good. Then I'll start giving orders right away. Meanwhile, there's a driver waiting to take you and General Mironov to your quarters.'

'I can assure you, we're not tired. . .'

'Nonsense.' Grigorenko slapped Kronkin's slim shoulders with a smile in which no friendliness showed. 'It's a hell of a flight from Moscow. You've had a long day. I'll have you woken as soon as the snow stops.'

Somehow Kronkin had been led to the door, Mironov at his heels. The meeting was very definitely over.

Kronkin had to wait until they were in the car before he

could vent his rage and disappointment. Fat Hermann heard him out patiently, saying nothing.

'He's phoning Moscow. That's what he's doing right now,' said Kronkin bitterly.

'Not necessarily, *mon cher*. He's probably talking to that moth-eaten crew we saw earlier. They're all scratching their heads and trying to make it out. Look at it from their point of view. We have no clout to speak of. In the GRU all we can do is make requests. Polite requests. If we feel strongly enough about it, we can ask Moscow for orders. But since, on this occasion, you and I can hardly approach Moscow, we're rather stuck, you know.'

Kronkin placed his hands on his knees and stared ahead. Mironov was right. There was nothing he could do.

'But you did well, *mon cher*.' Mironov spoke with gentle reassurance. 'We had no cards, no hand at all. Unless we can get hard evidence that those Americans represent a threat, a real threat, there is no reason to fear, after all. Grigorenko will double up the guards on the base. Everything will be all right, you'll see.'

Kronkin obstinately shook his head. He knew that everything was all wrong. But on one point at least he agreed with Mironov: there was absolutely nothing either of them could do about it.

Anna sat as close to the fire as she could, arms hugging her knees tightly into her chest. The glowing embers, last remnants of the small stock of dry wood which they had carried away from the hut, brought the only touch of living colour to a grey dawn in a white world.

She had survived. Over and over again she reminded herself of this miracle: she had survived. When she passed out they had been but a few yards away from the forest, without knowing it. Faber and Mannheim, patrolling the treeline, had found them within minutes. A miracle. There were such things, then. But after a mere few hours' sleep she still found it impossible to unravel the complicated skein in which the Americans' presence entangled her.

She had been telling Binderhaven of her near miss with the KGB in Irkutsk.

'I thought you'd take me with you when you left, that I could go with you. The man who brought the cases from Moscow, he said there was a plan. . .'

'What?'

'While we were riding in the car to the hut. . .he said to trust him. A plan. . .'

Binderhaven shook his head. 'I don't know what he meant, Anna. We have no contacts here in Russia. Maybe he was just trying to reassure you. Whatever he meant, we really have no choice now. You'll have to come along with McDonnell and me.'

'McDonnell?'

'Nat McDonnell, the one you know as Smithson. I'm Kirk Binderhaven.'

Kirk. Anna decided she quite liked the sound of that. Kirk and. . .Nat.

'You and he are very close, aren't you?'

Binderhaven picked up a twig and began to break it in pieces. Anna realised that there was something very hard at the back of those clear, disconcerting eyes.

'Pretty close.' He spoke gently, more to the fire than her, but Anna knew that inside him something had stirred.

'You have known each other a long time.'

'Yes.'

'But. . .you don't want to talk about it.'

Binderhaven hesitated. Anna, suddenly afraid of her own presumption, lowered her eyes. But she wanted him to tell, wanted desperately to hear the story of Nat McDonnell and . . .Kirk.

'I don't mind.'

Yet he still hesitated, dismantling another twig with mechanical, faraway movements while his mind hunted back over the past in search of truth.

'It was our first trip out together,' he said slowly; and again he was addressing the fire, the forest, the snow, anything but her. 'We scarce knew each other's names, then. That's how it used to be, out east. No names, no sorrows, it was supposed to happen easier that way. . .'

With a 'tchah' of disgust he flung the remnants of the twig into the fire and watched the flames leap up to consume them. Anna sat perfectly still, striving to catch the softly spoken words.

'We were on the river together, one night. On our way back to base camp, running with the stream. The boat was specially designed for. . .for our kind of work. Very light. A little movement was enough to overturn it. No moon, but a sniper saw us anyway. Some of those people can see at night.'

Deep inside Anna a chord vibrated a response to the quiver in his voice as he said 'those people'. A chord of emotion very close to terror.

'Nat took a bullet in the arm. He didn't cry out, just whimpered. I heard him. I should've stayed put. I didn't. I stood up. . .'

The silence that followed was very long. At last Anna, unable to bear the strain any more, whispered, 'Yes?'

'I near as hell killed us both. We went into the river. There were about thirty hostiles on the bank nearest where we tipped. If there'd been a moon. . .if they'd had a searchlight. . .'

Binderhaven rose and walked quickly over to the edge of the clearing, where he stood looking out at the forest. Suddenly he wheeled round and Anna, finding his eyes fixed on hers, started guiltily.

'I held him up. We swam. They must have fired two hundred rounds, more, I don't know. But they couldn't hit us. They couldn't hit us.'

It was very quiet in the forest clearing. Their voices sounded as if muffled by layer upon layer of cotton wool.

'It wasn't your fault,' Anna said weakly. 'It was a good

thought. You wanted to help your friend. . .'

'It was madness.' Binderhaven's voice sounded dull and flat: the voice of a man who could not be contradicted. 'Sheer madness. I should've been shot. McDonnell should've done it himself.'

Transfixed by those blazing blue eyes Anna could think of nothing more to say. She wanted to protest, to absolve him, speak words of forgiveness, but his eyes forbade any of it.

'So since then, I've been making up for it. Nat understands that. He accepts it. One day I'll've made up. We'll be quits. 'Til then. . .'

Binderhaven left the thought unfinished. He found Anna's round, awestruck eyes very troubling. For the second time he knew the eerie feeling that she alone in all the world had no unfavourable judgement to pass on him. 'We see,' the eyes said, 'but express no opinion. We accept. That's all.'

'And McDonnell?' Anna said quietly. 'Does he really know that all these years you've been "making up", as you call it? Does he need that? Does he want it? Or is it your idea of. . .'

Before she could complete the sentence they simultaneously heard the sound of footsteps slushing through the snow, and Faber and the rest were coming through the treeline. Binderhaven stood up.

'This is where we split,' he said. 'Joe, you and Frank Mannheim are going together with two of the missiles. Part company whenever you judge best. McDonnell, Anna and I'll take one case between us. Next, directions. The maps. . .'

'Engines!'

The noise overhead rapidly grew louder until it seemed to fill their senses. Each man looked up, as if some mysterious gift of X-ray vision could suddenly enable him to penetrate the thick, comforting layers of forest and cloud. Plane after plane roared over, the turbo-props leaving a long, whining trail to the north which seemed to take much longer to die away than to arise. As the last set of engines faded into the distance Binderhaven fancied for a moment that he could hear other planes, far away to the east, but he couldn't be sure.

'So that's it.'

His voice carried matter of fact conviction. He did not find the engines hard to interpret.

'Those planes were headed where we're headed. Must have been at least a batallion up there. Some of them may spread out to look for us, so be on the alert. Make sure you cover as much ground as possible today, before those troops can get properly organised. Now, maps. . .'

He unfolded the large-scale map and gave one edge to Anna to hold.

'We've been following the line of the river, here. . . During the night we covered about sixty miles. That leaves us with only twenty to do, give or take. We're here. . .'

Binderhaven stabbed at the map with his forefinger. Anna noticed that the nail was bitten down to the quick. From almost their first meeting, over lunch in the Hotel Angara, she remembered his hands: slim, pointed. . .and beautifully manicured.

'Take careful bearings and check them every half hour. It's hit or miss, but there must come a time when you start to hear air traffic going in and out: you can't hide an air base and use it at the same time. That's it. Questions?'

There were none. For a moment longer the four men looked at one another in silence, and Anna felt herself to be a spectator at some kind of moving ritual she didn't understand. She could sense that they were reliving common memories, common friendships, all in the space of a few seconds; she was aware, painfully aware, that they did not expect to meet again.

'See you all in Peking,' said Faber lightly. But nobody laughed.

240

26

The Lieutenant-Generals Kronkin and Mironov watched the last of the AN-12/CUBs take off from Irkutsk military airport before returning dejectedly to the control tower, where one of Grigorenko's staff officers had hot tea waiting for them. Unusually for a Russian Kronkin did not like tea, but his request for coffee was met with embarrassed prevarication. Kronkin, recognising a face-saving exercise, waved the man away with disgust.

'Here, *mon cher*, have a little bit of this.'

Kronkin looked down and saw that Mironov was discreetly pushing a square of dark bitter chocolate into his hand.

'Vladimir, Vladimir. . .always you have something to console me.' Kronkin smiled and began to suck slowly on the delicious brown nugget, making it last. Chocolate was one of his luxuries, but at this quality it was hard to come by. 'Where on earth did you get it?'

'Ah! Not me. . .our driver. Last night I made friends with the help of a bottle of scotch, and he showed me the town. You were asleep. I didn't want to wake you. . .'

Mironov eyed his chief from under lowered eyelids. Kronkin had been his friend now since childhood, they had no secrets from each other, but Mironov was careful not to try Kronkin's well-known puritan streak by regaling him with details of his less savoury escapades. Kronkin, however, merely smiled absently. He was distraught with worry. Seeing this, Mironov went smoothly on. 'He showed me where to buy some lemon vodka, and the chocolate. I have two whole bars, and I propose to ration you, *mon cher*. I shall make it last until dawn tomorrow. We will share the last piece between us as we mount the steps of the AWACS together . . .'

The door of the flight controllers' office flew open and Mironov looked up, startled, wondering whether the intruder had heard anything he shouldn't. It was Colonel-General Mishkin, Grigorenko's Chief of Staff. His face wore a polite, wary expression, as if the Lieutenant-Generals had gained a point or two since last they met.

'General Grigorenko presents his compliments, comrades . . .'

Kronkin raised his head. What was coming?

'There has been a telephone call this morning from the Ministry of Defence. Marshal Ustinov in person. . .'

Little Adolf and Fat Hermann exchanged rapid glances.

'You are to be afforded every facility in the pursuit of these American spies. Our troops are at your disposal.'

Kronkin leapt to his feet. 'You mean it! We can have that division?'

'You may have two divisions, if you wish.' Mishkin was all smiles; nothing was too much trouble. 'Of course, it will take a little time to mobilise, but. . .'

Kronkin careered round the table and grasped the startled Chief of Staff by his elbows.

'Time!' he shouted. 'We have no time! You must mobilise at once. But, General Mishkin, we shall never forget this. . .tell Grigorenko that. Tell him, he may have yet saved the Soviet Union from unimaginable defeat. And now, let's *move!*'

He was all but dragging Mishkin towards the door. As they reached it, however, he found time to look over his shoulder and, with an exultant expression on his face, mouth silently at his colleague, 'Kazin. . .*Kazin!*'

27

Faber lay face down in the snow, motionless. In his white clothing and silk face mask he was invisible even a few feet away. Only the merest hint of movement behind the eye slits indicated that he was alive at all.

He had been there now for twenty minutes, and in the whole of that time he had not moved. All his attention was concentrated on a squat grey blur in the tundra, half a mile away from where he lay on the treeline, facing east.

The blur was a helicopter, an Mi-6. It had passed high over Faber, secure under his belt of trees, wheeled back from the north and settled in a spray of snow to disgorge a full complement of troops, seventy men, give or take, armed and well equipped against the freezing weather. The American had thrown himself flat and crawled to the edge of the taiga, raised slightly above the level of the white steppe, so that he could look down on the enemy.

After a little disorganised stamping around the troops split up into three sections. The first moved off towards the north, and the next 'island' of taiga in the endless snowy sea, the very island to which Faber had been preparing to cross when he heard the clatter of the helicopter's engines. The second group struck out south-east, away from his hiding place, but towards the spot where he and Mannheim had separated an hour before. The third section was still by the helicopter, awaiting orders.

'Why don't they go?'

Faber's whisper was the merest hiss, but it was loud enough to betray the sick apprehension he felt. He was suffocated by the desperate desire that the troops should move, run, charge his position, even; do anything, in fact, except stay there in the wilderness of snow, undecided. Uncommitted. Free to act.

Suddenly the rotor blades of the helicopter began to turn, silently at first, then faster and faster with a mighty roar. The remaining troops scattered; the Mi-6 rose into the air, hovered for a moment, and began to drift northwards, as if in pursuit of the first section. Faber's gaze returned to the men on the tundra, and what he saw made him sweat.

There were now twenty of them spread out in a line, ten metres between each. They were armed with rifles; Faber couldn't identify the type at that range but he guessed the standard Kalashnikov AKM. That didn't worry him. It was their line of advance which made him almost sick with fear. They were coming across the steppe straight for the trees under which he was hiding.

He did a reverse crawl on his elbows and knees until he was hidden beneath the thick, black shadow of the low-drooping firs. What now? Faber licked his lips. Somewhere inside him a voice screamed, 'How the fuck do I know?' but he clamped down hard, furiously trying to think of a way out. It was no good leaving the protection of the trees: once he was on the tundra it could only be a matter of time before he was caught. Somehow he had to let those advancing men pass straight through the forest and out the other side, without making contact.

It could be done. During the Vietnam war they had found ways of becoming invisible, in dense jungle. Faber had done it several times, but never in snow. Never in terrain like this.

Cover those traces.

Faber considered the evidence of his recent crawl. He must back-track and smother the prints he made on the way in. *Fast*.

The patch of forest in which he was hiding was about a quarter of a mile thick. He worked at furious speed. Fortunately the technique was simple. As he moved through the taiga he had hugged the trees, avoiding clearings or anything approaching a path. By shaking the snow-laden branches it was often possible to dislodge enough to cover his light tracks. By the time he returned to the little clearing whence he started Faber was in poor shape: heart bounding painfully, body covered in cold perspiration.

The troops must be almost at the treeline. What now?

Dig in. Bury himself. . .

No. Climb.

He cocked his head. Somewhere through the dense shadows of the trees he had heard a human voice, raised in a tone of unmistakable command. He whirled round. Nothing. No trace of movement disturbed the peace of the forest. But his time had run out.

Faber snatched a few twigs from the nearest tree and retreated further into the densest part of the forest, sweeping the snow flat behind him as he went.

Now or never.

He bent to unstrap his snowshoes, clipped them together and wound the elasticated cords round his left wrist, using them to secure the precious briefcase at the same time. He looked up and for a moment studied the tree beneath which he had come to rest, assessing the relative strengths and weaknesses of the branches. Then he grasped the bole with his hands and knees, and began laboriously to haul himself up.

The climb was utter, unremitting hell.

It was the middle of the afternoon and Faber had already covered many miles that day. He had moved fast, dodging between the islands of taiga as rapidly as the snow would permit and using the patches of trees to rest up between the frantic bursts of travel across the exposed tundra. He had drawn deeply on his reserves of energy, and was very tired. Every muscle in Faber's body was shrieking in outraged protest before he had climbed ten feet. The tree boasted few solid branches, but on all sides of its slender trunk little sharp twigs stuck out to impede him, so that he was constantly having to protect his eyes from their spikes, and the briefcase was forever becoming entangled. But he dared not stop to rest. He had to get up high, so that as many branches as possible obscured the space between him and the troops on the ground, then hang there like a leech until they had passed by.

At last he could go no further. He clasped his hands together round the bole of the tree and fought to still his laboured breathing.

It was very quiet in the forest. No birds sang, no animal moved through the thick snow beneath. Faber strained his ears. Nothing. Had the voice he heard earlier been in his imagination?

He craned over his shoulder and looked down. From where he was he couldn't even see the ground. He began to count, making himself go slowly.

One minute.

His arms felt as though they were about to be wrested from their sockets. Cautiously Faber poked about with his boots, searching for a branch strong enough to bear at least some of his weight. Ah! A bunch of thick twigs, stronger than the rest, with a common root in the trunk. That should do. . .

This time the voice sounded very close, as though the speaker stood right underneath his tree. He nearly cried out at the shock of it, gritted his teeth. . . Then he heard it again, the voice of the officer, and the sound of men advancing slowly through the snow. . .swish, swish, swish.

Two minutes.

Cramp, sudden and fiery, darted along Faber's right arm. He flung back his head, teeth grinding at the invisible sky, huge drops of cold sweat dripping from his forehead.

Swish, swish, swish. . .

They were passing now. The sound of their snowshoes was diminishing towards the west. But the pain! Oh Christ, Christ, *Christ*. . .

Another ripple of pain. His left leg kicked convulsively and for all his efforts a low moan of agony broke through his clenched teeth. There would be a second wave. That was how it was in the jungle: a follow-up line of troops to catch the man who emerged from hiding too early, in the belief that the troops had gone. He must hold on. *He must!'*

The officer's voice was further away now. Through a red mist of pain Faber exulted. It had worked! They had not found him, or the case. Another few minutes and he would be safe, *safe*.

Faber yelped. A spasm of cramp, sharper than anything which had gone before, raced along both arms. He yelped again, chewing his lips in an effort to remain quiet. The pain in

246

his limbs, the salt blood in his mouth. . .his head was swimming. Surely they must have gone now. Surely, surely. . .

No sound rose from the forest floor. All was still. Faber's head lolled on one side, his bloodstained mouth emitting tiny gasps and whimpers of pain. With his left foot he prodded the fragile bunch of twigs which helped bear his weight, striving to ease the burden on his arms.

The sudden agony was like a streak of forked lightning. The main prong ran the whole length of his leg, sending off branches and sub-branches of lancing needle pain through his faltering flesh; his foot kicked violently against the tree; for a terrible second he fancied that all his toes were uncurling from off his foot. . .and then the last tattered shreds of strength left his arms and he was falling. . .

When he hit the ground he was travelling almost horizontally, and the impact broke his spine in two places. He died instantly. The main line of troops was already almost at the far edge of the taiga, preparing to cross the next patch of white plain, but, as Faber had surmised, some of the men had been detailed to follow up the main advance, treading with extra care and silence. As he fell to earth he did not cry out but countless twigs and tiny branches snapped under his weight, causing one of the rearguard to turn apprehensively. The empty forest yawned back at him, and the soldier frowned. Snow falling off a bough, that was all. Or was it. . .?

He raised his hand and looked swiftly to either side. Ten metres away he could dimly discern the form of his nearest colleague, who peered at him in curiosity. The soldier beckoned, raising a finger to his lips. Silently the two of them began to retrace their steps. Before they had gone very far the first soldier again raised his hand, and dropped to the crouch.

Through the trees he could just make out the form of a man lying in the snow. He raised his rifle, and with his free hand waved to his companion that he should work round on the flank. As he obeyed he disturbed a heavy weight of snow on a branch, but the noise of it slithering to the ground did not appear to attract the attention of the horizontal human figure.

The soldier gave his friend a minute in which to take up position. He used the time to investigate his quarry in more detail. The man was in a small clearing, he noticed, and beside him lay a dark brown object. A weapon, perhaps. The soldier moistened his lips. In front of him there unrolled a glorious vista of promotion and increased pay, a medal, a trip to Moscow to receive the medal. . . He had heard of the women who frequented the cafés of the Kalinin Prospekt, how they knew things no Siberian girl had ever dared learn, or so it was rumoured. . .

The minute was up. Ivan would be in position by now. The soldier drew a deep breath, stood up, raised his rifle to his shoulder and shouted, 'You! Stand up!'

The man in the clearing did not move. The trooper's finger twitched on the trigger and then he remembered. Alive. They were to be taken alive. He hurtled forward into the clearing, yelling 'Ivan!' at the top of his voice. Out of the corner of his eye he saw a flash of white movement where Ivan was emerging from the trees nearest the clearing. The stranger had not had time to draw a gun. With jubilant whoops the two Russian soldiers rushed forward to where Faber's body lay in the snow, waiting for them.

Senior Lieutenant Yuri Torokov looked impatiently at his watch. Two of his rearguard were missing and already they were late for the rendezvous at the next map reference. It was important not to screw this one up. This was Torokov's first proper assignment since receiving his commission. He had come up through the ranks, cursing the incompetence of his officers, until at last, after the statutory ten years as a *praporschik* they had given him his pips. Torokov was determined at all costs to make a good impression.

He was on the point of sending the Sergeant back to look for the missing troops when out of the trees there came a thunderous boom. Torokov was flung on to his back by a tremendous shock wave. He scrambled up and saw that his men were all at sixes and sevens, some of them on their hands and knees, others staring back into the patch of taiga which they had just finished searching. For a moment he hesitated, indecisively wondering what he had better do. Before he could make up his mind, one of the men extended his arm excitedly.

'Will you look at that!' he cried.

Wisps of yellowish smoke were starting to float through the trees at about the height of a man's head. For the best part of a minute, while they picked themselves up and pulled themselves together, the troops stared at these curious manifestations of what each man sensed to be something frightful, something eerie which had happened back there, in the woods. . . Torokov uneasily sized up the mood of his men, and called to his Sergeant. No use sending these dolts, in a minute they'd all be crossing themselves.

The two men passed rapidly through the trees, following the unmistakable trail of the wispy smoke. Torokov's stomach was beginning to churn. There was something unpleasantly sweet in the smoke, a mild stench of decay mixed with burning.

The journey did not take long. One minute he was among the dense firs; the next he had come straight out on to a clearing. But not a conventional forest clearing. In the middle was scooped out a great, regularly shaped bowl, from which the smoke seemed to emanate. Cautiously the two men approached the edge. Whatever it was had managed to soak through six feet of permafrost and reduce mature trees to smoking skeletons over a radius of fifty metres.

It took Torokov several seconds to break down the obscene mess inside the bowl into its constituent parts. A number of fir boughs lay there, still burning, even in the snow. But that was only a small part of it. What arrested the eyes, and drew them irresistibly down to the nadir of the bowl, was the sight of three human skeletons, charred, and in places broken, but nevertheless still recognisable as such. Here and there little blobs of flame attached themselves to the raw bone and hung resolutely on, burning merrily in the cold wet snow. There was also something that might once have been a rifle, minus its wooden stock, a twisted, smoking lump of metal. . .

Torokov looked up slowly in time to see his Sergeant hastily make the sign of the cross on his chest. And Torokov, without having the least idea why, did the same.

28

Night was falling. Kronkin stood looking out across the whitened runways, gloomily observing the pilots and crews as they disembarked from their Mi-6s. So far the helicopters had drawn a blank, and Weather had effectively closed down operations for the night by reporting more snow on the way.

Kronkin counted the helicopters again. One was still missing. He looked at his watch. If the pilot wasn't careful he was going to run foul of the blizzard which Weather had reported as blowing up over Mongolia. The Lieutenant-General gnawed his lip. Now that Grigorenko was co-operating at last, he didn't want any accidents, any aircraft lost on the GRU's say-so.

Arc lights fizzled into garish life, illuminating the airfield like a stage. Kronkin turned away from the triple-glazed window with a 'tchah' of impatience. Now there would be no more flying until dawn next day — if then. It all depended on the weather. Kronkin began to walk up and down, pounding one clenched fist into the palm of his other hand, while Mironov watched him with a complacent smile.

'The snow is something even you can't beat, *mon cher*. It's fate. Don't worry about what you can't change.'

Kronkin rounded on him with a snarl. 'You're so bloody thick, Mironov, there's times you make me want to spew. *Fate*. . .why not talk about God's will and have done with it? You and your bloody fate. . .'

Mironov's smile only widened. He looked past Kronkin and gestured at the window. 'There's the last chopper in now. I wonder why he's late.'

Kronkin resumed his angry pacing. Mironov took out a nail file and embarked on a manicure of impeccable thoroughness. To look at him you would have thought he had nothing to do except kill a few idle hours until the next meal.

The shrill ring of the phone brought Kronkin to a halt again. Mironov stopped filing, held out his hand for a brief examination, then made a long arm and removed the receiver from its hook while Kronkin looked on impatiently. He saw Mironov's face suddenly stiffen, and came quickly to his side. Mironov put his hand over the mouthpiece and whispered, 'That last pilot, they've got something. . . What? Hello, yes, I'm still here. . . We'll be right down.'

Mironov slammed the receiver back on its cradle and stood up. 'They've got a platoon commander in the debriefing room downstairs. He's in quarantine. Grigorenko's coming out himself, for the report. Something's broken. Let's go.'

The two Generals engaged in an undignified scramble for the door, and clattered down the narrow stairs at the run.

Lieutenant Torokov was sitting at a table opposite the Chief of Staff. His face was strained. In front of him was a steaming cup of tea, untouched, and in the ashtray an unclaimed cigarette burned slowly into grey ash. As Kronkin and Mironov entered the room the Lieutenant rose to his feet and stood rigidly to attention. Kronkin waved him down again, dragged a chair up to the table, threw himself into it and said curtly, 'Well?'

'We shall wait,' said the Chief of Staff smoothly, 'for the arrival of General Grigorenko. Smoke, gentlemen?'

Kronkin fought down his desire to smash something, preferably the Chief of Staff's jaw, and took a cigarette. Nobody spoke. Five, ten, fifteen minutes passed. Kronkin lit another cigarette from the butt of the first and embarked on another vain attempt to read Torokov's blank face. There was something behind that blankness, he thought. It was a cover, a blind. The man had seen something. And it shocked him.

At last there came the sound of voices in the corridor, and a second later the door flew open to reveal General Grigorenko. He seemed disturbed, that was Kronkin's first impression; he looked again, and saw that as well as being worried the

251

General was also half-seas over. Unconsciously Kronkin's clenched fist hit the table. He stared at it, then raised his eyes to find Torokov's gaze full on him. For a moment the two men looked at each other; Kronkin's glance was the first to fall.

Grigorenko took a chair and rested his elbows on the table in front of him. He was breathing heavily. He opened his mouth a couple of times to speak, but in the end merely succeeded in nodding. Thus encouraged, Torokov began his report.

At first he was nervous, but after a while he gained confidence and told his story well. Only when he came to what they had found in the remains of the taiga did his voice falter slightly, and his eyes look away from his superior's florid face.

When he had finished, for a moment all that could be heard was the sound of Grigorenko's laboured breathing. Then, 'You want to ask him anything?'

Kronkin looked at Mironov, who shook his head. The faces of the two Generals were equally expressionless, almost as if the Lieutenant's story had bored them.

'No, thank you. I commend you on the. . .clarity. . .of your report, Lieutenant. Perhaps I might suggest — ' a sideways look at Grigorenko — 'that you mention this to no one. Your troops and NCOs the same. We would prefer to avoid unnecessary gossip.'

Grigorenko appeared to wake from a half sleep. 'Eh? Oh, yes. . .talk to no one, you hear?'

Torokov nodded. 'Yes sir.' He realised that he had somehow stumbled on something secret, and terrible. For a Russian officer, that was bad. Torokov knew that from now on he would be watched, listened to, maybe even *suspected* — that word which all Soviet citizens, be they military or civilian, most dread. To be suspected is worse, in a way, than being found guilty, for at least the condemned criminal knows his fate. The man who is suspected has only fear to live with, a terrible apprehension that one night, when he is asleep, there will come a knock at the door. . .

Torokov was not going to talk to anyone outside this room about what he had seen on the steppe. None of his men were, either. Not if they knew what was good for them; not if he,

Torokov, could help it. So he nodded again, and repeated, with greater emphasis this time, 'Yes sir.'

'Then dismiss.'

Torokov was only too glad to obey. After he had left the room there was silence for a few moments, while Grigorenko eyed his unwanted guests with unmistakable malice.

'You want to tell me what the hell is going on?'

Kronkin turned to face him, very slowly, and with quiet deliberation blew a column of smoke past the General's right ear. 'No.'

Grigorenko's fist clenched and unclenched, but everyone in the room understood perfectly well what the position was. Since the phone call from the nameless one in Moscow, there had been a none-too-subtle shift in the balance of power. The GRU were, for the time being, masters of the Transbaikal Military District.

'Then I'm going back to my dinner.'

Grigorenko stood up and lurched heavily from the room, followed by Mironov's watchful gaze.

'Trouble brewing there,' he muttered. 'Don't let me forget. . .'

'Fuck Grigorenko.' Kronkin's voice was spiked with vitriol. When he managed to speak again he was almost spitting with rage.

'When I think of all the time we've wasted! You and I sitting here in Irkutsk, wrestling with that drunken oaf Grigorenko while all the time those Americans are getting nearer and nearer to target. . . Just a group of harmless, unarmed spies, are they? Like buggery!'

Mironov's forehead creased in a frown. 'I still don't understand what all the fuss is about.'

'*Fuss!*' Kronkin seized hold of Mironov's jacket and began to rock him to and fro like a doll. 'You great stupid mother-fucking idiot, don't you see? What do you suppose happened out there?'

'Some idiot loosed off a grenade, I suppose. . .'

'Oooh!' Kronkin clapped his hands to his forehead and closed his eyes. 'Lenin, give me patience! What sort of grenade sets a whole tract of forest on fire, eh? Come on, tell me. And what grenade smells *sickly-sweet*, eh? Mironov! Think! *Napalm!* Don't you realise yet. . .'

There was a knock at the door. With an almighty effort Kronkin got a hold on himself and released the lapels of Mironov's tunic. 'In!'

The door opened to reveal a Captain on Grigorenko's personal staff. If the man had heard anything unusual his face showed no sign of it.

'Excuse me, sir, but we have been collating the reports from the helicopter pilots. One of the last to land has reported seeing tracks in the snow, ninety miles from here, leading into a patch of taiga. We thought you ought to know.'

'Thank you, Captain. General Mironov and I will come to the operations room in just a moment.'

As the door closed behind the Captain, Kronkin swung round to face his colleague, face deathly serious, but when he spoke it was with his accustomed calm.

'Somehow, Mironov, we have got to persuade these *churkas* to get out on the steppe, tonight. We have to find the men who made those tracks. The sooner the better.'

Mironov threw back his head and laughed. 'You're out of your mind. If you think these goons are going to move off their fat arses. . .'

'Oh they'll move all right. Even if I have to get a signed order from Andropov himself.'

'*What?*'

For an instant Kronkin's face softened in a smile — just for an instant.

'You really don't see, do you? We've moved into another league. Forget all that's gone before. Concentrate on one thing only: this is war.'

'I still don't. . .'

'They are not unarmed. They have missiles. And unless we can flush them out of the taiga in the next ten hours. . .'

Kronkin drew a deep breath. He seemed to be having trouble in articulating his thoughts.

'They're going to blow up the AWACS.'

29

Even in the Soviet Union a man is entitled to assume, once he has reached a certain age and point in his career, that life will go on in the same old way. Therefore it did not occur to Frolov to worry about certain oddities which, in his younger days, would have caused him to break out in a cold sweat.

The lift was not working. The Frolovs lived in a stylish modern apartment block equipped with all the modern conveniences of life which their counterparts in London or Paris might expect to enjoy. There was, of course, a lift; it had never failed to work before. Frolov's eyebrows rose, but he was too engrossed in other things to pay much attention. He plodded up the three flights of stairs to the flat, latch key dangling from the fingers of his left hand, his mind still turning over and over the events of the past few days.

Things were rapidly getting out of hand. First there was the mysterious General Mironov with his fairy tales of Christian mothers. With some difficulty Frolov had succeeded in tracking Mironov down to the upper echelons of the GRU — which still didn't explain why he should seek out Frolov for the apparently express purpose of destroying Povin. Then there was the debacle over Kazin's address, and the hearse. Frolov, in his usual state of perplexed fear, couldn't decide what to do for the best.

On paper it was easy. He had the dirt on Povin. When he had the dirt on someone he turned him in. But the person to whom he turned him in was — Povin. Frolov felt the time had come to do something about his boss, was keen to do so in fact, but he hadn't got the faintest idea of how to go about it.

The Kommandant? Frolov shuddered at the thought. Kazin? A possibility, yes, but any approach to that quarter was recognised as having potentially suicidal overtones. It was a problem, and one of which Frolov was by now almost desperately anxious to relieve himself. Suppose someone else — Mironov, for example — was closing in on Povin and got there first, only to discover that Frolov had been collecting the same information but had kept it to himself. Wouldn't that be incriminating? What if Mironov was a crony of Povin's, planted to test Frolov's loyalty? Or a crony of someone else, planted to test Frolov's loyalty to the Party line?

Frolov tightened his grip on the stair rail. He had to do something. Fast.

The lights on the landing were off. Frolov mechanically stretched out his hand to the plunger of the automatic timer switch on his way past. Nothing happened.

It was then that the first tiny alarm bell sounded a warning in Frolov's brain. He lifted his head and looked swiftly from right to left. The passage was empty. In the same second he raised his knee, ready to run. Then something heavy and suffocating was flung over his head; something else hard and gnarled pistoned into the small of his back; hands grasped his ankles. . .and Frolov was being carried swiftly to the back stairs which led down to the little street behind the block.

His assailants were very efficient. A car was waiting right at the foot of the stairs, its engine turning over quietly. Frolov was bundled into the back seat and as the door slammed the driver let in the clutch, easing smoothly into the flow of the rush hour traffic.

Looking back on it afterwards the thing which most depressed Frolov was that in the whole of the thirty seconds or so it took to kidnap him he had not managed to summon up the initiative either to shout or to struggle.

When they ripped the blanket off his head, however, it was a different matter. For a split second Frolov sat there gasping in huge breaths of fresh air; then he started.

'What the *hell* do you think you're doing? Who are you? Have you any idea who I am?' His voice took on its customary dangerous note of harshness. 'You'll pay for this in Siberia.

Stop this car. Let me out.'

No one said anything. The driver ignored his request. Frolov was becoming more and more enraged with every passing second. When nobody answered him he reached across to the nearside door handle, but before he could lift it a hand closed around his wrist and, to his astonishment, Frolov found he could not move. His jaw dropped. Somewhere close by a man laughed very softly.

'We know who you are, Colonel Frolov. There is really nothing you can do about this. Nothing at all. The journey takes about an hour. Sit back in your seat and relax.'

Frolov did as he was told. The quiet voice was coming from the front seat, he realised, and the speaker was young. For a moment the wild thought crossed his mind that this was some weird offshoot of his meeting with Olga Michaelov, that her friends had decided to risk this incredible escapade for a reason known only to themselves. . . But it only had to be stated to be dismissed at once as rubbish. Frolov swallowed. He did not much care for the quiet voice. Its owner might have been passing on a weather forecast or a football result, imparting information of trivial, transient interest. An indifferent voice.

'Where are you taking me?' He tried to make it sound bored, and failed. He was not resigned.

'To see the Chairman of the KGB.'

'Don't be ridiculous.' It was on the tip of Frolov's tongue to retort that there was no Chairman at present, but his natural sense of caution suddenly inhibited him. Perhaps they didn't know that.

'The appointment does not take effect for a day or two,' said the quiet voice. 'I anticipate a little.'

Frolov's eyes were slowly growing accustomed to the darkness inside the car. One man sat on his right, another on his left. There was a driver, of course, and the owner of the only voice he had heard so far sat in the front passenger seat. The occasional flash of a street lamp revealed two pale, rigid young faces on either side, and that was all.

The quiet voice spoke again.

'I should tell you what my instructions are, Frolov. I am to deliver you where we are going alive or dead. That's all. No indication was given me as to which was preferred. So shut your mouth, and keep still.'

Frolov swallowed again. His mouth was very dry. He was conscious of an acrid, sweaty smell, and with a start he realised that it was emanating from himself. Fear. Frolov had smelled it before, in others. Now it was here, in this car, rising up to his nostrils from his own pores.

He found he was no longer angry. Rage had drained away for lack of support. With a sudden, nauseating rush it suddenly came over him that he was just a man, alone, in the power of other people stronger than he was — and that being a Colonel in the KGB was, in such a situation, merely an irrelevancy.

The car sped on towards the west. Frolov did not know they were going west; he had spent the first ten minutes in the car learning his place the hard way, and now he found it was too late to identify landmarks which might have helped him guess where they were going. But they were leaving the city behind, that much was obvious. There were fewer cars about and the quality of the roads was deteriorating. Frolov's brain wouldn't function. What did it mean, 'the Chairman of the KGB'? Who in his right mind would be capable of such macabre humour? The very thought was treasonable, worth a life sentence in a labour camp if uttered aloud.

Who in his right mind?

Fear. . .

Now the car was slowing. They turned off the road and started to bump down a rough track. It was pitch black outside; Frolov couldn't see a thing. The car turned a corner and straight ahead a solitary light appeared in the middle of the track. As they approached Frolov saw that it was suspended from the middle of a red and white bar across their path. Beside it stood a sentry cabin.

A torch was shone in Frolov's eyes. He squeezed them shut against the unexpected assault; when he opened them again the barrier had risen and they were moving forward once more. Another bend in the track, a lurch, and the car was back on a metalled surface. A few more minutes and they were pulling up outside a large, sprawling *dacha*.

Frolov's heart was beating uncomfortably fast. He realised

that for the last quarter of an hour he had been wanting the journey not to end. The car seemed to be surrounded by men carrying torches, and somewhere there was the yelp of a dog. As they hustled him out he was dimly conscious, amidst all the hurry, of a stone façade, dark and cold, of the presence of many men, of torch beams criss-crossing virgin snow. Then he was inside a huge hall, brilliantly lit, and quite alone.

He could not quite believe it. He looked to right and left; then he swung round on his heels. Behind him were two vast double doors through which he must have come a moment before. Now they were shut, and ominous-looking wires led neatly away from solid-looking locks. Frolov chewed his lower lip. Electronic gadgetry. Impressive.

He turned round again. The hall was huge. Red damask lined the walls, and everywhere was brass ornamentation of the most extravagant kind, even down to the ornate little beads which dangled at the ends of tassels on the pleated lampshades. A lot of the uncarpeted floor was taken up with cluttered little tables, their knick-knacks glittering dully in the artificial light from the huge candelabra overhead. Only the back of the room remained in darkness, and suddenly that too was flooded with light.

Frolov gasped.

The whole of the far wall was covered by an enormous portrait. Recognition was instantaneous. Frolov took a step nearer, then another. He could not take his eyes off the painting. It mesmerised him.

The subject sat at a table littered with papers, his right forearm resting on the wood, his left hand grasping the arm of his chair. It was as though he had pushed his chair away for long enough to give the artist his chance, and that any minute the paint would writhe, allowing the sitter to resume his interrupted tasks, those pressing matters of high state policy from which he had allowed himself to be temporarily diverted. His eyes, black flecks, seemed to stare off the canvas at Frolov. As he advanced they followed his progress. Frolov had never heard of the technique whereby the sitter is made to stare straight at the artist, so that the eyes of the finished portrait seem to move as if alive; to Frolov this was all black magic.

The portrait was possessed of the most extraordinary vitality, as though the oil was still wet. Every detail of it was familiar to Frolov from countless photographs, and more ...from some inherent, inbred, atavistic sense of history, of belonging to the nation which this man had ruled so thoroughly and for so long. The black, shaggy hair swept straight back from the forehead, the drooping black moustache, the mouth that seemed to be almost on the point of a smile but not quite, as if the sitter could not even now quite tear himself away from the cares of managing *rodina*, the Motherland. . .His eyes fell to the bottom of the frame, and the neat gilt plate, knowing already what they would see.

IOSIF VISSARIONOVICH STALIN

And as he read the inscription a current of electricity seemed to run from Frolov's feet right up to the crown of his head before settling in his lower stomach, a ripple of such intensity and force that his knees sagged and next moment he might have fallen.

'Done at the very height of his power.'

Frolov swung round. Above the doors through which he had entered was a gallery. In the exact centre of it stood an elegantly tailored figure, his hands behind his back, eyes fixed on the portrait. Although he had not raised his voice every vibrant syllable penetrated Frolov's brain with the most perfect clarity. His eyes widened, his jaw dropped; for a moment the figure in the gallery continued to stare at the livid portrait on the wall, and then his gaze refocused on Frolov.

'Krubykov!'

Frolov's knees, momentarily relieved by the unexpected sound of the voice, started to tremble again. For he recognised the man in the gallery: Major Krubykov of the Kremlin Kommandant, principal liaison officer for the Politburo's Central Inspectorate of the KGB, a shadowy all-powerful body feared even by the Heads of the Main Directorates. The spies who watch the spies, that was how Povin once described them, and now, looking up at Krubykov's grave face, Frolov at last understood something of the awesome dread which the very name of the Kremlin Kommandant could inspire in the hardiest of Party servants.

260

'Come up here, Frolov.'

Krubykov's quiet voice carried effortlessly over the vast space which separated him from the man by the portrait of his spiritual master. Without taking his eyes off Krubykov's face Frolov made his way slowly towards the right wing of the huge staircase which led up to the gallery. When he was half a dozen paces from the Major he stopped. A tiny spark of self-respect urged him to protest, ask questions, demand explanations, only to die away unnurtured. Krubykov removed his right hand from behind his back and Frolov saw with a jolt of renewed fear that he was holding a gun.

'To your left, Frolov. The door at the end.'

But even before they reached the end of the corridor Frolov knew who he was going to find there. From the moment he first set eyes on the portrait in the hall downstairs a part of him had already made the vital deduction. There was only one candidate. Even the mysterious reference to the Chairman of the KGB now made sense.

By contrast to the magnificent hall the room at the end was very sparse. Everywhere seemed white: the ceiling, the walls, even the tiny square of rug before the white marble fireplace. The effect was antiseptic, and cold. It reminded Frolov of a hospital. Or a morgue.

At one end of the room was a desk, with a wooden chair set before it. On the far wall behind the desk was a smaller version of the portrait. Beneath it sat a man, nearly bald, his eyes greatly magnified by the thick pebble-lensed spectacles which covered the top part of his fresh, pink, rather plump face. He sat with his hands folded on the white blotter in front of him, his face turned slightly towards one side, as if in inquiry. Blue cigarette smoke shimmered upwards from the little cane holder resting in the white stone ashtray at his right elbow, column upon column, collapsing only to form over and over again.

Kazin.

His voice, when he spoke, had no music in it.

'Sit down, Frolov.'

Frolov obeyed in silence. He could not speak. He knew he was alone with the man they called 'Stalin's baby', a veiled

261

reference to the scandal and rumour which surrounded his birth; the last and most loyal of the Great Father's disciples, preserver of the sacred flame in all its white-hot omnivorous purity. And Frolov could not speak.

For what seemed an eternity the two men sat and looked at each other, and did not move.

The old stories came flooding back into Frolov's mind like a massive tidal wave. How he was supposed to have smashed his own daughter's head with a hammer for siding with the Mensheviks. How he had taken the machine gun in his own hands, tripod and all, to shoot down line upon line of women and children after the Kiev uprising. How he had boasted of building bones, the bones of slave labourers, into the Belomor Canal, so that it would last for ever. How he had insisted on riding with the first tanks to enter Hungary, and Czechoslovakia, and then stormed at Brezhnev himself for not allowing him to complete the hat-trick with Poland. All rumour, nothing provable. . .all true.

Frolov looked into the eyes of the man opposite him on the other side of the desk and knew for certain that he was in the presence of a madman.

'You're a meddler, Frolov.'

He spoke with the cracked voice of a harsh old man. It grated against the ear, like the clamouring whine of the chainsaw when first it touches the proud young tree.

Frolov's body temperature was dropping rapidly. A fire blazed in the hearth but somehow he could not get warm. He knew that if once he let his teeth chatter his last pretence at self-control would have gone.

'First the Confidential Registry. Then Baku. The Michaelov whore.'

Kazin picked up the cane holder and inhaled deeply, his next words blowing smoke into Frolov's eyes.

'What's it all about, Frolov? No, don't answer, not yet. Let me tell you something. You see Krubykov? He's going to cover you. There. . .that's right.'

Krubykov moved round to stand by Frolov's side, the gun held out so that it was almost touching the Colonel's earlobe. Frolov averted his eyes, only to feel them inexorably drawn back towards the gun muzzle.

'You know who this house used to belong to, Frolov. Don't you.'

Kazin took another savage drag on his cigarette. Frolov was dumb.

'You won't be the first one to die in that chair. In his lifetime or in mine. Answer truthfully, Frolov. Answer me *now*. What exactly are you up to?'

Krubykov took a step forward and Frolov felt a cold ring of gunmetal rest against his temple. He tried to speak and could not. He tried again, but still the words refused to come. Kazin took another swift draw on the cigarette, and into Frolov's mind came an image from a book he had seen as a child, a picture of an ogre tearing off the head of his victim with his teeth: Kazin smoked in just that way.

'I. . . I n-ne. . .'

'Yes?'

Frolov took a great gulp of air, squeezed his eyes tight shut and began to speak.

'I never believed Michaelov was the traitor, not even when Stanov made it official and the Politburo published that internal Order, and so I decided to find out for myself; it's all there, it's in the records, it wasn't Michaelov at all, it. . .'

'It was Povin,' said Kazin calmly. 'Of course. We know that, Frolov. I've known it for years. But what's that to you, eh?'

'I. . . I. . .'

'I, I,' mimicked Kazin. 'You'd do anything for power and promotion, wouldn't you, Frolov? Anything at all.'

It was as though a great weight suddenly lifted off Frolov's shoulders. All his instincts shrieked at him that at last they had come to the crossroads, that from now on he could plunge down even deeper into the darkness which surrounded him, or at a single bound leap into the sunlight. Without in the least understanding why, he tossed back his head, looked Kazin straight in the eye, and said, 'Anything, comrade. Anything at all.'

And for several moments there was silence.

Kazin continued to regard him with that sly, sideways gaze of his, the expression on his face unchanged. Underneath the desk one leg had begun to jog in a regular nervous rhythm: Frolov was conscious of the quiet sound the material of his trouser leg made against the wood. The first inkling he had that he had chosen well was the removal of the gun barrel from his forehead. Hardly daring to look, Frolov made himself cast an upwards, sideways glance at Krubykov. The Major's hands were once more behind his back. Of the gun there was no sign. Krubykov was smiling.

Krubykov was smiling.

'You've been a long time on the road, Boris Andreyevich.'

Cautiously Frolov turned his head. It was not his imagination. Kazin really had spoken those words. He, too, was smiling.

'And then again, perhaps not. After all, you chose the right time to arrive, given a little help from General Mironov. Krubykov was right about you, after all.'

Kazin stood up and came round the desk to stand in front of Frolov, who looked up uncomprehendingly.

'Stand up.'

After a struggle Frolov was able to do as he was bidden. Kazin hugged him close and kissed his cheek. As he let go the bewildered Colonel sank down again into his chair, overwhelmed.

'Very much the right time to arrive, Boris Andreyevich. Oh yes. I have need of your services.'

'Of. . .of me?'

'Certainly, yes, of you. Krubykov, get the file.'

As the elegant Major left the room Kazin picked up his cigarette case and offered it to Frolov, who accepted with trembling hands. He could not hold the tip still in the flame of the lighter.

'I require commitment from my men, that is all. Commitment *now*, rather than after they see how the wind blows, you understand me?'

Frolov shook his head.

'Things are happening in this glorious Motherland of ours. Very shortly, the times are going to change for the better. That cannot happen without human help. The helpers must declare themselves now if they are to share in the glory to come. I need

264

men who put their money, themselves, on the table.' Kazin smiled glacially. 'I think you have that kind of commitment, Frolov. I need greedy, dissatisfied men like you, because while things remain as they are you're never going to amount to anything, whereas once I. . .'

He checked himself, then went on in quieter vein.

'There is shortly to be a monumental shake-up. Until quite recently we all thought there might be a war as well, but tonight we learned that the President of the United States has been overruled by his military chiefs. Not that I give a damn about any of that, but the shake-up. . .that's another thing. The question of my role in the new regime has recently become the subject of certain delicate discussions. I've never made any secret of my desire to control the KGB. After it was suggested that I take an early, well-deserved retirement — ' again the icy smile — 'that desire seemed destined to remain unfulfilled. Now it's a possibility again. But there's the question of my contribution, my. . .price, if you like. I need a ticket, Frolov. Tickets cost money.'

Krubykov re-entered the room carrying under his arm what looked like a stiffly-bound book which he handed to Kazin.

'This is my ticket, Boris Andreyevich. You're familiar with some of it. A twenty-page report and one hundred and fifty or so pages of supporting documentary evidence. The Povin file.'

Frolov took it from Kazin's outstretched hand and began to examine it.

'It proves three things. One, Michaelov was loyal and was executed for crimes he did not commit. Two, Povin has been betraying the Soviet Union almost since he learned to talk. Three, Povin — himself a Christian — has for years been living in the shadow of a scandal involving his devoutly Christian mother, whom he should have reported to his superiors but did not.'

'These are photocopies?'

'Of course. The originals can be provided. You remember the desecrated page in the Confidential Register?'

Frolov leafed through a few more pages. To his satisfaction he noticed that his fingers were once more supple and in control of their task. The trembling had stopped.

'It is my contribution, my ticket. Yours too, in a way.'

'Mine?'

'You're going to deliver it. Tomorrow. First thing. There is a certain committee meeting of the Politburo, consisting only of those persons who intend to bring about the shake-up I mentioned earlier. They will be very interested in that file. Apart from the obvious thing, it contains much incidental material to discredit Stanov for the grossest inefficiency. Certain factions in the new regime will like that.'

'You want *me* to deliver this?'

Frolov looked at Kazin, then at Krubykov. His meaning was obvious.

'Krubykov stays on the sidelines. He's not KGB, for one thing. I need an emissary from inside, someone who by his presence will indicate a certain willingness on the part of the KGB to have dealings with me.' Kazin's lips twisted into a bitter smile. 'And in any case, he's too valuable to lose. If anything goes wrong, I need him for the next time.'

Frolov looked down at the file on his knee. Where his fingers held it steady, the knuckles were white.

'May I ask a question?'

'That depends. It depends on whether you're going to put your stake money down on the table.'

Kazin expelled the stub of his cigarette from its cane holder and inserted a fresh one. Frolov had the overwhelming impression that his answer was a matter of complete indifference to the man who sat opposite. He put into his next words all the conviction they could carry.

'I shall do that. Without fail.'

Kazin's lighter flared. Through the flame Frolov saw the ironic, slightly mad eyes flicker upwards from the cigarette to meet his own, and again sensed that curious feeling in the pit of his stomach which he had first known downstairs, in the presence of the portrait of Stalin.

'Then ask your question.'

But for Frolov it was not as simple as that. A medley of conflicting emotions threatened his very sanity. They were using him, that much was obvious, using him in an intrigue which was by its very nature treasonable. For the first time in a

266

long time Frolov did, in fact, recognise quite clearly what the price of a particular failure would be: the death penalty. But against that there was overweening ambition, greed, lust for power; yes, Kazin had been right about that. There was nothing Frolov would not do for power. Yet so much as to think these things within the Soviet Union. . . It was unreal, a dream.

Kazin was not a dream.

'What do you have in mind for me?'

Kazin yawned, his mouth opening wide enough to show Frolov the gold fillings inside.

'I shall need deputies.'

'You mean. . .I would keep my present job. As Deputy Head of the First Main. . .'

'Don't be an idiot, Frolov. I shall need deputies of the KGB. Deputy chairmen.'

Frolov gawked at him. He could not speak.

'Well, was that your question?'

'I have another.'

'Be quick.'

'Why has this file never seen the light of day before? When Michaelov was disgraced, for example? You had made a deal with him. . .'

Frolov tailed off. Kazin was rising to his feet, very slowly. The terrified Colonel felt Krubykov stiffen beside him, as if preparing to jump aside. Kazin came round the desk until he was standing opposite Frolov, his face mere inches away from the Colonel's own. For a moment he regarded Frolov through narrowed, hostile eyes; then, very softly, he began to speak.

'You think I cared about Michaelov. . .you think I cared if Povin blew them all up? Good riddance! Scum!' His voice, still calm, was steadily rising in pitch. 'Filthy, degenerate, bourgeois greasy *scum*! The whole of the KGB riddled with it, from top to bottom. What if Povin did cleanse a few of them? You think they were missed? You think they *mattered?*'

Kazin had grasped hold of Frolov's jacket and was casually tossing him from side to side like a piece of luggage.

'What was one petty traitor more or less to me, to Kazin? Michaelov . . .'

Kazin turned his head and for a second Frolov thought he was going to spit, but instead he laughed: a controlled, almost thoughtful chuckle, voicing unspeakable contempt. Frolov sat transfixed, incapable even of fear. All his senses had deserted him, closed down until the storm passed and it was once again safe to emerge from hiding.

Kazin gave Frolov a final shake and turned away, muttering to himself. Frolov shot a look at Krubykov, who stood impassively by the side of the desk, and wondered how many of these incomprehensible rages the Major had witnessed in his time. Was he ever scared, Frolov wondered? Or did he know himself to be so invaluable to this old, mad wizard that he was immune to fear?

Kazin had resumed his seat behind the desk and was once more speaking normally.

'Things were not as easy as you appear to think. I was under a cloud then, you know. Not for the first time. Stanov fooled them all with that report of his. He'd found his traitor; that was the end of it. He was on the up and up, towards the end. Things are different now. Stanov's gone, finished. The climate's changed. . .'

He tailed off. Frolov saw that his mood was altering. His face, which had become blotchy during the recent tirade, was its old pink self. The storm had blown over, leaving the world a fresher place.

'Anyway, you had one thing right, Boris Andreyevich. I wasn't about to trust Michaelov with hard evidence. Clever of you to spot that. Oh yes, the girl talked, told us all about your conversation with her . . .'

The memory of it seemed to please him. There was a long pause while he savoured it.

'But now we must think of you. You will be my messenger tomorrow. We must build you up, give you some credentials.'

Kazin smiled. He had retrieved his cane holder from the floor and was busy fitting a new cigarette into it.

'Something that is not yet in the file. We shall conspire together a little, you and I. There is a piece of additional evidence you can give them, all by yourself. Something I have kept specially for this moment.'

Frolov licked his lips, fear giving way once more to greed. 'Povin intends to go out with a bang. Tomorrow he will leave for the West. Or so he thinks. He has negotiated a bargain with the Americans and betrayed a vital part of the coming shake-up to the British. I could overlook much from Povin: when he was around, Stanov never kept very far out of the shit, and that suited me fine. But when he is so foolish as to meddle with my own affairs. . .no. So tell them tomorrow that Povin told SIS about the plane. Just that. It'll mean something to them, don't worry about *that*.'

'Yes. But. . .'

Kazin's lips twitched. 'But what?'

'It's just that. . . I'm asked to take so much on trust.'

'Remember what I said earlier. Money on the table. In this game there is no credit given by the bank.'

But this time Frolov's innate sense of self-preservation was too strong.

'This thing about the plane,' he said urgently. 'When they ask me for proof, what am I to say?'

Kazin and Krubykov exchanged glances, and smiled.

'There is some proof,' Kazin observed. He lifted the receiver of the white phone which stood at a corner of his desk and spoke into it. 'Bring him in.'

The minutes passed. Kazin continued to sit at his desk, head turned slightly to one side, blue columns of smoke rising at his elbow. Krubykov gazed ahead of him, his face bare of expression.

The door behind Frolov's chair was flung open, making him jump, and he turned to see two men half drag, half carry a heavy weight into the room. He stood up. Something about the burden was disturbingly recognisable.

'On the floor.'

At Krubykov's command the two men dropped whatever it was they were carrying, and Frolov, in spite of himself, moved closer.

It was a man. Blood soaked his face and torn clothes but the figure on the floor was undoubtedly human. Frolov knew the face. Only days ago he had spent long hours studying photographs of it. Winner of the Lenin Prize, Hero of Soviet Labour, Pyotr Stolyinovich. . .

'Povin trusted him completely, with everything down to the last details. He told us a great deal.'

Kazin's voice seemed to reach Frolov as from a great distance, muffled.

'Show him the hands.'

One of the two guards lifted Stolyinovich's right hand, and through the same muffled distance Frolov heard a voice cry out. His own.

The fingertips had been smashed into red pulp. Frolov could see little splinters of bone mixed in with the scarlet of blood. For a second his brain refused to analyse the significance of what he saw. Then he looked up to see Kazin's face behind the desk, and he spoke. 'You. . .have. . .destroyed. . .yes, *destroyed*, one of the greatest artists the world has ever seen. . .'

Frolov tailed off. From the look on Kazin's face it was apparent that he considered Frolov's statement entirely fair and reasonable. Frolov's eyes strayed again to the mess on the floor. As he did so Stolyinovich moaned, retched, and vomited blood on to Kazin's white rug. The thin trickle of red came to rest close by Kazin's foot.

'Russians need broad backs. And a strong master.'

Strong master, *krepki khozyain*. Frolov had not heard the phrase for years, perhaps not since 1953, and the death of the man for whose name the phrase had been a synonym, the one whose portrait hung in the hall downstairs.

'But, the world! What will they say. . .?'

Frolov was aghast. He understood now. There was to be no going back. This was the 'commitment' which underlay Kazin's power, the determination that no one was above the call to sacrifice. Not even poor, queer Stolyinovich, the pianist.

'The world,' said Kazin comfortably, 'will shortly have other things to worry about. Take him away.'

The guards came forward and lifted Stolyinovich from the floor. As the door closed behind them Frolov turned to Kazin and was about to speak when the telephone rang, which was convenient, for otherwise Frolov might have had cause to regret the words which welled up inside him.

'Hello, yes. . . Kronkin! What in the name of. . .'

Kazin fell silent. While Frolov watched his face underwent a subtle change. Cruelty and malice were replaced by craft and intelligence. Evil by itself was nothing, he realised. It requires direction, and direction itself comes only from ability. At a sign from Kazin, Krubykov bent low to catch the voice at the other end of the line. His face too hardened in concentration. Frolov was growing more and more curious, his earlier anger forgotten. He recognised the atmosphere. A wheel was coming off.

'Stay where you are. I'll do what I can but it won't be easy. Send Mironov to talk to Grigorenko's Chief of Staff, maybe he can swing something for us. Promise him anything, anything at all, you understand? Good. I'll ring you back. Oh, and Kronkin. . .there is something from our end you had better know. . .Victor slipped through tonight's net. He's on the loose, we don't know where, but it's occurred to us that he might be with you. If you see him, don't hesitate: obliterate him forthwith. Understand?'

Kazin replaced the receiver and turned to Frolov. 'Have you see Victor lately?'

'Victor?'

'Don't play the buffoon at a time like this, Frolov. You knew the Povin set as well as anyone. Victor, Victor, Povin's bodyguard, thug, call him what you like. The one who always attended to sensitive "wet" affairs.'

'No, I. . . No. I haven't seen him in a long while.'

Kazin subjected him to a long, distrustful look.

'I hope that's right,' Kazin said slowly. 'For your sake, Frolov, I really do.'

All through this colloquy Krubykov had been making illdisguised gestures of impatience. 'Can we change the rendezvous?' he said urgently.

For a long moment Kazin continued to stare at Frolov; then he turned away, and Frolov felt himself go limp like a puppet whose master has released the strings. 'No. It's far too late. Everyone is in place. Once we are committed there is nothing anyone can do, and we're committed up to the hilt.'

Frolov was obviously forgotten. The two men spoke as if he did not exist.

'But if those Americans have missiles. . .'

'If, if, if! There's less than eight hours to go. Nothing can change. We must just hope that Kronkin manages to organise a proper search.'

'And if not?'

Kazin was silent. And Frolov remembered, too late, that he had already put his money down on the table.

The GRU Captain's face hardened as he saw the three figures materialise at the top of the steps. He consulted his clipboard. This was the last plane-load of troops due in from Irkutsk. Everyone was accounted for. Nothing in the manifest said anything about extra passengers.

As the three men descended to the concrete apron he motioned to a rifleman, who ran forward. The Captain drew his pistol. Orders were explicit. Maximum security procedures were to be observed at all times.

The officer knew a killer when he saw one. The first of the three men now coming towards him across the apron was an unpleasant piece of work. Those scars on the neck, now, where had they come from?

'Halt!'

The leader moved to put his hand inside his coat and the Captain's pistol jerked. 'Keep your hands where I can see them. Stand over there by the. . .'

Suddenly the Captain and his rifleman were looking at a little red-covered pass bearing the State seal; their eyes began to distinguish the letters of the signature beside it; the Captain got as far as Y-u-r-i A-n-d. . .'

The graceful, self-contained gesture with which the Captain

holstered his gun, snapped to attention and saluted confirmed what Victor had surmised ever since he reached the top of the steps and looked down at him, namely, that here was an officer of the Red Army who would one day go far.

Binderhaven lay on his stomach and swept the landscape with his night glasses for the umpteenth time. Every detail of the luridly lit scene below was already impressed on his memory but tomorrow there was no second chance. He had to be sure.

He was positioned approximately three quarters of a mile from the single runway, in the middle. By crawling to the very edge of the nearest patch of taiga he could look down a gentle slope to the perimeter fence, beyond which stood the control tower and a few single storey buildings. He recognised it from his study of the aerial photographs. TDM-13.

Target.

The day had gone well. They were closer to the base than they had realised when they first set out, and their route had taken them almost entirely through thick forest, with only one short detour to avoid a village. They had seen troops on several occasions, but always moving away from them, or behind them. By late afternoon they were only a mile from target, but then it had been necessary to work round the boundary to the opposite side, always hugging the protective mantle of trees, where it seemed quieter, and further away from the main buildings where the troops would be housed. Even after darkness fell it was not difficult to keep going in the right direction. The base hummed with activity, an immovable point of reference.

The scene below Binderhaven was brightly lit with powerful arc lamps placed at regular intervals round the perimeter fence. At five-minute intervals guard patrols passed to and fro, many of them with strings of dogs. On the base itself there was a lot of movement, mostly in GAZ field cars but with some heavy transport also.

Air traffic had been light at first but in the past hour, since Binderhaven took up station, it had greatly increased: helicopters, troop carriers, MiG fighters. Planes landed in droves;

few of them took off again. To Binderhaven the message was plain: the Russians were stuffing their base to capacity with troops. Next day, at first light, the search would resume with even greater intensity. He wondered what had become of the others. Were they already in place on the other side of the airfield? Had they been captured? Did the Soviets know their plans? He shook his head angrily — no point in speculating.

Binderhaven began to edge backwards on his knees and elbows, the smell of kerosene and the constant whine of turbo-engines pursuing him into the forest. If the Russians stuck to their timetable, so that the AWACS flew in at dawn, it might be possible to make the shot. But he would have to stand on the very edge of the treeline in order to preserve a clean line of sight, and remain there for at least ten seconds. If a marksman happened to be looking in his direction. . .

Binderhaven, now deep in the shelter of the forest, stood up and dusted the snow off himself. He didn't think the Russians would send men out into the taiga during the night, especially since the sky had been heavy with snow since midday, but he'd have to post a sentry just in case.

Although there was no moon and it was very dark in the forest, Binderhaven found his way back to the others without difficulty. His sense of direction was unimpaired. When he was still a few feet away from their hiding place he called out quietly, to let them know it was a friend, and Anna answered.

His face softened. Throughout the gruelling day she had kept up with the two men without complaining. He wished he had met this girl before, in other circumstances. How could he tell her that, with the troop build-up he had witnessed over the past hour, their slim chance of escape had wasted away to nil? Better to say nothing.

The other two were waiting for him in what remained of a trappers' hut. During their journey across the steppe they had found many such. This one had obviously been abandoned long ago, and Binderhaven guessed the building of the air base would have had something to do with that. But it was still used: some empty tins, not yet rusting, lay between two broken floorboards, and a half-burned sheet of newspaper sticking out of the stove was still legible, notwithstanding the cold and wet.

Perhaps the troops who in normal times manned the air base liked to use the cabin for a weekend's hunting. Although they could not make a fire, it was several degrees warmer inside the wooden hut. Anna and McDonnell lay in their sleeping bags, conserving energy. Binderhaven went to kneel beside them.

'One of us'll stay down by the treeline,' he said quietly. 'That's the direction they'll come from, if they do. Two hours on, two off. We've got to try and catch a little sleep if we can.'

'I'll go,' said McDonnell. 'You got the glasses?'

As he handed them over Binderhaven gave crisp instructions. 'Familiarise yourself with the lay-out. When I move up to the firing point tomorrow I want you near me but back a way. If a sniper gets me you'll have to be ready to take over.'

'Check.'

'On your way, fellah.'

As Binderhaven turned away he felt a hand descend on his own, and the girl spoke.

'Have you. . .eaten?'

He grinned at the pause. 'Yes, it's funny, isn't it? Those damn pills, more like medicine than food.'

'I can't get used to it. But you know what I mean.'

Beneath the low roof of the hut it was so dark that he could not see her face, although they were touching each other. Her voice was firm, and more than firm; for some reason he couldn't explain the word 'peaceful' came into Binderhaven's mind. But that was silly.

'I'm chewing glucose. Want some?'

She accepted the thin tablet from him and a second later he heard her crunch it.

'Suck it. Make it last.'

Still leaving her hand over his she pulled him down to the ground.

'We laid out the sleeping bags, Nat and I. They are wonderful. I have never seen anything that resembles them.'

'Light but warm. And the bottom's sealed with waterproof material so that you can even sleep in the open if you have to.'

He slipped inside his and zipped it up to the chin. They were still very close. Through the layers of wadding he could feel the

275

hardness of her body all along his own.

'In Russia we have nothing like that.'

'You don't live in a technological society. You have other things.'

She snuggled a little closer to him and he heard a low, bitter laugh.

'Such as?'

'Beauty. Tradition. A fabulous history.'

'But you are joking?'

'No. America's a young country. I don't approve of how your government manages your affairs, but I couldn't be a Russian and yet not feel pride in my country.'

The silence went on for a long time while she wrestled with his thoughts.

'I think you are right about the country. It is only the men who rule her that I despise. How strange that it should need an American to show me that. What drives you to say such things, Kirk? What has brought you to this place?'

He took time to consider her question.

'I saw the fight that had to be fought,' he said at last. 'Even though no one else seemed to. I studied Communism in all its manifestations in the world today, and saw only evil. I asked myself, why are they building those missiles, those tanks, far above any capacity needed for mere defence? And I received no answer. At that point it became simpler. But the world is full of people — I'm talking about *our* people now — who spend their time trying to make it sound complicated.'

'And Nat? The others?'

Binderhaven smiled and shrugged.

'I never asked. Oh, I guessed. Joe Faber and I met up in Africa, doing some pretty wild things for a pretty weird bunch of people. He used to be in the Army, but nowadays even that's starting to get complicated. Nat — he left the Army about the same time I quit the CIA, and for pretty much the same reasons. He wanted a crack at the real thing before it got too late. Frank Mannheim's the same — only he wants to go back.'

'Back — to America, you mean?'

'To the CIA. He's found it's lonelier in the big wide world than he thought. That's why I let him in on this. If we can pull it off, they'll have to take him back. Out of sheer gratitude.'

A corpse, he was thinking. They'll take back a dead body. . .

But Anna was still puzzled. 'How have you lived, all of you? What do you do when you're not lying in a Russian hut, with me?'

He laughed. 'It's kind of hard to remember,' he said, and was silent. Her body wriggled against his and he became aware of desire, dull but insistent.

'We all have skills that can be hired, often very expensively. We guard things. We protect people. Sometimes we destroy things, and people too. All that unites the four of us is that we're picky about who signs the pay checks. We like to examine a proposal all ways before we buy it.'

He had been lying on his back, looking up at the ceiling. Now he turned his head, so that he was facing her.

'That's why I feel so sorry about this, Anna. For you, I mean. You never had a chance to decide.'

'But I did! Listen, Kirk, there is something I want to tell you.'

'Oh, Anna, I. . .'

'No! It is not what you think. I must tell you how all today I have been wanting to ask you, what will happen tomorrow? And I have not, because I know there is no answer to my question, so why trouble you with foolishness when you have so many other things to worry you. But. . .this is what I want to tell you. . . It — tomorrow — doesn't matter. Do you understand that, Kirk?'

He wanted to comfort her but was forced to shake his head. 'No.'

'Oh, how can I explain it! Listen. You remember the woman I told you about, the woman on the train?'

'Yes.'

'And my cousin, the one who went to America.'

'I remember.'

'The woman told me so many things. It was all so glib and slick. But then I began to think about it. Believe me, Kirk. . . I really thought. Until at last I saw how she had tricked me.'

Binderhaven thought she had made a rare mistake in her normally faultless English. 'You mean, how the Soviets tricked you?'

'No. The woman.' She laughed softly. 'What a fool they must have thought me. It was hard at first, very hard. But deep inside me something had always known that when Aleksei, my cousin, went to America, he would forget me. He never did write, you see, not after a first letter just to say they'd arrived.' She paused. 'Actually, it was not a letter. A card only.'

'Oh, my dear, my dear. . .'

'No, listen. Please listen. You see, I lied to you just as I lied to the woman on the train. Out of pride, I suppose. It mattered, then. Not now. But the important thing is that, once I'd seen through the trick, once I'd learned to accept the truth — I was glad.'

'*Glad?*'

'Oh, yes. Because, you see, although they — the Russians, the Americans — had taken my Aleksei away from me, between them they'd given me something else. Something to fill the emptiness inside me. A legend. A story that I could go on believing for ever, until I died. A loyalty. A *cause*. The freedom which Aleksei had but which was always going to be denied to me. I wanted my cousin to have that, even though there was nothing else I could give him. The gift of myself. Of my understanding. My. . .assent.'

She chuckled softly.

'And so you see, whatever happens tomorrow, it does not matter. I chose it, therefore it is right. Now do you understand?'

'Yes. A little. But I wish I could have your peace of mind.'

'It is not so hard once you have decided that you will never be taken alive.'

'That's a foolish thing to say.' Binderhaven meant to go on and explain why, but the words weren't there.

'For you, perhaps. For the American imperialists, for the spies, there is always the exchange, the deal. They keep them out of the papers, but we know about such things. You'll make out. But for me, for the Soviet citizen willingly lending assistance. . . No. Face the truth, Kirk. I must not be caught. If there is any danger of it, you and Nat must. . .must. . .'

'Oh, Anna. . .'

The temperature had fallen way below freezing. The silence

and the darkness were total, so that Kirk Binderhaven could not quite convince himself that he was still in the world. When her lips descended on his it was as though a ring of scalding fire touched his skin, making it smart against the bitter winter cold all around him. The kiss lasted a long time. It went through many phases. At first it was soft, tender, exploratory, like gentle sparring between two strangers. Then his tongue touched hers for the first time and their mood changed. The dull desire flared up into a demanding need. Their hands began to dare the freezing gap between the two sleeping bags, revelling in the rich warmth of the other's body after the brief intervening shock of cold. By contrast with the snow and ice of the forest, their bodies exuded fire, and they began to be hungry for the flame: their hands pressed, stroked, caressed with growing urgency. They had one night left. The last night.

For what might have been five minutes or fifty they lay in each other's arms, marvelling at something they would never know again; then reluctantly they parted, afraid lest McDonnell should come back through the forest silently and find them there, together.

They lay quietly in their sleeping bags, eyes open, scarcely touching, talking not at all. Every time words came into Binderhaven's brain he discarded them, because they had nothing significant to say about what had just occurred. And between them there was no sadness.

It was not until McDonnell had returned, and Binderhaven was once more lying on his stomach in the snow overlooking Base TDM-13, that he remembered he had not asked Anna about Aleksei, the cousin, and Boychenko: their relationships, what those men meant to her. Binderhaven had wanted to ask all these things, but now it was for ever too late. And he was glad.

31

'Will you shut that fucking thing *off?*'

Little Adolf had to scream to make himself heard by the helicopter pilot, who took no notice anyway.

'I said. . .'

Mironov plucked his arm. 'It's no *good*,' he shouted. 'They have to keep it going or it'll freeze up. He could not start the rotors again. That's why he's leaving us here.'

He's *what!*'

'Leaving us. To *refuel*. If he keeps the engine going much longer he'll run out of gas, and then. . .'

Kronkin raised his clenched fists to heaven and swore comprehensively. Nobody could hear him over the appalling din of the engines. Mironov tugged at his greatcoat. 'Better get on with it.'

Down on the steppe a company of troops drawn from the 61st Motor Rifle Brigade was lined up in the snow. It was pitch dark except for the feeble light cast by the officer's torches. In the beam of one of these Kronkin tried to study the map.

'How far do you say we are from where the pilot saw the tracks?'

'About a quarter of a mile. We didn't want to land too close and alarm them if they're still in that patch of taiga.'

'Alarm them!' Kronkin looked meaningfully at the helicopter behind him, then turned back to the Colonel in charge with a snarl. 'Frighten them to death, more like.'

The helicopter pilot chose that moment to take off, showering Kronkin with powdery snow. It was a long time since either of the Lieutenant-Generals had been in the field, and Siberia was a completely new experience for both of them. Kronkin quivered in the slipstream and fought to keep hold of the map. 'This place is too close to TDM-13. Damn and blast...' Mironov took him aside. It was easier to talk now that the Mi-6 had gone. 'What did he say in Moscow?' Kronkin shook his head. 'He'll do what he can. But it's too late to change anything. I knew that'd be the way. The scientists have already arrived, the Army's ready to roll, everything's set for tomorrow morning. We *have* to find these fucking Americans.'

'But surely we could divert the plane somewhere else?'

'Kazin says not.'

'Then to hell with Kazin, that's what I say!'

'Well, please don't say it too loud when I'm around. You want to get us all shot?'

Kronkin cast an uneasy glance in the direction of the Colonel, who stood where they had left him, patiently awaiting his orders. Mironov started to speak, changed his mind, and shut his mouth with an audible snap.

'All right, Colonel.' Kronkin waded his way back to the company commander, arms flailing as he fought to keep his balance on the uncomfortable snowshoes they had given him in Irkutsk. 'Do you reckon the other units will be in place by now?'

'Oh yes, comrade General. We're in touch by radio. This taiga's effectively surrounded.'

'Then let's move!'

The Colonel made a sign to his radio operator, who nodded and spoke anxiously into the microphone of his chest set. The company formed up in three lines and after a brief interval began to move across the frozen steppe.

Little Adolf and Fat Hermann travelled with the O Group, which brought up the rear. Before very long both men were struggling, and swearing like good troopers. After a while the company commander was moved to intervene. Keeping the career soldier's contempt for the GRU well under control he said, 'If you saved your breath for walking, comrades, you'd feel better.'

The two Lieutenant-Generals took his advice, at least for a

while. But when they reached the treeline, and suddenly there were concealed roots, and bushes, to deal with, they soon fell back into their old ways. After a few moments the Colonel was forced to halt O Group and talk to them with quiet urgency.

'We must have silence, comrades. Or we lose the advantage of surprise. Perhaps you would like to remain on the treeline?'

Kronkin glared at him. Stumbling through treacherous forest was bad enough; the prospect of being left alone, in the darkness, with American spies somewhere close by, was genuinely frightful.

'We'll go on,' he snarled. 'Quietly.'

Progress was very slow. The troops were highly trained in search and destroy tactics, but the exercise of those skills requires peace and patience. They were using hand-held night 'scopes with phosphor screens, which conferred an overall light gain of 40,000-x and frequent halts were necessary for their efficient use. After about a mile of slow plodding Kronkin and Mironov felt that they would never be warm again.

It was during a brief rest-halt that the message was passed back through the lines: the 'scopes had detected something.

'About two hundred metres to the left,' said the Colonel thoughtfully.

'What is it?' asked Mironov.

The Colonel hesitated. 'It could be an animal. Something large, a wolf maybe.'

Kronkin shuffled his greatcoat a little more thoroughly over his shoulders and looked around him. The forest, he noticed, was unpleasantly quiet.

'Or it could be a man.'

'So what do we do?'

'Nothing, for the moment. I'm going to back off with my radio operator and make contact with the other units, well out of ear-shot. I don't propose to investigate further until at least one other unit is ready to converge on that location.'

Kronkin opened his mouth to speak but the company commander had already disappeared into the surrounding darkness. Kronkin and Mironov instinctively moved closer together. For several minutes, neither spoke.

'Wolves,' said Kronkin suddenly. 'I hear they don't attack

unless they're provoked. Did you hear that?'

'No.'

'Shit. Have you got any more of that chocolate?'

'One piece. For tomorrow morning, remember.'

Kronkin was about to argue when the company commander materialised out of the gloom as silently as he had gone. 'Another unit is in range. They have established an infra-red source in the approximate position I indicated to them. Their image is clearer than ours. They report a single figure, standing. I suspect he was alerted by the sound of our helicopter.'

Kronkin was fired by excitement. 'So we go on. . .'

'A moment, comrades. Please. You remember what happened last time. An explosion. . .'

'Well?' Kronkin was impatient.

'Do you want to withdraw?'

'No,' interjected Mironov roughly; then, turning to Kronkin he shrugged and said, 'If we can't catch those bastards. . .'

He left the sentence unfinished but his meaning was obvious. Faced with the choice between a quick death, and the labour camp that was the price of failure, he was still enough of a soldier to prefer the former. Kronkin nodded. 'I agree. But, Colonel, I want to examine this man. And anything he's carrying. You understand? I want him taken *alive*.'

Kronkin peered through the darkness, striving to penetrate the gloomy forest. He found it hard to believe that a whole company of soldiers, and more, was lost in the trees somewhere up ahead. Everything depended on the next few minutes. Surely the American would realise he was surrounded: a twig must snap under a boot, a branch shed its load of snow, a hundred-and-one tell-tale signs must give them all away. And then? What would the American do? Did he have another missile? Would it explode?

Kronkin dashed these uncomfortable thoughts from his mind. Let them just get through the next few minutes.

The Colonel was re-grouping his men into assault positions. It took a long time, since orders had to be passed in a whisper and the troops were spread out over a considerable area of forest. To Kronkin and Mironov, their feet growing colder by the minute, it seemed to take for ever. But not quite for ever. At

last there came a moment when the Colonel dispatched a final
runner with the simple, monosyllabic order: Go.

Kronkin found himself unwittingly counting the seconds.
The tension was appalling. Somewhere in the lower part of his
stomach the nerves were remorselessly mashing away at the
shit in his guts, turning it to fiery fluid. With a start he realised
that he had almost stopped breathing. He opened his mouth to
draw in a deep gulp of cold air when from in front of him there
seemed to come a confused shout, followed by many voices
raised in the yell of attack. Then he heard shots, two quick
bursts of fire from the company's Kalashnikov RPK, and he
shut his eyes tight in anticipation of the blast.

There was no blast. About a hundred metres ahead lights
suddenly flickered into life, and Kronkin opened his eyes
again. Several officers in O Group switched on their own
torches; the beams lanced out to enmesh and grapple with
those of the assault force approaching down the track.

A Senior Lieutenant came on to report to the company
commander. Kronkin listened avidly. The American had made
a dive for the case beside him; the machine-gunner, mindful of
the case's likely contents, cut him down. Kronkin elbowed the
Colonel aside and pounced on the Lieutenant.

'And the case?'

For answer the young man merely turned round and pointed
to the ground, where two soldiers were gingerly laying a rectangular black object on its side. Kronkin grabbed the nearest
torch and directed the beam downwards.

'Stand back!'

He was surrounded by a ring of curious troops, many of
them breathing heavily from their recent exertion. He made
them give ground until he was at the centre of a human circle
some ten metres in diameter. Only then did he kneel down to
inspect the case. He did not touch it, but the beam of his
borrowed torch darted into every nook and cranny of the by
now heavily scored leather. The inspection was very thorough.
When at last he stood up his face was grim.

'We'll have to leave that here, Colonel. I want a guard
mounted. No one to come closer than they are now, not on any
pretext whatsoever. It stays put until the bomb disposal squad

get here. It's certainly booby-trapped. If what's inside goes up, it'll take most of this forest with it.'

Kronkin shone his torch rapidly round the ring of faces to see if they understood. They did. The apprehension was almost tangible.

'Where is the man you found?'

Someone led him over to where a human shape lay on the ground. A cursory flash of the torch was enough to satisfy Kronkin that the American was indeed dead, most of his face having been blown off. He swore with disappointment, and then was glad to divert his torch beam away from the mess. He had seen nothing as unpleasant as that since the defence of Moscow more than forty years before.

'We're going back to Irkutsk. As for you, Colonel, now you're out here you might as well press on. There's still two more of them to track down, and they'll have a case like that one. Every bit as lethal. You understand?'

'I understand, comrade General. We'll radio for a chopper and then be on our way. But. . .'

'But?'

'These men are tough, sir. But they've already had a long night. Just how much more of this is there?'

Kronkin chuckled. 'Keep them going until 0700 tomorrow, Colonel. If you haven't found anything by then, it doesn't matter any longer.'

He linked his arm through Fat Hermann's, and Mironov grinned.

'That's right,' he confirmed. 'After that, it really doesn't matter at all.'

32

Kruger had been living in a kind of limbo since his arrival in the USSR. He spent his time playing chess with Control, or taking long walks in the frozen tracts of forest which surrounded the dacha. They fed him well, he had no other wants, and yet he was scared out of his wits.

The landing had unnerved him.

He knew that some time soon he was going to have to return to that mad strip of ice, they would dig out the huge AWACS and de-ice her, and say to him: All right, she's yours, fly her. And then. . .

He was dreading it. To call that flat lake of ice and impacted snow an airstrip was a joke in poor taste. There was no proper ancillary equipment for miles: no fire tenders, no snow-ploughs, no warning flares. The thought of a night take-off made Kruger sick to his stomach.

Control smoked his pipe contentedly and watched the American from under his shaggy eyebrows. Every so often he would say something to reassure him, such as, 'It will be all right, Mitch', or, 'Trust me, you'll see,' but his words made no impression.

Until, that is, they stepped out of the helicopter in the clearing and the miracle was made plain.

Straight in front of him stood one of the most extraordinary things he had ever seen: a helicopter on stilts. Kruger stared at it uncomprehendingly.

'The Mi-10 Harke,' Control murmured in his ear, knocking the dottle from his pipe. 'Helicopter crane. With those tall legs of his he can straddle a load as big as a house. Come, I'll show you. . .'

He led Kruger underneath the mighty helicopter and on the other side the American found that the scene had been transformed. Arc lights lit up the clearing, runway flares stretched away into the distance, a snowplough was racing up the strip towards them. Everywhere was bustle and activity. It would be no worse than, say, a night take-off from Buffalo in the middle of December.

'Incredible!' breathed Kruger, and Control laughed.

'I told you to trust me,' he said.

Kruger turned reproachful eyes to him. 'You might have told me.'

'But you had no need to know. How many times have I told you about that, eh? The famous "need to know".'

'But I've been worried out of my mind. . .'

Control clapped him on the back. 'I know you have. And I felt for you. But see how much we trust you, Mitch. We knew that for all your worrying you'd be all right. Even without this. . .'

He waved his hand, allowing it to come to rest in the direction of the AWACS itself, recently dug out of its snow overcoat and now in the process of being de-iced. Kruger counted a dozen men under the lights. Nothing was being spared.

'Your boys work fast.'

'Everything you see arrived here after five o'clock last evening. When it was dark. It's a long shot, but we didn't want to give the Americans the chance of picking any of this up on a satellite. You think this looks busy? Three-quarters of the men and most of the equipment have already dispersed. That's the last Mi-10 over there. The rest have gone.'

The two men walked slowly over to the AWACS. Kruger inspected the nose wheel for damage and found none.

'Don't worry, they've fixed all that. Let's go up. It's time we started the pre-flight checks.'

'We?'

'Sure. I never told you, but I'm a qualified Boeing pilot.'

The cabin was empty. So was the cockpit. Orders had been given that no one was to set foot inside the Boeing until after it landed near Irkutsk. Everything was just as Kruger had left it three days before, except that the bodies had been removed. He took his seat and tested the headset. Immediately it crackled into life, but the voice at the other end was Russian. Control took the head-set from Kruger and briefly requested permission to start up.

The pre-flight checks were soon completed. All four engines fired smoothly and quickly settled down to their usual roar. As Kruger taxied the short distance to the end of the runway he threw all his concentration into establishing the 'feel' of the plane. Everything seemed fine. The heavy aircraft held the icy ground perfectly, with no sign of skid.

The runway, this time brightly lit, stretched away into infinity. Kruger reached up to extinguish the cabin lights and let his eyes grow accustomed to the soft violet glow of the instrument panel. Control was talking to the men on the ground. Kruger trimmed the engines a fraction and put his feet on the brakes, ready for the run-up.

'You see?' Control pointed through the windscreen. 'There really was a surface under all that ice. Concrete. The real thing.'

Kruger grunted. Instead of being reassured he felt unsettled. Why couldn't they have taken this trouble when he landed?

'OK, Mitch. We go now.'

Kruger eased the throttles up to full power, did some last fine tuning to the engine pressure ratios, and took his feet off the brakes. The runway began to fall away beneath the windscreen. Seventy. . .eighty. . .ninety. . .

'V-one.'

And now the runway lights were ending. They had fooled him, after all. Kruger's jaw dropped, his heart seemed to pound in his chest, his eyes grew round with terror. They had duped him. *It was a con!*

'Rotate.'

Control's calm voice cut through the haze of panic which threatened to rise up and engulf him; mechanically he pulled back the stick, obeying the promptings of deep-seated instinct; the sky turned black, he felt the sudden spring as the weight came off the wheels, and they were up.

As soon as he had levelled off Kruger took his hands from

the stick and wiped his forehead. He felt as if he was going to throw up.

'Hands on the controls, please, Mitch. There will be no automatic pilot on this flight.'

Grudgingly he did as he was told. Out of the corner of one eye he could see Control ripping open a large cardboard envelope.

'Here are our orders, Mitch. We are to fly to an air base near Irkutsk, known as TDM-13. And Mitch. . .'

When he did not continue Kruger turned his head, expecting to be given the detailed bearing. To his surprise he saw that Control was staring at the papers in his lap. The expression on his face was hard to read, but Kruger thought he detected perturbation, and surprise.

'Yes?'

At the sound of his voice, Control turned to face him directly. Now his face bore only its usual gentle smile.

'As we make the approach, be ready to abort the landing.'

Kruger's hands tightened on the controls. 'What the fuck . . .?'

'There may be a little difficulty. At the last moment. That's all.'

33

Two and a half thousand miles and five time zones away, Povin stood before the high plate glass windows of the VIP lounge in Vnukovo II airport, sipping champagne. It was not a drink he much cared for but the occasion was special and he also felt, in a vague sort of way, that he needed to prepare himself a little for 'The West' in advance. Veuve Clicquot was a trifle sweet for his taste, he concluded; probably he would stick to scotch in his new home.

From the placid expression on his face none of his fellow passengers could have guessed at his melancholy thoughts. He was a Russian to his fingertips, to his soul. Scratch a Russian deep enough and he had a soul; they all did. Povin always understood very clearly that the dissidents' dread of exile outweighed their fear of the camps. Why, then, was he doing this? What foolishness prompted him to give up everything he loved, all that moved him, made him weep?

He continued to regard the scene below him with an expression of polite boredom on his face, occasionally taking a sip of champagne. At this late hour the only aircraft on the apron was the Ilyushin-62 which was going to fly him and thirty other distinguished passengers to Tbilisi. Povin could see some of those other favoured passengers reflected in the glass. At a rough guess he doubted whether the entire lounge held a single item of clothing that had been manufactured in the Soviet Union. Even the stewardesses' outfits were made in Paris.

With a guilty start he realised that he was going to miss this. In America you queued up with the rest of them and took your chance of a place. There was no Chaika to run you to the airport in warm, overfed comfort; no KGB guard waving you through the security check with an obsequious smile; no dispensation from customs by genial Major Avdeyev. Where he was going there were no privileges, no free lunches.

There was one thing, and one thing only, which Russia lacked, and it had to be worth all the rest.

Peace.

Down on the tarmac they had finished refuelling. A minibus slowly approached the foot of the aircraft's steps and the crew got out, the girls automatically putting their hands to their ridiculous little hats to prevent them blowing off in the wind. As they climbed the steps a young man steadied one of the stewardesses and Povin felt a pang the nature of which he didn't care to investigate. He turned away and placed his half empty glass on a table. Suddenly he wanted to go.

As if in response to his unspoken wish a bell rang and Aeroflot announced the departure of its flight No. 674 to

Tbilisi and Baku. At once there was a general scramble for luggage. Povin carried only a small grip, which he could put under his seat. Everything else he had left behind. The *dacha* was just as it always was, clean and tidy as if to await his return. The Moscow apartment had been shut up for a few days, 'while I am away', he told the surly *dezhurnaya* in the caretaker's flat. He found it surprisingly easy to give away all that he had.

As Povin reached the automatic glass doors which led from the lounge into the covered stairwell he felt a hand pluck his sleeve. He looked up and to his astonishment recognised Major Krubykov of the Kremlin Kommandant.

His eyes dilated, just for a second; but the Major saw.

'Good evening, General. I'm sorry about this but a matter has come up which requires your personal attention. It won't take a moment. I have already arranged for your flight to be held.'

He moved a step or two towards the half-open door of a nearby office, hand raised in a beckoning gesture, but Povin did not move. He could not.

It was beginning. He had always believed that he would know when it began. For an instant Povin bowed his head and closed his eyes, like a man hearing the name of Jesus spoken aloud in church. And Krubykov, who had beckoned to so many hapless individuals in his time, understood.

The first thing Povin saw on entering the office was a doll. He stared at it, shocked from awareness of his surroundings. The painted grin on the face of the toy was malignant with barely-suppressed satisfaction.

Mishka.

Very slowly Povin's stare shifted to the office's other occupant.

Colonel Frolov was sitting with his accustomed ease, legs crossed and propped up on the table. He did not rise. The General said nothing. Frolov folded his hands across his stomach, waited until Krubykov had closed the door, and smiled.

'I'm afraid you're not going anywhere, Stepan. Nowhere nice, anyway.'

For a moment Povin allowed his eyes to dwell on the bloated, self-satisfied face of his former deputy and in those instants he came close to feeling a kind of sympathy with Frolov; it was impossible to look on such a triumph and not take some share in it. Then his glance strayed to the clock on the office wall. Stolyinovich had been in Athens for six hours now. Not all the triumphs belonged to Frolov.

'These mistakes have happened before,' he said casually. 'They are always sorted out, in the end. I don't propose to give you the satisfaction of an argument, Frolov.' His lips twitched in a half smile. 'That can wait. For later.'

Frolov raised one eyebrow, his sole concession to a coolness he had not expected, and took his feet off the table. The effect of the champagne on Povin was wearing off. He suddenly felt sick, and swallowed hard. He must not vomit. He must not vomit.

They led him out by another stairwell. As they crossed the broad pavement he had ample time to look over his shoulder and see where, fifty metres away, the passengers with whom he had shared the VIP lounge were boarding a very different kind of vehicle. Fifty metres. A quick break, a dash and then. . . nothing. They would catch him, and chain him under the astonished eyes of the other passengers, some of whom would turn their children's faces away, and take him back to the van parked in the shadows. In the West he could have done it. In the West he could have mingled with the holidaymakers fifty metres away, knowing that the police would not shoot, he might even have found helpers, support, a friend. Not here. Here the country *was* the prison.

Povin had expressed that thought to himself many times over the years: the country was the prison. But tonight, for the first time, he saw with penetrating clarity the inevitable consequence. The *narod*, the ordinary people. . .they were the jailors.

As they threw open the door of the van and shone a light inside Povin became aware that he was not alone, but they pushed him in before he could catch a proper look at the face of his companion.

'Stepan.'

At the sound of that terrible voice, half whisper and half groan, Povin let out a gasp of pure anguish. It was a voice he knew.

'Stepan. . . I told them. I *told* them. . .'

A heavy form collapsed against him, sobbing uncontrollably, and Povin absently began to stroke Stolyinovich's hair, soothing him into silence, looking straight ahead, seeing nothing. Outside a guard swung one of the rear doors to. As he reached out for the other one, Povin heard for the first time in his new role the dreadful words which had haunted every day of his working life in the old.

'Prisoners! The convoy shoots without warning!'

The second door clanged shut, plunging the interior of the van into total darkness.

'Forward!'

Binderhaven lay on his stomach and watched the file of grey-clad men fan out across the steppe, rifles held diagonally across their chests.

It was barely light. He had been on watch for nearly two hours when he first caught a glimpse of something moving by the perimeter fence. A platoon of troops, marching through a gate in the wire. He raised his glasses. The steppe was still shrouded in semi-darkness and it had recently begun to snow again, a gentle shower of huge flakes which drifted across his field of vision, making surveillance difficult. But there they were, perhaps a kilometre away or less. Moving. Moving towards where he lay face down in the snow, to monitor their steady progress.

Binderhaven pushed with his elbows, using his hands to

brush a layer of snow over his tracks. As soon as he was well back from the treeline he leapt to his feet and began to run.

McDonnell and Anna were already up when he arrived back in the tiny clearing. McDonnell took one look at his face and said, 'What the. . .?'

'Russian troops. They're headed this way. Not many, not yet. A platoon, maybe. We've got to stay ahead of them, keep moving.'

While he spoke the other two hurried to pack up the few bits and pieces of essential equipment.

'Somehow we've got to divert them, play every damn trick in the book. Make sure your snowshoes are on back to front.'

Seconds later they were trudging through the forest.

Kruger was flying west, away from the dawn. The sky was a dark star-studded blue. So far the flight had been smooth and without incident, but in the last few minutes he had become increasingly puzzled by one of his instrument read-outs.

'Do we have a fighter escort?'

'No. We are far from any frontier. That would be a waste of fuel.'

'I'm picking up something I don't understand on my primary radar. We've got company. A shadow.'

'A shadow,' said Control quietly. 'You describe it better than you know, I think.'

He craned his head to look out of the starboard windscreen. 'From where you are sitting I do not think it will be possible to see anything, but there is just enough light on my side. I will take over the controls while you come and look out of the plane.'

Kruger unstrapped himself and moved over behind the co-pilot's seat, straining to see out. At first it seemed too dark for anything to be visible above the thick layer of grey cloud which carpeted their route; then his eyes began to accustom themselves to the twilight thrown by the first rays of the rising sun.

His eyes widened in astonishment and Control felt his hand tighten on top of his seat.

'Well I'll be damned,' said Kruger.

*

Captain Litvak carefully examined the marks in the snow, like a man preparing for a medal-winning putt. He walked up to them, round them, away from them, all the time keeping his head down and his knees bent.

'Could be a mink. Or a sable.'

The Captain liked to test his opinions aloud, to see how they sounded. His Sergeant said nothing, but Litvak knew what he was thinking: Fucking big mink, to do all that.

He raised his eyes and scanned the edge of the forest. Apart from the curious marks in the snow, everything seemed normal enough. He took a few steps into the undergrowth, and crouched down. Here something had disturbed the snow and the bushes too: several twigs had snapped off. Litvak stood upright and extended his sphere of observation. No, there was nothing there, nothing over there, either, and as for over there. . .

'A footprint,' he said. 'Sergeant, come and look at this.'

The NCO came to his side and looked down. Almost at once he spotted another bootprint which Litvak's first examination had missed.

'Looks as though he ran off into the forest, sir. Shall I get the men?'

'Yes. And, Sergeant. . .'

'Sir?'

Litvak did not answer immediately. He stood with his brow creased in thought, trying to establish in his own mind what the man in the forest had been up to. Why had he been in that particular spot in the first place? What had he seen to make him leave in such a hurry? Suppose he had been watching the perimeter, and had seen troops advancing towards him. . .

'Get some of the dogs, too. And see if you can lay your hands on a square of that material they brought up last night. You know, the scrap of clothing they took from the spy. I want to know if the dogs can make a connection.'

Without waiting for his men to catch him up Litvak proceeded into the forest. It was an easy trail to follow but still he advanced with the utmost caution. There were too many rumours in circulation, and not enough hard facts; plenty of talk of spies and mysterious explosions on the steppe but nothing detailed, nothing *concrete*. The men had caught the mood. They lacked assurance. By the time Litvak reached the clearing and its abandoned hut his platoon were spread out behind him. When Litvak stopped, they stopped too.

Here the marks were even more puzzling. Outside the hut it looked as though there had been a struggle of some kind, to judge from the irregular bumps and hollows which someone or something had formed in the snow. And those tracks, coming in from the north, what did they mean?

Litvak walked round and round the clearing. Suppose these people, whoever they were, had come down from the north, and then one of them had gone down to the treeline before returning and proceeding on south with the other two? But the tracks to the south were fainter than the rest, as if made yesterday. How could that be?

Litvak beckoned to his radio operator and ordered the man to make contact with batallion HQ at the air base.

'Captain Litvak reporting, Major. I'm in the taiga to the west of the runway, approximately halfway along it and a hundred metres beyond the treeline. We've found some tracks, leading north-south. I think it might be worthwhile for you to put some men into the forest at both ends of the runway. . . You have? Ah, well then. . . Yes, I'll keep a good look-out. I've ordered up the dogs. . . Out.'

Litvak removed the headset and handed it back to the radio operator with a shrug. A clever bastard, that Major Subotin. Trust him to have thought of everything first. If it was the two Americans and the girl, which Litvak, who had long ago ceased to believe in fairy stories, was inclined to doubt, then they were shortly going to encounter the best part of a company secreted amongst the trees. And good luck to them, thought Litvak, who liked to hunt in his spare time and had a hunter's instincts.

'What is that thing?'

Control smiled. 'It is a Tupolov Moss-126, the nearest thing we have had to an AWACS. Until now. Same shape, same radar signature. Three of them have been specially equipped with jet engines, to maximise the deception of United States spy satellites.'

'That's incredible,' breathed Kruger. Then a frown creased his forehead. 'But one thing I don't understand. Why here? If the idea is to deceive surveillance, why have one of those things sit on our tail?'

'It will land first. In case there is any problem on the ground, it will act as a decoy.'

'Problem? What kind of problem?'

'Sit down, Mitch. Take over flying the plane.'

'Now look. . .'

'Sit. . .down.'

Reluctantly Kruger did as he was told. Only when he was once again strapped into the pilot's seat did Control speak.

'You've trusted me for a long time now, Mitch. This isn't the time to start having doubts.'

'Simon. This isn't the time to start having *problems*.'

Control did not reply. For mile after mile the two planes flew on, almost wing to wing, until as they approached TDM-13 the decoy Tupolov pulled ahead of the AWACS and gradually sank below the thick clouds which still shrouded the aircraft from watchers on the ground. For the first time Kruger could remember, Control showed signs of being under strain. He held the headset in place with one hand, constantly tuning and retuning the radio as if willing Ground Control to speak. In the early morning sun his face looked white and sickly. When Kruger opened his mouth to speak Control snapped his fingers impatiently to silence him.

Suddenly his flickering eyes became still, and Kruger knew that at last they had made contact with the ground.

'The Tupolov is established,' hissed Control. 'He's entering the glidepath now.'

There followed another long silence. Kruger gripped the controls and stared out of the forward windscreen. What exactly were they worried about? Here they were in the middle of Russia, surrounded by friendly airspace on all sides. Why the apprehension? Why the delay?

'He's down!'

Control's face lit up, but seeing Kruger about to speak he raised his hand. Ground Control was still talking. Control listened, his lips slightly parted, face immobile. At last he slowly replaced the headset and stretched out his legs with a long, luxurious yawn.

'He's taxied in. No problems. Now it's your turn, Mitch. Ground Control will talk to you in English from now on. She's all yours.'

Kruger donned his own headset. Seconds passed. Then suddenly a voice was murmuring in his ear, 'Come in, Colonel Kruger, come in please. . .'

'Roger. Kruger here.'

'There is a cloud ceiling of nine hundred feet but the snow has now stopped and visibility at ground is fair. The runway is clear.'

'Roger.'

'Descend to two thousand and reduce to one-seven-oh knots. You are fifteen miles from touch-down.'

'Roger.'

They began to sink through the cloud layer. Kruger realised that he was going to need all his considerable skills as a pilot: strange air base, low cloud, visibility only fair. The stick was slippery with the sweat from his palms, his body was becoming stiff with tension.

'Colonel Kruger, you are established on the localizer and just twelve miles from touch-down.'

'Roger. Confirm establishment now, and am leaving two thousand on the glidepath.'

Snow flecked the windscreen. But for the heavy cloud tearing past the plane Kruger would scarcely have believed they were moving. He set the flaps and reduced throttle still further, until the AWACS seemed to hang, almost motionless, in the grey pall around it.

Then suddenly his eyes caught the first glimmer of the approach lights, and the sequence flashers directing him towards the runway centre-line. He heard Control say, 'Outer marker. . .middle marker. . .fifteen seconds. . .ten, nine, eight. . .'

'Flare-out.'

Kruger lifted the aircraft's nose and felt her settle gently, hover: a second before the main gear touched the runway he said, 'We're down.'

By McDonnell's watch it took Binderhaven four minutes and thirty-eight seconds to unpack the Stinger and assemble it ready to fire. As he stood up carrying the long, ungainly launcher a movement from the forest caught his eye.

'Get down!'

McDonnell seized Anna and pulled her to the ground next to him.

'What is it?'

'Something white moved in the trees behind you.'

'Troops in snow gear?'

'Could be.'

'Shit! What do we do now?'

Binderhaven thought for a moment. 'Down to the treeline. Across their line of advance. It's our only hope.'

Using every scrap of cover they could find the three of them crawled through the undergrowth. Anna's muscles soon gave out under the unnatural strain. She felt she could go no further, but then pride and stubbornness drove her on. Every movement was an agony to her. As she was about to lie down and tell them to leave her, Binderhaven stopped and cautiously raised his head. For a second, no more, he held his position before dropping down again and swivelling through 180 degrees to face the other two.

'We're ten feet from the open steppe,' he murmured. 'Soldiers are advancing through the trees from the north, but they're still a good way off and they're taking it real slow. Now what I. . .'

He broke off, his face suddenly galvanised with amazement. 'Listen!'

For several seconds the other two could hear nothing. Then McDonnell picked it up: the far-off drone of a powerful turbo-jet.

'That's it,' he breathed, his lips scarcely moving. 'The AWACS. My God, Kirk, we made it. We really made it!'

'Not yet we didn't.'

In the ensuing silence the sound of the advancing plane grew rapidly louder. The pilot was coming in fast and low. Binderhaven felt his heart pump wildly and tried to make himself think, *think*.

'We'll wait until it lands, if we can. A perfect level shot.'

'But will there be enough heat left in the engines to attract the missile?'

'Yes, yes. But the troops. . . In a minute we'll be able to hear them.'

As if prompted by Binderhaven's thoughts a dog howled, sounding unpleasantly close to their skimpy hiding place. Anna shivered and drew closer to Binderhaven. Things were happening around her, terrible things, and she could not look, she did not want to see.

The drone of the turbofans had risen to an ear-shattering scream.

'She's coming in!'

As Binderhaven rose McDonnell thrust him violently aside and leapt to his feet, grabbing the missile launcher. The dog howled once more and broke into frantic barking. Several voices shouted at once and among them Binderhaven heard the order to fire.

'*Pli!*'

Then McDonnell was dodging between the trees at the crouch, and to his horror Binderhaven saw that the soldiers were firing tracers from their automatic weapons, so as to pinpoint the target and guide the mens' aim. He began to follow, but more slowly, keeping his head well down. The girl cried out at that, and tried to restrain him, but he roughly shook her off and left her, suddenly careless of what might happen to Anna Petrina.

On the other side of McDonnell's stumbling figure he could see the plane. It had landed and was taxiing away from them, the hot jet-vents gaping wide. Still a dozen yards behind, he saw McDonnell raise the launcher to his shoulder and steady it there while he aligned the barrel with the AWACS, now less than half a mile away from where he stood, his legs apart, heedless of the sizzling white chains which converged upon him.

Then he fell.

The launcher dropped from his hands. McDonnell clasped his stomach, rocked backwards and forwards, sank to his knees. For a second he hung there, silhouetted against the background of the monstrously deformed aircraft, before keeling over in a little shower of snow.

Binderhaven picked himself up and hurtled across the few yards which separated him from his friend's body. As he skidded to a halt the Stinger seemed to fall into his hands as if by magnetism and his scrabbling fingers found the trigger. The voices were very close now, and he could hear the sound of men trampling through the undergrowth, dogs barking and howling at their heels. He rolled over and pointed the barrel towards the by now fast-retreating plane.

Something was wrong.

In the fraction of time left to him Binderhaven never registered in his conscious mind what it was. Something about the lines, the paint, the cut of the engine cowling, a dozen things like that. They were enough to make him hesitate. In that dreadful split second of indecision, a white-hot tracer bullet struck his hand. Binderhaven screamed in agony and dropped the launcher in the snow, where it lay with its muzzle towards him, gaping wide open as if in horrified condemnation of his failure.

When the first wave of troops caught up with Binderhaven he was on his hands and knees, almost up to McDonnell. To his amazement he saw that his friend was still alive. His body temperature was dropping rapidly, though, and it must be only a matter of time before he died. Binderhaven stared in fascination at the terrible wound in his chest, from which rich dark blood still flowed to stain the surrounding whiteness.

'Kirk. . .the girl. She's. . .great. That's why I. . .you and her. . .'

'Don't try to talk, Nat. Don't say any more.'

As Binderhaven stretched out his injured hand to touch McDonnell's face, a soldier kicked him with brutal force in the small of his back; he gritted his teeth in agony and sank down, defeated.

'You two. . .carry him. The girl's not hurt, she can walk.'

Captain Litvak had belatedly arrived on the scene. It was, he reflected, perhaps the most satisfying moment in a hitherto not very distinguished career. Now it was just a simple matter of

301

clearing up. But as the two troopers knelt down to lay hands on Binderhaven another voice spoke.

'You there! Leave him alone. Which one of you is Litvak?'

Binderhaven raised his head and saw the Soviet officer salute rapidly. By following the Captain's gaze he at last made out a dark figure down by the treeline. Pain made it hard for him to concentrate but in the rapidly gathering light he could see blue shoulder boards, three stars. . .full Colonel. . .

In the hands of the KGB Colonel a 7.62mm AK was pointing at the ground approximately halfway between Binderhaven and Captain Litvak.

'Those people are now the responsibility of the KGB. I have a helicopter waiting down by the treeline. My men will take over.'

Two men dressed in the winter uniforms of KGB troops ran forward to lift Binderhaven, who groaned at the sudden burst of pain. The Colonel himself stepped towards Anna and grasped her roughly by the arm.

'No!' Binderhaven tried to protest.

'Do as he says, Kirk.'

Something in the girl's voice made him twist round desperately as the troops carried him towards the open steppe, and see that her face was strangely calm. Too late, he remembered her dread of being taken alive, and groaned again.

'Wait a minute. . .'

Litvak emerged from the trance into which the Colonel's dramatic appearance had thrown him in time to realise that he was witnessing the imminent collapse of his greatest ever achievement, the capture of the American spies.

'Colonel, I want to see your identification. These prisoners are *mine*. By what authority. . .'

'Stand back, Litvak. I haven't the time.'

The Colonel threw a glance over his shoulder. Binderhaven and the girl were being bundled into the Mi-6. He stooped, and picked up the missile launcher.

Suddenly they all heard the sound of jet aero-engines. Another plane was coming to land.

The Colonel began to back down the path, never taking his eyes off Litvak's face. By this time the Captain's rage had passed the point of no return.

'You have no *right*,' he shouted; then, turning to his Sergeant, 'Stop them!'

Before anyone could move to obey the Colonel tucked the missile launcher a little more firmly under his arm, raised his AK to the horizontal, and shot Litvak dead.

For a moment the Captain hung there in space, as if suspended by invisible wires, with a look of the most intense astonishment on his face. As he collapsed in a heap the Colonel loosed off three quick bursts of fire, killing the Sergeant and two of the nearest troops, still locked in the grip of amazement; then he was running for the helicopter like an Olympic champion.

'Up,' he screamed as he threw the missile launcher into the Mi-6 and scrambled after it. '*Up!*'

While the Colonel's boots still scrabbled on the ground the pilot twisted the collective pitch lever and the helicopter shot upwards in a shower of snow. As soon as the Colonel was safely on board he looked around for Binderhaven.

'You know how to work this thing?' he hissed, tossing the missile launcher towards the dazed American. Binderhaven looked up at him incredulously. The Colonel's voice was a cold rasp, perhaps something to do with the ugly scar on his neck. . .

'Yes.'

'Then *look!*'

The helicopter lurched. Binderhaven rolled towards the still open hatch, managed to save himself in time; but something else was dislodged. As it fell to earth, spinning in the slipstream, Binderhaven thought it looked like a hat, a large fedora hat. . .then his attention fastened on the troops, their weapons raised and firing white hail. . .and the plane. . .

Binderhaven gasped. Far below him another aircraft seemed to settle across his line of sight, just barely floating over the perimeter fence a dozen feet above the ground; and this time no warning signals flashed in his brain.

'Hold her steady!' he shrieked, and the Colonel relayed an instantaneous translation to the pilot. Binderhaven raised on one knee and lifted the heavy launcher on to his shoulder. His

303

injured hand was nearly crippled, the pain was excruciating. He gasped, and nearly dropped the launcher as a bullet ricocheted off the rim of the open hatch.

'*Pli!*' screamed the Colonel in his ear. '*Pli! Pli! Pli!*'

'Stand away. . . Open the hatch on the other side! Backfire. . .*Remember the backfire!*'

The Colonel hurled himself to one side and shouted an order to one of his men, who clambered forward to wrench open the hatch on the other side of the helicopter.

As the main gear of the AWACS scraped the concrete, sending up a shower of snow crystals, Binderhaven pulled the trigger. For a second he was aware of the almighty roar of the missile and the stream of thick red smoke which seemed to trail away from him into the grey sky; behind him the helicopter endured a second of almost unendurable heat and noise; the red smoke-trail seemed undecided, uncertain. . .

And then it hardened.

A decision, based on all the available information, had been taken. There was no more hesitation, no more doubt. Instead, the ground-to-air missile darted straight through the mesh of white-hot tracer bullets and, drawn by the heat of the Boeing's engines, homed inexorably on to target.

'McDonnell,' Binderhaven screamed. 'Nat. . .!'

A great cry went up from the advancing soldiers, a cry in which mingled awe, and despair, and terror; but McDonnell did not hear it. He did not see the red and orange and black cloud blossom outwards, nor feel the blast, nor the rain of white-hot metal fragments which exploded into the forest, setting it on fire to burn like a torch drenched in petrol, nor the grey hat which lightly brushed his hand before settling, upside-down, in a snowdrift. He lay on his back, sightless eyes open to the sky, one hand thrown casually across his chest, indifferent to all these things.